Ayhan Kaya
»Sicher in Kreuzberg«

Ayhan Kaya (MA, MSc, PhD.), Lecturer at the Department of Political Science and International Relations, Istanbul Bilgi University; specialised on the Berlin-Turkish youth cultures and the construction and articulation of modern diasporic identities; received his PhD and MSc degrees at the University of Warwick; has various articles on Berlin-Turkish youth cultures, ethnic-based political participation strategies of German-Turks, Berlin-*Alevis*, and historians' debate in Germany; currently working on Circassian diaspora in Turkey, globalisation, diaspora nationalism, German-Turks, and multicultural clientalism in the west.

Ayhan Kaya
»Sicher in Kreuzberg«
Constructing Diasporas:
Turkish Hip-Hop Youth in Berlin

[transcript]

Die Deutsche Bibliothek – CIP-Einheitsaufnahme
Kaya, Ayhan:
Sicher in Kreuzberg : constructing diasporas;
Turkish Hip-Hop youth in Berlin / Ayhan Kaya
    Bielefeld : Transcript, 2001
    ISBN 3-933127-71-8

© 2001 transcript Verlag, Bielefeld
Cover Design: Kordula Röckenhaus, Bielefeld
Cover Photograph: Ayhan Kaya
Typeset by: digitron GmbH, Bielefeld
Printed and bound in Great Britain by
Marston Book Services Ltd, Oxfordshire
    ISBN 3-933127-71-8

Contents

Acknowledgements 11

Introduction   13

RESEARCH FRAMEWORK AND INTEREST 15
THE UNIVERSE OF THE RESEARCH 18
    Naunyn Ritze Youth Centre 19
    Chip Youth Centre 20
    BTBTM Youth Group 21
DEVELOPING RAPPORT WITH YOUNGSTERS 22
THE IMPLICATIONS AND THE SCOPE OF THE STUDY 26

Chapter 1   31
The Notions of Culture, Youth Culture, Ethnicity, and Globalisation

NOTIONS OF CULTURE 33
GLOBALISM AND SYNCRETICISM 38
GLOCALISED IDENTITIES 41
SUBCULTURAL THEORY 44
OUTSIDERISM: ETHNIC MINORITY HIP-HOP YOUTH CULTURE . . 48

Chapter 2   55
Constructing Modern Diasporas

THE CHANGING FACE OF ETHNIC GROUP
POLITICAL STRATEGIES 55
   The Migratory Process 56
   The Formation of Ethnic-Based Political Strategies 58
   Migrant Strategy 64
   Minority Strategy 66
DIASPORA STRATEGY 72
DIASPORA REVISITED 72
DIASPORIC CONSCIOUSNESS 79

Chapter 3   87
Kreuzberg 36: A Diasporic Space in Multicultural Berlin

A TURKISH ETHNIC ENCLAVE 88
'KLEINES ISTANBUL' (LITTLE ISTANBUL) 91
INTERCONNECTEDNESS IN SPACE 96
MAJOR TURKISH ETHNIC ASSOCIATIONS IN BERLIN 100
INSTITUTIONAL MULTICULTURALISM IN BERLIN 105
ESSENTIALISING AND 'OTHERING THE OTHER' 108
   The Case of Manifest Alevism in 'Multicultural' Berlin 111

Chapter 4   127
Identity and Homing of Diaspora

LIFE-WORLDS OF THE WORKING-CLASS TURKISH YOUTH
IN KREUZBERG 127
   Life in the Youth Centre 128
   Life in the Street 129
   Life in the School 133
   Life in the Household 136
'SICHER IN KREUZBERG': THE HOMING OF DIASPORA 138
MIDDLE-CLASS TURKISH YOUNGSTERS AND THE QUESTION
OF IDENTITY 144
MIDDLE-CLASS TURKISH YOUTH: COSMOPOLITAN SELF
AND 'HEIMAT' 146
LANGUAGE AND 'CODE-SWITCHING' 147

Chapter 5 — 155
Cultural Identity of the Turkish Hip-Hop Youth in Kreuzberg 36

CULTURAL SOURCES OF IDENTITY FORMATION PROCESS
AMONG THE TURKISH YOUTH 155
   Orientation to Homeland 156
   Religion and Ethnicity 158
   Reception of Diasporic Youth in Turkey:
   German-Like (Almanci) 160
WORKING-CLASS TURKISH YOUTH LEISURE CULTURE 162
HIP-HOP YOUTH CULTURE AND WORKING-CLASS
DIASPORIC TURKISH YOUTH 165
   Graffiti 166
   Dance 169
   'Cool' Style 170
HIP-HOP YOUTH STYLE: A CULTURAL BRICOLAGE 172

Chapter 6 — 179
Aesthetics of Diaspora: Contemporary Minstrels

RAPPERS AS CONTEMPORARY MINSTRELS, 'ORGANIC
INTELLECTUALS' AND STORYTELLERS 180
   Cartel: Cultural Nationalist Rap 182
   Islamic Force: Universalist Political Rap 188
   Erci-E: Party Rap 197
   Ünal: Gangsta Rap 200
   Azize-A: Woman Rap 202

Conclusion — 209

Appendix — 215

GLOSSARY 215
BIBLIOGRAPHY 218
DISCOGRAPHY 234
FIGURES 235

List of Tables

Table 1　Germany's Non-German Population and Turkish Minority 57
Table 2　Demographic Structure of Kreuzberg, 25.07.1996 89
Table 3　Turkish Population in Berlin District, 30.06.1996 95
Table 4　Turkish TV Channels in Germany and the Rate of Audience 97
Table 5　Turkish Newspapers Printed in Germany 99
Table 6　The Number of the German and Non-German Students in Kreuzberg. 133
Table 7　Major Turkish Football Teams in Kreuzberg 158

Abbreviations

AAKM	Anadolu Alevileri Kültür Merkezi (Anatolian *Alevis*' Cultural Centre)
AMGT	Avrupa Milli Görüs Teskilati (European National Vision Association)
BA	Bundesanstalt für Arbeit (Federal Labour Agency)
BIVS	Berliner Institut für Vergleichende Sozialforschung (Berlin Institute for Comparative Social Research)
BTBTM	Berlin-Turkiye Bilim ve Teknoloji Merkezi (Berlin-Turkish Centre for Science and Technology)
DITIB	Diyanet Isleri Türk-Islam Birligi (Turkish-Islam Union, Religious Affairs)
EU	European Union
FRG	Federal Republic of Germany
TGB	Türkische Gemeinde zu Berlin (Turkish Community in Berlin)
TRT	Türkiye Radyo Televizyon Kurumu (Turkish Broadcasting Association)

Dedicated to the youngsters of Kreuzberg

Acknowledgements

This volume is derived from my Ph.D. dissertation submitted to the Centre for Research in Ethnic Relations, University of Warwick, England, in 1998. Many people helped me throughout this work. For stimulating and sustained intellectual responses and for his guidance all the way through the process, I am indebted to Steven Vertovec. I am especially thankful to Martin Greve for his support, thoughtful insights about Berlin and Kreuzberg. Clive Harris and specially Birgit Brandt contributed immeasurably by close reading of parts of the book. They were untiring in their supply of ideas and bibliographic references about German-Turks and ethnic minorities. I thank them both for their interest. I am deeply grateful to Marta Guirao Ochoa for the time, effort and support she devoted to my entire work. She read the whole work with good humour and enthusiasm, and helped editing the book. I learned an enormous amount from Robin Cohen, Kevin Robins, Tom Cheesman, Ayse Çaglar, Jochen Blaschke, Werner Schiffauer and Ahmet Ersöz whose concerns, intellect, and support shaped this work. I thank them for their serious interest. Thanks very much, too, to Mel Wilde and Graham Bennett for their valuable proof reading and editing.

The youngsters I interviewed enthusiastically shared their experiences and thoughts, and I want to thank all the youngsters in *Naunyn Ritze* and *Chip* youth centres. I am also grateful to the *BTBTM* youngsters. For their support and warm welcome I thank the youth workers Neco, Elif Düzyurt and also Nurdan Kütük. A separate and special note contains my thanks and acknowledgements to the Berlin-Turkish rappers Islamic Force (Kan-AK), Ünal, Azize-A and Erci-E, whose thoughts, experiences, lyrics and music precisely shaped this work. In the course of my research in Germany there were many others who helped and guided me. Serdar Coskun, Baki Zirek, Levent Nanka, Claudia Wahjudi and Yüksel Mutlu are just some of them. I want to express my grateful thanks to them.

Acknowledgements

Iam grateful for the institutional support and encouragement provided by the department of Political Science and International Relations, Marmara University. Thanks, too, to Zig Layton-Henry, director of the Centre for Research in Ethnic Relations at the University of Warwick, who generously provided a supportive academic environment for the preparation of this work. I should also acknowledge my gratitude to *Berliner Institut für Vergleichende Sozialforschung* (BIVS) for their unique database on transnational migration. Emre Isik, Penny Masoura and Adem Nergül were always there, good friends and actively involved when I raised issues for their consideration. This research was supported in part by funds from the European Union Jean Monnet Awards Scheme, German Academic Exchange Programme (DAAD), British Overseas Research Students Awards Scheme and University of Warwick. I would like to express my gratitude to these bodies. Of course, none of those mentioned here are in any way responsible for the ultimate outcome; it is I who must take final responsibility.

Finally, I acknowledge my parents who have provided me with an essential moral support throughout all those years. I want to express my deepest gratitude for their love and support.

Introduction

Bu dünyada beraberce yasiyoruz	We live together on planet earth,
Dogu ve batiyi birlestiriyoruz	and if we want to grow in peace
Sinirlari asiyoruz	We need to erase our borders,
Kültürler kaynasiyor	share our rich cultures.
Birbirini tamamliyor.	Yes, connect and blend the West
	with the East.
Azize-A	*Azize-A*[1]

In her rap song *'Bosporus Bridge'*, the Berlin-Turkish rapper Azize-A, attempts to locate the descendants of Turkish migrants in a hybrid space where cultural borders blend, where the periphery meets the centre, and where the West merges with the East. She perceives these transparent cultural border crossings as sites of creative cultural production, not as what Renato Rosaldo (1989: 208) calls 'empty transitional zones.' So far, Turkish immigrants in Germany have been regarded by most Turkish and German scholars as culturally invisible because they were no longer what they once were and not yet what they could become. Only recently some scholars have begun to inquire into the creative character and potential of newly emerging syncretic cultures.

We can identify three stages in the studies on Turkish migrants in Germany. In the early period of migration in the sixties, the syncretic nature of existing migrant cultures was not of interest to scholars analysing the situation of Turkish *Gastarbeiter* (guest worker) in Germany. The studies carried out during this period were mainly concerned with economics and statistics, 'culture' and the dreams of return (cf. inter alia Abadan, 1964; Castles and Kosack, 1973). As Ayse Çaglar (1994) has rightfully stated, the reason behind this neglect is twofold. First, at the beginning of the migration process, Turkish workers were demographically highly homogenous, consisting of either single males or females, and were not visible in the public space.

Second, workers in this period were considered temporary, and they themselves regarded their situation as such (Çaglar, 1994: 16-17).

The end of recruiting foreign labour to Germany in 1973 and the beginning of family reunion mark the beginning of the second stage. The number of studies on Turkish migrants' culture increased with the visibility of Turkish migrants becoming more evident in the public space after the family reunification. Faced with the choice of leaving Germany without a possibility of returning, most migrants decided to stay in Germany for the time being and were joined by their families. The transformation from being a rotatable workforce to becoming increasingly settled went hand in hand with the emergence of community structures (development of ethnic small business, sport clubs, religious organisations and meeting places), which made Turkish migrants more visible to the German populations. Furthermore, the rising presence of non-working dependants, women and children, necessitated the provision of some basic social services, such as education and housing. Against this background, studies of this period concentrated on the reorganisation of family, parent-child-relationships, integration, assimilation and 'acculturation' of migrants to German culture (cf. inter alia Abadan-Unat, 1985; Nauck, 1988; Kagitçibasi, 1987). The key words in these studies were 'cultural conflict,' 'culture shock,' 'acculturation,' 'inbetweenness' and 'identity crisis.'

The third stage – starting in the 1990s – is characterised by a wide diversity of approaches. In this last stage, questions pertaining to the relationship between structure and agency, and interest in cultural production have come to the fore. Studies have dealt with such questions concerning citizenship, discrimination and racism, socio-economic performance and increasingly with the emergence of diasporic networks as well as cultural production (cf. inter alia Çaglar, 1994; Mandel, 1996; Schwartz, 1992; Zaimoglu, 1995; Faist, 2000b).

This study is critical of conventional approaches that followed a holistic notion of culture. Rather than reducing Turkish-German youth cultures to the realms of 'ethnic exoticism,' this work claims to be evolving around the notion of cultural syncreticism, or bricolage, which has become the dominant paradigm in the study of transnational cultures and modern diasporas. The formation and articulation of the German-Turkish hip-hop youth culture will be investigated within the concept of cultural bricolage. The main framework of such an investigation should, of course, consist of the question of 'how those youngsters see themselves': as *'Gastarbeiter,'* immigrant, *'gurbetçi'* (in exile), caught 'betwixt and between,' as with no culture to call their own, or as agents and *avant-garde* of new cultural forms.

Research Framework and Interest

As I began to search the Turkish diasporic youth in Berlin, my attention often wandered to some more particular aspects of diasporic youth culture. I became fascinated with the hip-hop youth culture, undoubtedly because Turkish hip-hop has represented an adequate model of cultural bricolage and diasporic consciousness. This book focuses on the processes of cultural identity formation and articulation among the Turkish male hip-hop youth living in Kreuzberg, Berlin. My main hypothesis is that Berlin-Turkish hip-hop youth has developed a politics of diaspora to tackle exclusion and discrimination in their country of settlement. As a response to those boundaries that have been erected to keep them apart from the majority German society, these youngsters have created symbolic boundaries based upon parental, local and global cultures that mark their uniqueness. Apparently, these symbolic boundaries have been created through diasporic networks and modern means of communication and transportation.

The politics of diaspora is a product of exclusionist strategies of 'differential incorporation' (Rex, 1994) applied by the Federal Republic of Germany *vis-à-vis* migrants. The politics of diaspora, which I shall call diasporic consciousness in the following chapters, or diasporic identity, is comprised of both particularist and universalist constituents. The particularist components consist of an attachment to homeland, religion and ethnicity; and provide these youngsters with a network of solidarity and a sense of confinement. The universalistic constituents include various aspects of global hip-hop culture such as rap, graffiti, breakdance and 'cool' style; they equip the youngsters with those means to symbolically transcend the discipline and power of the nation-state and to integrate themselves into a global youth culture. In this sense, the notion of modern diaspora, as I shall suggest in the following chapters, appears to be a useful concept for the study of contemporary labour migrants and their descendants: it embraces and conceptualises two of the main antithetical forces that characterise modern times, namely localism and globalism.

Introduction

My main interest lies upon the creation of diasporic cultural identities amongst the working-class Turkish hip-hop youth in Kreuzberg, Berlin. I am not concerned with generalised external pronouncements about the 'problems' or 'crises' of Turkish identity, but focus on the form and content of these identities as they are experienced in everyday life. In doing so, I try to move away from a predominantly macro-structural approach, in which Turkish youth constitutes a social category considered only in its relation to institutions.

The research for this work has been carried in a Turkish enclave. However, it does not claim to shed light on the situation of all youngsters living in this enclave. In this sense, my work is rather illustrative, not representative. Various other youth groups such as Islamic youth, middle-class youth and *Alevi* youth will be touched upon in order to provide the reader with a deeper analytical insights for understanding the distinct situation of Turkish hip-hop youth. Far from constituting a culture of despair and nihilism, I intend to demonstrate that Turkish hip-hop youths are concerned with the construction of new cultural alternatives, in which identity is created and re-created as part of an ongoing and dynamic process. By focusing on a specific group of Turkish youths, I seek to compose an alternative picture of Turkish youth, commonly portrayed as destructive, Islamic, fundamentalist and problematic by the majority society (cf. inter alia *Der Spiegel* 1997; *Focus* 1997; Heitmeyer, 1997).

Flagging up the notions of cultural bricolage, diasporic consciousness and globalisation, my research draws from and contributes to the fields of migration studies, 'race' and ethnic relations and diaspora studies (cf. inter alia Clifford, 1997, 1994, 1992; Hall, 1994; Gilroy, 1995, 1994, 1993; Cohen, 1997, 1996, 1995; Vertovec, 1997, 1996b). The growing research on transnational migrant communities and their descendants suggests that the notion of diaspora can be considered an intermediate concept between the local and global, thus transcending narrow and limited national perspectives. The material analysed in this study provides further evidence that the contemporary notion of diaspora is a beneficial concept in order to study the formation and articulation of the cultural identity among transnational communities.

Much of the current research on the Turkish migrants and their descendants in Germany has focused on socio-economic issues, emphasising their labour relations, residential patterns and 'acculturation' difficulties. No research has yet been undertaken to explore the formation and articulation of both cultural identity and political participation strategies among German-Turks, based on the notion of diaspora. One of the central claims here is that working-class Turkish hip-hop youth culture in Berlin can adequately display how cultural bricolage is formed by the diasporic youth in collision, negotiation and dialogue with the parental, 'host' and global cultures. The idea of cultural bricolage, thus, contravenes those problematic terms such as 'deculturated,' 'inbetween' and 'degenerated,' attributed to the German-Turkish youth.

In addition to investigating how the Berlin-Turkish hip-hop youths have constructed and articulated a form of diasporic consciousness and cultural bricolage, this study also scrutinises how the Berlin-Turks, those allegedly least autonomous and influential actors of the German social system, have hitherto developed two major strategies for political participation. These two strategies are namely *migrant strategy* and *minority strategy*. These political participation strategies have been built up by migrants along ethnic lines as a response to the exclusionist and segregationist regimes of incorporation applied by the Federal Republic of Germany *vis-à-vis* migrants. Migrant strategy was formed at the beginning of the migratory process as a need to cope with the destabilising effects of migration. Minority strategy, on the other hand, emerged sometime after the family reunion started and the labour recruitment ceased in 1973. While the former strategy was based on a non-associational community formation, ethnic enclave, *hemsehri* (fellow citizens) bonding, and a *Gastarbeiter* ideology (see Chapter 2), the latter was based on the idea of permanent settlement and the discourses of culture and community. Shedding light upon these two strategies, my work will also demonstrate how the modern diaspora discourse appears to be replacing, or at least supplementing, these ethnic strategies.

Before describing the details of my field research in Berlin, let me briefly touch upon some of the terms I will be using in the book. The terms such as Turkish hip-hop youth and/or Berlin-Turkish hip-hop youth, which I will interchangeably use throughout the work, primarily refer to the working-class male Turkish diasporic hip-hop youth. Hip-Hop, in general, has its roots in urban American ghettos and represents a form of youth culture that expresses the anger, visions and experiences of black and/or Latino 'underclass' youngsters. Although there are some successful female hip-hoppers such as Queen Latifah and Sister Souljah, hip-hop remains a predominantly male domain. Against this background, I choose to focus in my research on male, working-class youngsters. During the course of my research, I did, however, meet and converse with a number of Turkish women hip-hoppers, who provided me with a valuable insight into their experience both as a comparison with, and contrast to, the experience of Turkish men. Clearly, an analysis of female hip-hoppers is necessary in the future in order to gain a fuller picture on cultural forms created by diasporic youth.

A separate note is also needed for the contextual use of the term 'German-Turk' in this work. The notion of German-Turk is neither a term used by the descendants of Turkish migrants to identify them, nor is it used in the political or academic debate in Germany. I use the term German-Turk in the Anglo-Saxon academic tradition to categorise diasporic youths; the term attributes a hybrid form of cultural identity to those groups of young people. There is no doubt that political regimes of incorporation applied to the immigrants in Germany are very different from those in the United States and England. Accordingly, unlike Italian-American or Chinese-British, Turks have never been defined as German-Turks or Turkish-German by the official discourse. They have rather been considered apart. That is why, practically, it does not seem appropriate to call the Turkish diasporic communities in Germany 'German-Turks.' Yet, it is a helpful term for my purposes for two reasons: the term distances the researcher from essentialising the descendants of the transnational migrants as 'Turkish;' furthermore it underlines the transcultural character of these youths.

The Universe of the Research

The main body of my research took place among three separate youth groups in Berlin. Two of the groups are located in the Turkish ethnic enclave in Kreuzberg 36^2, spending their leisure time in two different youth centres. The first one, which was the focus of my research, is called *Naunyn Ritze Kinder & Jugend Kulturzentrum* located in *Naunynstraße*. The second one is the *Chip Jugend, Kultur & Kommunikationszentrum* located in *Reichenberger Straße*. Both centres are quite close to each other, so that the youth workers and some of the youngsters are in contact. Both centres are financed by local organisations and Kreuzberg municipality.

The third youth group is comprised of youngsters living mostly outside Kreuzberg and attending the gymnasium. These middle-class Turkish youths were approached in order to build, by way of contrast, a fuller view of the life worlds of the working-class Turkish hip-hop youngsters, and to indicate the heterogeneity of the Turkish diasporic communities. Inclusion of the middle-class Turkish youth will also provide us with a ground where we can more precisely differentiate between the strategies of cultural identity formation undertaken by various Turkish youth groups in the diaspora. In what follows, I shall briefly describe these groups.

Naunyn Ritze Youth Centre

Naunyn Ritze youth centre is situated in *Naunynstraße*, a street that is predominantly inhabited by the Turkish migrants originating from the eastern rural parts of Turkey (see Chapter 3). The centre is run by the Kreuzberg municipality and a Kreuzberg neighbourhood organisation, *Mixtur 36 e. V.* The main activities in the centre are breakdance, *capoeira* (Brazilian dance), mountain climbing, graffiti, painting, photography, bodybuilding and taekwondo. The Turkish youngsters in the centre, who number between forty-five and fifty, are mainly involved in breakdance, graffiti, painting, body building and taekwondo. Some of them have won many prizes in Berlin's breakdance and graffiti competitions. The other activities are dominated mostly by Germans. The centre is open from Tuesday to Saturday between 15.00 and 22.00 o'clock. The proportion of girls and boys coming to the centre is almost equal. There is a *café* in the centre where the youngsters usually congregate; in addition, the girls have a separate room for themselves.

The centre employs approximately ten youth workers, three of whom are Berlin-Turks. The youth workers have the controlling power over the youngsters. There is some tension between the German youth workers and the Turkish youngsters, and the Turkish youth workers, Neco (25), Elif (25) and Ibo (28), try to absorb this tension since they are more respected by their co-ethnic youngsters. Incidentally, the presence of the Turkish female youth worker, Elif, encourages the Turkish girls to come to the centre and to become involved in the activities.

Naunyn Ritze is the most popular centre for Turkish minority hip-hop youth. This is the centre where the previously active *36ers* and *36*

Boys gangsta groups, and the local rap group *Islamic Force*, which I shall examine more fully in Chapter 6, originated. It is also the place where interested parties of the German media come in order to collect trendy material on Turkish hip-hop youth culture. There is always American music in the background. It is the head youth worker, Peter, who decides which music to play, not the youngsters. Yet, the girls and boys, when they meet up in their private rooms in the centre prefer listening to Turkish *arabesk*, Turkish folk music, Turkish pop music and *Islamic Force* (see Chapter 6). *Arabesk*, hip-hop, Turkish folk music and Turkish pop music are respectively the most popular types of music amongst the youngsters. The pessimism of *arabesk*, the romance of the Turkish pop, and the 'coolness' of rap match the feelings they have. They call *arabesk* '*isyan müzigi*' (rebellion music). *Arabesk* is a protest style of music in itself, but it has always had a passivist beat and a pessimist content, which leads to what Adorno (1990/1941: 312) called 'rhythmic obedience' (see Chapter 6).

The youngsters in *Naunyn Ritze* are mainly *Alevis* (see Chapter 3) – few are *Sunnis* – and their parents migrated mostly from the eastern parts of Turkey. This group is a relatively homogenous group in terms of ethnicity compared to the other 2 youth groups examined in this study.

Chip Youth Centre

Chip is located in *Reichenberger Straße*, a street that is situated on the other side of the *Kotbusser Tor U-Bahn* station and which is inhabited by mixed ethnic dwellers such as Turkish, Lebanese, Yugoslavian and German (see Chapter 3). It is also administered by the municipality. Activities in the centre include music, graffiti, photography and computing. It is smaller than *Naunyn Ritze*; there are only five youth workers, none of whom are Turkish. The research was carried out with approximately twenty Turkish youngsters. The centre is mostly dominated by Turkish and Lebanese male youngsters. Turkish girls participate only in the vocational training activities, and rarely spend their spare time in the centre's *café*. In these respects, *Chip* is quite different from *Naunyn Ritze*.

The controlling power resides in the hands of the male youngsters, especially of the Turks. There is always a tension between the youth workers and the youngsters; even I, myself, could feel this tension during the course of my research. Furthermore, the relations between the Turkish and Arabic youths are problematic and sometimes violent. The youngsters and the youth workers told me that an Arab killed a Turkish youngster in front of the centre in 1994. Thus the tension between the groups has continued since. It should be noted that *Chip* is another important centre like *Naunyn Ritze*: *Chip* has previously been a meeting place for one of Berlin's *gangsta* groups – the *Fatbacks*, a group that was mostly composed of Turkish and Arab youngsters. Tension between the *Naunyn Ritze* boys and *Chip* boys still exist, however sometimes alliances are formed to fight against other Arab or German youngsters.

The Turkish youngsters coming to the centre are mainly *Sunnis*. Their parents originate from various regions in Turkey. It is a more heterogeneous centre in terms of parental origins. It is the youngsters themselves who decide which type of music is played in the *café*. They mostly choose the melancholic and pessimistic Turkish *arabesk*, which plays in the background. Wolfgang, a youth worker, indicated that the youth workers in the centre have been trying to adopt a democratic understanding in *Chip*. Although they have granted the youngsters the freedom to choose their type of music, they were not happy with the pessimist and passivist *arabesk* music. Two months after my first visit to the centre, the youth workers had made some rearrangements in the organisation, i.e. they took over the running of the *café* from the youngsters, and now they play hip-hop music to attract also German youngsters to the centre.[3]

BTBTM Youth Group

This is a group of between fifteen and twenty middle-class youngsters, living mostly outside Kreuzberg. They all attend Gymnasium. In addition, they take some additional courses at the *Technische Universität* delivered by a Turkish student organisation called Berlin-Turkish Science and Technology Centre (*BTBTM*).[4] Courses that they are taking include Turkish, Maths, Physics, Biology and German literature. These youngsters decided to form a group that meets regularly and gives them the opportunity to exchange ideas about their problems. Their meetings were organised by a university student, Nurdan who was then the head of the *BTBTM*. Discussion topics include identity, sexism displayed by Turkish men, youth, racism, xenophobia and nationalism. At the end of these meetings, which lasted nearly one year, they initiated a *Jugendfest* (youth festival) in the *Werkstatt der Kulturen* located in the neighbouring district of Neukölln. They presented their own works to German and Turkish audience (see Chapter 4). I joined their meetings as an observer and also participated in the festival and their entertainments.

While doing the research, I spent time with several political activists in their community organisations, with a few families in their homes, with many first generation male migrants in their traditional Turkish *cafés*, and with many youth social workers in the youth centres. However, I spent most of my time with youths in the street, at their other 'hangouts' and in their youth centres. Of these three distinct aforementioned youth groups, *Naunyn Ritze* youths became the core of my field research. Accordingly, in the following section I will narrate the story of my acceptance into the *Naunyn Ritze* youth centre.

Developing Rapport with Youngsters

At the very beginning of my research, I was a stranger for the youths, coming from a place that they did not know. I was obviously a Turkish citizen, but what kind of Turkish? Was I Kurdish, or *Alevi*, or *Sunni*, or what? They were initially extremely sceptical about me, as they always are about any stranger. However, as the social workers of the Naunyn Ritze Youth Centre, Neco and Elif, had introduced me to them, they had a slightly more positive first impression of me. Beyond their introductions, our rapport depended on my own ability to communicate with them. Should I act as a researcher asking many questions, or as a participant observer scrutinising everything, or should I interact with them as 'myself'? These were the questions with which I struggled in the beginning. Actually, it seemed extremely difficult, and not at all reasonable, to decide on which role to choose at the very beginning of the research. I merely endeavoured to avoid the formalism of research methods.

I was at the centre almost every day, except on holidays. I introduced myself as a student coming from England and doing research about experiences of Turkish hip-hop youngsters in Kreuzberg. Their first reaction, or first confirmation, of what I was doing, was that I had come to the right place to research such a subject. *Naunyn Ritze* has hitherto been the most popular place for German and other international journalists who want to find out about the daily life of Turkish youngsters and *gangsta* groups living in Kreuzberg. That is why I was also treated as a television or newspaper journalist at first sight and was even asked by the youngsters where my camera or tape-recorder was. Since I avoided using any mechanical equipment to record, to videotape, or to take pictures, I convinced them that I was not a journalist. Although they were at first slightly disappointed, it did not take long for them to get used to the fact that I was just a student. They immediately wanted to know what kind of student I was. Apparently, I did not match the type of student they had in mind – according to them 'I was a bit old to be a student.'

Repeatedly, they asked me questions about England and the Turkish youths living there. They wanted me to make a comparison between themselves and the British-Turkish youths. I let them question me as much as possible in order to balance our positions. My transnational identity – or, in their perceptions, cosmopolitan identity – obviously worked in my favour and facilitated a rapport with them. They found my English connection more interesting to play with than my Turkish connection. I was trying, at all times, to avoid being received as merely an academic researcher. Rather, I was presenting myself as a student doing his PhD., or doctorate, which they failed to understand clearly. To make it clear for them, I told them that this research would, at the end, lead to a book about them. It was pleasant for them to imagine their stories printed in a book. Then, they all agreed to help me.

While I never concealed the fact that I was doing research, these youngsters did not generally define my identity as merely a researcher. I was seen as an elder brother (*agabey*) and a good friend who would understand their problems and help them obtain their goals. Accordingly, my relationship with the youngsters developed on a friendly basis. If the researcher makes friends with the actors of the research and considers them 'interlocutors' rather than 'informants' and/or 'respondents,' and if the actors trust the researcher, they will also be honest with him/her (Horowitz, 1983, 1986; Adler et al., 1986; Alasuutari, 1995: 52-56). My personal background is working class and I am of Turkish-*Alevi* origin, therefore quite similar to those of the youngsters. Accordingly, I was not relegated to a marginal position in the course of the research. Rather, I was considered an insider to a certain extent, though they maintained a fragile distance.

In the course of the field research, I did not need to apply any of the formal participatory roles established by various schools of research. For instance, I refused to implement both the Chicago school of symbolic interactionism, whereby the researcher attempts to take the most objective and detached position, and the ethnomethodological way of subjective interactionism, whereby the researcher takes the most radically subjective and involved position. I tried to refrain from a variety of research postures differing in the degree of researcher's involvement. Hence, I tried to abstain from the use of two polar field research stances: *the observer-as-participant* and *the participant-as-observer*. Rather, I eventually maintained a balance between involvement and detachment. I was spending time with the youngsters, getting to know them informally, but also trying to avoid becoming personally or emotionally involved with them to retain my objectivity.

Developing close relationships with the youngsters still made me aware of the severe pitfalls associated with losing detachment and objectivity: 'going native' (Berg, 1995; Rosaldo 1989, Chap. 8; Adler et al., 1986; Hammersley and Atkinson, 1983). 'Going native' refers to developing an overrapport with research subjects that can harm the data-gathering process. Overrapport may also bias the researcher's own perspectives, leading him/her uncritically to accept the views of the members as his/her own (Adler et al., 1986: 364). The rapport I developed with the youths never involved making repeated overtures of friendliness, artificial postures to attract the attention of the youngsters, or exploiting the norms of interpersonal reciprocity to build a research web of friendly relations and key informants. Because playing roles and using deceptive strategies in the interest of sociological inquiry do not constitute a good faith commitment.

Another crucial point to be raised about gaining rapport among the youngsters is the advantages and disadvantages of being an 'ethnic' researcher. As an ethnic minority researcher I acquired privileged relations with both Turkish youngsters and adults. Familiarity with the language and physical space of the Turkish minority in Berlin provided me with an easy access to the youth groups that I worked with. I had more advantages compared to German researchers because of the negative perception that the working-class Turkish youths have of the Germans. The youngsters assumed that I empathised with them – an empathy that they would not expect from a German researcher. But as well as providing a crucial advantage in facilitating the process of 'getting in,' being an ethnic researcher brings about some disadvantages. It might accelerate 'going native,' and it might also lead to the sentimentalisation of the research due to the close effective links established with the people researched. Above all, sometimes the minorities might expect the ethnic researcher to solve their problems, or at least to mediate between the governmental authorities and themselves. Having in mind all these disadvantages of being an ethnic researcher, I tried to abstain from developing an overrapport and giving an impression, which might lead them to think that I was there to find a solution to their problems.

I had a theoretical and ethical difficulty in treating the youngsters in the process of social inquiry. Was I going to treat them as 'respondents,' 'informants' or whatever? After spending some time to get into their worlds, I realised that treating the youngsters as 'respondents' was not relevant and ethical at all because it was the parents, youth workers and the police who asked questions in their world. These were the social actors who signified power to be obeyed by the youngsters. Accordingly, I tried to refrain from adopting the power to ask questions as granted. Above all, the researcher who has the power to ask questions attempts to place himself/herself on a higher position than that of the people s/he searches. Such a positioning might lead to the manipulation of the research on the sidewalk of the researcher. In other words, this notion might invite the risk of praising the scientific dogmatism or pure sociological investigation.

Unlike 'respondents,' the term 'informants' might, at first glance, seem a more reasonable role to give the youngsters because, then, they are considered to narrate their own life stories to the researcher who supposedly stands on a neutral, or rather assimilated, positioning. Although this term ethically seems more accurate, the researcher ceases to exist as a subject. Contrarily, this term might invite the risk of 'going native,' which is contemplated as the end of scientific knowledge. Thus, I also tried to avoid purely ethnographic approach, praising the youngsters and their narratives more than necessary. As Rosaldo (1989: 180) put it I had to dance "on the edge of a paradox by simultaneously becoming 'one of the people' and remaining an academic."

Bearing in mind the limitations of these two terms, I prefer using the term 'interlocutor' that locates the researcher and youngsters as separate subjects, who are free from ideological manipulation of each other and open to dialogical interaction. In doing so, I tried to distance myself from pure sociological and ethnographic puritanism, or from what Rosaldo (1989) calls 'sociological and ethnographic monumentalism.' Treating the youngsters as 'interlocutors' is also an attempt to minimise the question of power between the researcher and the people 'researched.' This term, at the same time, situates the researcher in a middle position where s/he can utilise both his/her objective and subjective dispositions in his/her attempt to capture and explain the full meaning of the social life of the people 'researched.' Without objectivity, researching particular/local cultures and identities is out of the question because objectivism attempts to prevent the subjective researcher to romanticise his/her subjects. Identically, it is also accurate to claim that the subjective character of the human beings that collect and interpret the knowledge influences all human knowledge. Therefore, social analysts should explore their subjects from a number of different positions, rather than being locked into any particular one.

I spent approximately eight months in Berlin, from January to August 1996. Afterwards, I had a few more trips to Berlin for a couple of weeks, one of which was in December 1996, and the others in June 1997, September 1998 and August 2000. Besides interacting and making participant observation, I also carried out semi-structured in-depth interviews with ten members of the each youth group, five of whom are girls and five boys. My intention was to obtain a summary of the experiences utilising some 'key questions' suggested by an examination of the data. However, these interviews remained semi-structured in that the replies by the youngsters led to the generation of further questions as I sought explanations and elaboration of the events. In the course of the research I did not use any tape- or video-recorder to record the interviews or informal chats I made with the youngsters. Since there were many journalists visiting these two youth centres, especially *Naunyn Ritze*, the youngsters seemed to develop a fixed way of representation of themselves to the media. Being equipped with no electronic recorder, I aimed not to be received as a journalist by the youths.

The Implications and the Scope of the Study

As pointed out before, my work mainly reflects the stories and narratives of the two working-class youth groups who took part in the field research in Kotbusser Tor, Kreuzberg 36. During the course of the study, it has become evident that the processes of cultural identity formation of these youth groups primarily revolved around two significant constituents: *diasporic cultural consciousness* and *global hip-hop youth culture*. Accordingly, this work explores these two constituents in order to map out the landscape of these youths' cultural identity. To do so, these Berlin-Turkish hip-hop youth groups should be situated in a broader social and cultural framework highlighting their ethnic enclave, their parental culture, middle-class Turkish youth culture, majority society culture and contemporary global youth culture.

Thus, this study is built on three principal phases. The first phase portrays the diasporic urban space created by the Turkish migrants and their descendants in Kreuzberg. The second phase of this study considers teenagers as they interact and develop identities in various social settings: in their homes, in the schools, on the streets, and in Turkey. The third phase of the study examines the process by which the Berlin-Turkish hip-hop youth develops a diasporic consciousness in collision, negotiation and dialogue with the majority society. Hence, the main theme, which these three phases aim to reveal, is the cultural bricolage and diasporic cultural identity constructed and articulated by the Berlin-Turkish hip-hop youths that are subject to the streams of globalisation.

The first chapter explicates the debates over the relative importance of theoretical notions such as culture, youth culture, 'subculture,' ethnicity, globalism and hip-hop in the study of German-Turkish hip-hop youth. In a first step, two distinct notions of culture namely the *holistic notion of culture* and the *syncretic notion of culture* are put forward. Departing from this differentiation, I summarise the main trends that characterise studies on German-Turks. Highlighting the limits of these conventional studies, I base my argument on the idea of cultural bricolage through which the youngsters construct their identities. In this chapter, where I question some theoretical conceptualisations, I also try to develop a theoretical frame that allows differentiating the hip-hop youth culture from the traditional concept of 'subculture.'

The second chapter explores the migratory process in the Federal Republic of Germany, which has resulted in the formation of a diasporic consciousness by the Turkish labour migrants. Prior to describing the formation of diasporic consciousness, it discusses ethnic-based strategies of political participation developed by the Turkish migrants in Germany since the beginning of the migratory process in 1961. In drawing up the main framework of *migrant strategy* and *minority strategy*, I also outline the migratory process and the incorporation regimes in the Federal Republic of Germany, leading to the 'ethnic minorisation' of the labour migrants.

Chapter 3 begins with delineating the importance of Kreuzberg for migrants, refugees and asylum-seekers, and demonstrates how Turkish migrants and their descendants in Kreuzberg 36 have created a modern diasporic space, or what they call *'Kleines Istanbul'* (Little Istanbul). Thus, it portrays the images, symbols, sounds, views and traditions carried by transnational migrants from their homeland to form a diasporic space which provides them with a protective symbolic 'fortress' against institutional discrimination, assimilation and racism. Subsequently, the major constituents of this diasporic space are displayed: the Turkish media and ethnic associations in Berlin. Eventually, this diasporic space and its cultural constituents are evaluated in the broader setting of multicultural Berlin with special reference to the Turkish *Alevi* community. This final section aims to raise the question of ideology of multiculturalism and its discontents for the Turkish diasporic communities.

Chapter 4 examines the process of 'homing of diaspora' by the working-class Turkish male youths in Kreuzberg that experience a socioeconomic and political marginality. Being subject to structural outsiderism, working-class Turkish diasporic youth develops a 'demotic' discourse and a language of fatalism against exclusion and discrimination. This chapter also delineates the principal life-worlds of the working-class diasporic Turkish youth: youth centre, street, school and household. The male peer groups construct their identities in negotiation between these distinct worlds. To understand the working-class Turkish diasporic youth, this chapter also explores a relevant side of the identity formation processes among the middle-class diasporic Turkish youth.

Chapter 5 investigates the major constituents of 'third culture' and/or cultural syncreticism developed by the working-class Turkish hip-hop youth in Kreuzberg. Their cultural syncreticism becomes apparent in their leisure culture, which is characterised by both particularistic and universalistic constituents. The particularist components of their leisure culture are *'âlem'* (meeting with friends), *düğüns* (wedding ceremony) and *arabesk* music, while the universalist ones are rap, graffiti, dance and 'cool' style. Defining the main framework of the cultural identity formation processes and of leisure culture of these hip-hop youngsters, this chapter underlines the multicultural competence of ethnic minority youths.

Chapter 6 calls attention to the issues of cultural syncreticism, 'double diasporic consciousness' and transculturation. It explores the discourses and social identities of the Berlin-Turkish rappers whom I consider *contemporary minstrels*, 'organic intellectuals' and 'storytellers' of their own communities. What they call 'Oriental' hip-hop provides these youngsters with a ground where they can express their imagaginary nostalgia towards 'home' and 'already discovered country of the past' as well as to manifest their attachment to the 'undiscovered country of the future.' In other words, 'Oriental' hip-hop as an expressive cultural form represents the symbolic dialogue undertaken by the diasporic youths between 'past' and 'present,' between 'tradition' and 'translation,' between 'there' and 'here,' and between the local and global.

Finally, I conclude that a diaspora can be created through cultural artefacts and a shared imagery that symbolically connect the new country of settlement to homeland. These symbolic links between the diaspora and homeland can only be produced through modern means of communication and transportation. I am aware that in rapidly changing world all generations are transitional, but I am convinced nonetheless that Turkish hip-hop youngsters in Berlin have constructed something unique – a 'third culture,' which transcends conventional binary understandings of cultural interaction.

Notes

1 Orientation (1997). *Bosporus Bridge*. Berlin: GGM Orient Express. The project of 'Orientation' run by the Oriental Express, is a mix of 'oriental hip-hop' and 'arabesk soul.' It aims to introduce an amalgamation of various musical forms to the Berlin audience. Meryl Prettyman made the translation of this song. I made the English translations of all the other Turkish rap songs in this book.

2 The number 36 refers to one of the pre-reunification postal area codes of the Kreuzberg district which is densely populated by Turkish migrants. Kreuzberg 36 comprises the three *U-Bahn* stations Kotbusser Tor, Görlitzer Bahnhof and Schlesisches Tor. Kreuzberg 36 can be defined as a Turkish ethnic 'enclave,' not a 'ghetto.' Peter Marcuse (1996) describes enclaves as 'those areas in

which immigrants have congregated and which are seen as having positive value, as opposed to the word 'ghetto,' which has a clearly pejorative connotation.' In this sense, enclaves refer to symbolic walls of protection, cohesion and solidarity for immigrants and ethnic minorities. Kreuzberg as an ethnic enclave is rather different from those black and Hispanic ghetto examples in the United States, where the poor, the unemployed, the excluded and the homeless are most frequently concentrated.

3   *Chip* was temporarily closed in June 1997 due to some violence among the youths.

4   Berlin Türk Bilim ve Teknoloji Merkezi (BTBTM) was founded in 1977 by a group of Turkish university students in order to provide technology transfer to Turkey from Germany. Although it was established in the very beginning as an initiative aiming to contribute to the technological development of Turkey, it has recently become a social democratic student initiative dealing with the problems of the second and third generation Turkish students. It has become more oriented to the Turks living in Berlin rather than to Turkey. Since 1992 they have conducted a project in Berlin, called *'Project Zweite Generation'* (Second Generation Project). Through this project they aim to assist Turkish students with their problems whilst studying in the high schools in Berlin.

Chapter 1

The Notions of Culture, Youth Culture, Ethnicity, and Globalisation

As the main theme of this work is to explore the construction and articulation processes of the diasporic cultural identity among the working-class Berlin-Turkish hip-hop youths, the concepts of culture, minority youth culture, ethnicity, globalisation and diaspora must also be examined. Accordingly, this chapter aims to redefine the concepts of culture and minority youth culture by departing from the conventional definition of culture in order to provide a theoretical ground for understanding diasporic youth culture. Raymond Williams (1983: 90) has defined culture in three different ways that are in fact complementary to each other. Firstly, culture could be used to refer to 'a general process of intellectual, spiritual and aesthetic development' (anthropological definition). Secondly, culture might be used to suggest 'a particular way of life, whether of a people, a period, or a group' (sociological definition). Finally, culture could refer to 'the works and practices of intellectual and especially artistic activity' (humanistic definition). While culture was previously defined as the received high culture of various literary and philosophical canons, now it is characterised in a broader sense as any expressive activity contributing to social learning.

The expansion of the notion of culture affects the way in which popular culture is now conceptualised as a broad ensemble of everyday discursive practices that may fall outside the traditional parameters of official high culture. Over the past three decades the dominance of high culture over popular culture has depreciated. Popular culture is articulated as a structured terrain of cultural exchange and negotiation between forces of incorporation and resistance: a struggle between the attempt to universalise the interests of the dominant against the resistance of the subordinate (Storey, 1993). The upsurge of popular culture in alliance with global culture crosscuts with the rapid industrialisation, urbanisation, domestic/international migration and social mobilisation since the 1960s, when the periphery started to infiltrate the centre. Popular culture has mainly been formed in urban spaces in which many kinds of cultures and life forms have to intermingle. It is also evident that much of the impetus behind the expansion of the notion of culture springs from the sweeping transformations in information technology after World War Two – a point to which I shall return shortly.

The study of youth cultures has recently gained a remarkable space within the field of popular culture. The expansion of the ideology of consumerism, leisure industry, post-Fordist economic production, the extension of the adolescence period through raising of the school leaving age, and the globalisation of Western urban culture turned the concept of youth to be one of the significant fields of study in social sciences. Topics that receive scholarly attention include definitions of style, musical tastes, unemployment, delinquency, sexuality, resistance, difference and ethnicity. Beginning with the Chicago School of sociology and continuing throughout the 1960s, interest on youth began to emerge. In the 1970s, the Centre for Contemporary Cultural Studies (CCCS) became the site of a great deal of research on youth 'subcultures.' These studies examined working-class youth subcultures as social groups through analyses of class structures (Cohen, 1972; Hall and Jefferson, 1976). While these works were highly influential in determining how youths were to be conceptualised, it remained at the level of the examination of facets of youth cultures as expressions of class conflict or the position of youth in future adult roles. Furthermore, these studies also helped to reinforce the view of youth as primarily passive.

In this context, particular cultural forms have been produced and articulated by minority youths, a group that emerged after the settlement of migrant labour in the 1970s in the continental Europe.[1] The cultural forms produced by minority youths provide a number of facilitating conditions for the creation of new ethnic cultures and identities, which celebrate specificity, difference and distinction (Hannerz, 1989; Appadurai, 1990). More recent studies on the minority youth cultures involve notions such as globalisation, diaspora, *'youthnicity,'* multiculturalism, cultural agency, leisure, transnationalism, transculturation, bricolage, syncreticism, *différance*, racism, exclusion and hegemony (cf. inter alia Gilroy, 1993; Keith, 1995; Amit-Talai and Wulff, 1995; Wilpert, 1989; Liebkind, 1989; Pamgren et al., 1992, Ålund, 1996; Ålund-Schierup, 1991; Schwartz, 1992; Mandel, 1990; Vertovec, 1996a, 1995). The primary difference of these works from those of the Chicago School and of the CCCS is that youths are not considered victims of technology and consumerism, or passive receptors of parental culture, but active agents who are capable of producing, reproducing and articulating their cultures. Much of my work shall follow the recent approach to portray the expressive cultures of the Berlin-Turkish hip-hop youth. Yet, some aspects of the CCCS scholars will necessarily be taken into consideration in the course of analysis.

Contemporary scholarly works on minority youth cultures also refer to the notion of modern diaspora in order to describe the complexities of simultaneous processes of cultural localisation and transculturation by the respective youths. The diaspora idea invites us to explore expressive minority youth cultures in relation to their 'roots' and 'routes' without essentialising them (Gilroy, 1987, 1993, 1994, 1995; Clifford, 1992, 1994; Hall, 1994). Diaspora studies, as I will demonstrate, provide us with a convenient framework to display cultures of bricolage, which exist in mixing rather than in static ethnic lines. In what follows, I will elaborate various notions of culture in relation to the literature on Turks in Germany. Thereafter, the literature of the earlier schools working on youth cultures will be briefly reviewed. Consequently, I will locate the minority hip-hop youth culture in the framework of modern diaspora studies.

Notions of Culture

There are two principal notions of culture that I will briefly summarise in this section. The first one is *the holistic notion of culture*, and the second is *the syncretic notion of culture*. The former considers culture a highly integrated and grasped static 'whole.' This is the dominant paradigm of the classical modernity, of which territoriality and totality were the main characteristics. The latter notion is the one, which is most obviously affected by increasing interconnectedness in space. This syncretic notion of culture has been proposed by the contemporary scholars to demonstrate the fact that cultures emerge in mixing beyond the political and geographical territories.

The term culture came to the fore in Europe during the construction of cultural nationalist identities. As the main constituent of the age of nationalism was territoriality, culture was defined as the cumulative of 'shared meanings and values,' which manifested itself in that particular territory throughout history. This is the holistic notion of culture that has provided the basic for the emergence of the myth of distinct national cultures. To quote Eric Wolf,

The demonstration that each struggling nation possessed a distinctive society, animated by its special spirit or culture, served to legitimate its aspirations to form a separate state of its own. The notion of separate and integral cultures responded to this political project. Once we locate the reality of society in historically changing, imperfectly bounded, multiple and branching social alignments, however, the concept of a boxed, unitary and bounded culture must give way to a sense of the fluidity and permeability of cultural sets. In the rough and tumble of social interaction, groups are known to exploit the ambiguities of inherited forms, to impart new evaluations or valences to them, to borrow forms more expressive of their interests, or to create wholly new forms in answer to changed circumstances (1982: 387).

The idea that cultures exist as separate and integral entities clearly supported the project of defining the 'imagined communities' (Anderson, 1983) of nations struggling for independence or dominance. The holistic notion of culture resembles the usage of the German Romantics, as in '*Volk* culture' imprisoning cultures within distinct social compartments containing separate sets of 'shared meanings and values.' This understanding attributes a time, context, territoriality, space, unity and memory to culture. According to this approach, modernity, which appears in the form of electronic communications, transportation, deterritorialisation and cultural imperialism, has disrupted the 'unity and authenticity of culture' (Smith, 1990, 1995; Bell, 1978).

The main claim of the holistic approach is that 'shared meanings and values' are the principal constituents of each distinct culture. The focus on 'shared meanings and values' may sometimes make culture sound too unitary, homogeneous, holistic and too cognitive. The disturbance of this unity and holism is considered to result in crisis, breakdown or degeneration. The themes of 'identity crisis,' 'in-betweenness,' 'split identities' and 'degeneration' raised by some scholars in the study of ethnic minorities – a point to which I shall return in the next chapter – is the product of such an assumption. This assumption claims that culture emerges in discrete ethnic lines, and holds no place for syncreticism and bricolage. Syncreticism could merely be considered, in this approach, nothing but an impurity polluting the 'authentic culture.'

Although some researchers working on Turkish migrants' culture in Germany note emergent syncreticisms, they dislike these 'cultural impurities,' to use James Clifford's term (1988). The common trend amongst these scholars in the context of Turkish migrants in Germany is either to label the cultures of bricolage as 'degenerate' (Abadan-Unat, 1976, 1985; Kagitçibasi, 1987), or to diagnose the situation as 'fragmented cultural world leading to a crisis of identity' (Mushaben, 1985). These scholars regard the Turkish migrants as the victims of transnational capitalist process. This is why those 'victims' have been considered to be incapable of coping with the new circumstances and obstacles emerging in the diaspora. This approach negates the subject-centered analysis. Ironically, this notion of culture also provides the ground for the formation of multiculturalist polities. Multiculturalism, as I shall explore in the coming chapters, assumes that cultures are internally consistent, unified and structured wholes belonging to ethnic groups.

Most of the studies on Turks and Turkish culture in Germany are based on a notion linking ethnicity and culture. This approach mainly rests on the assumption that Turkish migrants carry their own distinct cultural baggages all the way along from home to the country of settlement. Underestimating the situational and instrumental nature of ethnicity, these scholars went back to the place of origin of migrants to find out the main parameters of their social, cultural and ethnic identifications. These analysts took the 'traditional culture' of Turkey as their basis to ascertain the migrants' social and cultural identities in their new social milieu. The emphasis is usually placed on the norms, values and codes that predominate in rural areas of Turkey. Islam, on the other hand, comes to the fore in these studies as the core of this 'traditional culture.' Moreover, this group of scholars approaches the issue through the lens of an 'identity' framework in which identity is considered stable, fixed, centred and coherent (Abadan-Unat, 1976, 1985; Kagitçibasi, 1987; Mushaben, 1985).

On the other hand, *the syncretic notion of culture* claims that mixing and bricolage are the main characteristics of cultures. In this approach, culture does not develop along ethnically absolute lines but in complex, dynamic patterns of syncreticism (Gilroy, 1987: 13); and cultural identity is considered a matter of 'becoming' as well as 'being' (Hall, 1989, 1994). It seems more appropriate for this perspective to treat migrant cultures as mixing their new set of tools, which they acquire in the migration experience, with their previous lives and cultural repertoires. The major challenge to the scholars who are bound to the holistic notion of culture comes from those who reject the idea of viewing ethnic groups as pre-given social units.

The problematisation of ethnicity and culture of Turkish migrants in an anti-essentialist perspective is relatively new. The *Berliner Institut für Vergleichende Sozialforschung* (BIVS) focuses on the ethnic group formation processes and shifting boundaries between ethnic groups (Blaschke, 1983; Schwartz, 1992). Ruth Mandel (1989, 1990, 1996) emphasises the construction of new ethnicities amongst the Turkish diaspora, and sheds light on the formation of what Avtar Brah (1996) calls 'diasporic space' (*gurbet*). She considers this space heterogeneous, whether articulated as *gurbet* or as a potential *Dar al-Islam* (Land of Islam). Similarly, Thomas Faist (1991, 1995, 2000b) is concerned with the exclusion of Turkish youth from the labour market and schooling. Herman Tertilt (1996) did a research on the life-worlds of a Turkish gangsta group located in Frankfurt. Bridging the theories of sociology and ethnology, and referring to the 'subculture' notion of the Chicago School of Urban Sociology, Tertilt tries to portray the individual members of the gang, *Turkish Power Boys*, and the significance of parental culture, migration, peer groups, masculinity, drug and violence in their expressive culture.[2]

There are some Turkish scholars and intellectuals who also start off from the syncretic notion of culture in their interpretation of the cultural formation processes of the Turkish migrants and their descendants. Ayse Çaglar (1994, 1990 and 1998) prefers exploring the cultures and life-worlds of the first generation Turkish migrants in the context of their own social spaces rather than within a framework encapsulated in a reified ethnicity and/or an immutable 'Turkish culture.' She denies the conventional holistic notion of culture and considers the cultural practices of German Turks like any other 'culture' in today's world:

The product of several interlocking histories and cultural traditions mediated and transplanted by the media and the host society. The traces of different cultural traditions and languages are visible in these new forms, created by the fusion of these distinct traditions, but the emergent forms are reducible to none of them. Hence, they can neither be explained in relation to a fixed, unitary, and bounded traditional Turkish culture, or within an acculturation framework. In fact, migration is one of those processes that aggravate the flow of images and cultural forms bringing about results in surprising combinations and crossovers of codes and discourses. The emergent cultural forms and practices of German Turks need to be understood first as products of such processes (Çaglar, 1994: 7).

Likewise, Gündüz Vassaf (1982) refuses some conceptualisations, which are attributed to the children of Turkish migrants in Europe especially by the Turkish 'experts' – concepts like 'in-betweenness,' 'lost generation' and 'split identities.' Rejecting the treatment of migrants' children as problematic, he rightly claims that those children have developed their own cultural space. "This is the new cultural space," says Vassaf "which has been recently built up in the West by all the constituent ethnics of Europe such as Austrians, Algerians, Turks, Germans, Surinamese, Norwegians, Moroccans, Swedes" (1982: 155).

In the same manner, Feridun Zaimoglu (1995 and 1998) who is a German-Turk, attempts to conceptualise the way the German-Turkish youth speaks. He calls this newly emerging language *Kanak-Sprak* (*kanake* language), which forms a 'creole art.' Giving examples of this language, Zaimoglu demonstrates the main characteristics of this language: sentences without comma, full stop, capital letter, or any kind of punctuation, with frequent switches between Turkish and German – a point which I will touch upon later. All these scholars, whose notion of culture springs from the principle of syncreticism, call attention to the creative and hybrid aspects of migrants' practices rather than seeing them as symptoms of a long list of problems and crises. The consideration of diasporic cultures in the framework of syncreticism is linked to the process of globalisation leading to cultural heterogeneity and bricolage. In what follows, I will demonstrate the link between globalism, syncreticism and identity.

Chapter 1

Globalism and Syncreticism

Modernity has resulted in 'cultural flows in space' loosening up of social and cultural boundaries, migration, expansion of global culture, cultural melting-pots known as 'global cities,' cultural variety, transculturation, transnationalism, syncreticism and new social movements (Berman, 1983; Hannerz 1992, 1996; Melucci, 1989; Ålund-Schierup, 1991). All these features and aspects of late-modernity are known as constituents of the age of globalism. Many scholars in various social, political and economic fields (cf. inter alia, Robertson, Giddens, Hall, Appadurai, Hannerz, Brecher et al., Sklair and Robin Cohen) have raised globalism as one of the primary conditions of modernity.[3] In this book, I shall limit my focus to the social impacts of globalisation and with what Brecher et al. (1993) have called 'globalisation from below.' In this sense, globalism indicates, as Roland Robertson (1992: 8) has posited, 'the compression of the world and the intensification of the consciousness of the world as a whole' by means of communications and transportation. What comes out of the compression process of the world as a whole is a global culture, which is unlike conventional culture, i.e., timeless, memoryless, contextless and translocal. As Arjun Appadurai posits that the global culture consists of five significant flows moving in non-isomorphic paths:

Ethnoscapes produced by flows of people: tourists, immigrants, refugees, exiles and guest workers. Secondly, there are *technoscapes*, the machinery and plant flows produced by multinational and national corporations and government agencies. Thirdly, there are *finanscapes*, produced by the rapid flows of money in the currency markets and stock exchanges. Fourthly, there are *mediascapes*, the repertoire of images of information, the flows, which are produced and distributed by newspapers, magazines, television and film. Fifthly, there are *ideoscapes*, linked to flows of images, which are associated with state or counter-state movement ideologies, which are comprised of elements of freedom, welfare, rights, etc. (1990: 6-7, as paraphrased by Featherstone, Introduction).

With reference to the global cultural flows displayed by Appadurai, an interest in 'diaspora' has been equated with anthropology's now commonplace anti-essentialist and constructivist approach to ethnicity (Hall, 1994; Clifford, 1994; Hannerz, 1996; Vertovec, 1996b). In this approach, the fluidity of constructed styles and identities amongst generic diasporic communities is particularly emphasised. These contemporary studies partly focus on the construction of diasporic youth cultures that emerge in the crossing of local-global and past-present. These cultural forms are sometimes called syncretic, creolized, translated, crossover, cut 'n' mix, hybrid or alternate (Vertovec, 1996b: 28). In this work, I will interchangeably refer to the notions of 'bricolage,' 'hybridity' and 'creolization' in order to demonstrate transnational and transcultural formation and articulation of culture in Turkish diaspora. I shall briefly clarify these terms.

Hybridity – etymologically linked to animal husbandry and crop management – may presuppose the 'pure' origin of elements prior to their hybridisation. As one of the definitions found in *Oxford's English Dictionary* clarifies, a hybrid is 'an animal or plant that is the offspring of individuals of different kinds.' On the other hand, the etymology of bricolage points to the construction or creation from whatever is immediately available for use, as exemplified in *The Savage Mind* by Levi-Strauss (1966: 17) to define 'bricoleur':

> The bricoleur is adept at performing a large number of diverse tasks; but, unlike the engineer, he does not subordinate each of them to the availability of raw materials and tools conceived and procured for the purpose of the project. His universe of instruments is closed and the rules of his game are always to make do with 'whatever is at hand,' that is to say with a set of tools and materials, which is always finite and is also heterogeneous because what it contains bears no relation to the current project, but is the contingent result of all the occasions there have been to renew or enrich the stock or to maintain it with the remains of previous constructions or deconstructions.

The process of bricolage involves a 'science of the concrete' as opposed to our 'civilised' science of the 'abstract' because the 'bricoleur' attaches more importance to the 'things' rather than to the 'thoughts.' Unlike hybridity, bricolage foregrounds political – rather than natural – paradigm of articulation and identity. To put it differently, the notion of bricolage, unlike hybridity, presumes the individual as a social agent who is capable of making decisions. As far as Turkish hip-hop youths in Kreuzberg are concerned, the act of bricolage as a conscious action of diasporic subject will be readdressed in terms of lingual code-switching, graffiti painting/writing and daily life-worlds in the following chapters.

In the same way, creolization takes place in the process of interchange between the cultural centre and periphery (Hannerz, 1989, 1996). Ulf Hannerz uses the term, creolization, to refer to the process of globalisation, which is what Roland Robertson (1992: 6) calls 'the compression of the world into a single place.' To paraphrase Hannerz (1996: 12), 'The third world is in the First World, and the First World in the Third; the North is in the South, and the South is in the North; the centre is in the periphery, and the periphery is in the centre.' Speaking on such a conceptual basis, Hannerz (1996: 153-154) introduces another concept to demonstrate the two-way character of creolization in the European context: 'double creolizing.' Berlin, for instance, is subject to two quite separate forms of creolization processes. On the one hand, there is the creolization of German national culture in the form of what Hannerz calls 'Americanization;' on the other, there is that multifaceted creolization process, which involves the greater majority of immigrants, coming in as labour migrants and refugees, and mostly having to adopt to German circumstances.

Creolization was once something that happened to the colonial others of the world, and now, it happens to a larger world population by means of global telecommunications systems and global market forces (Friedman, 1994: 208).

Although the process of creolization in the age of colonialism was based on the introduction of 'high cultures' and 'civilisation' to the 'uncultured' and 'uncivilised' lands, the new form of creolization is different from the previous one in the sense that it introduces what Clifford calls 'post-culture.' Clifford (1988: 95) proposes the notion of 'post-culture' in his apprehension of a postmodern condition:

In a world with many voices speaking all at once [...] where American clothes made in Korea are worn by young people in Russia, where everyone's 'roots' are in some degree cut [...] I evoke this syncretic, 'postcultural' situation only to gesture toward the standpoint (though not so easily spatialised), the condition of uncertainty from which I am writing.

It is evident that globalism and localism are two simultaneous phenomena of the late modern times. On the one hand, globalisation of the world in the form of the dominance of global mass media, mass education, monetary economies, identical clothes, household goods, ideas, fantasies, books, music and communication networks spreads all our identities all over the map (Berman, 1983: 35), and brings about deterritorialisation.[4] On the other hand, localisation, in the form of desperate allegiances to ethnic, national, cultural, religious, class and sexual groups, is thought to give us a kind of 'firm' identity (Berman, 1983: 35). The simultaneous intensive flows of global and local dynamics seem to have an essential influence on the construction of new identities and cultural forms. Henceforth, the link between globalisation and new identities will be expounded upon.

Glocalised Identities

The relationship between 'local' and 'global' has become increasingly salient in a wide variety of intellectual and practical contexts. The compression of time and space in the age of globalism has led to the formation of new identities. These identities have been grounded on the paramount antithetical forces of 'local' and 'global,' or on what Featherstone (1990) calls *'glocal'* (*glo*bal and lo*cal*). It is evident that the increase in knowledge and interaction between the social and individual agents through the modern means of communication and transportation have awakened individuals, minorities and nations to differences, and repositioned them in a new social setting. As Hall (1991a: 21) rightly emphasises, "when you know what everybody else is, then you are what they are not." In other words, intense contact with new social and political environments, confrontation with personalities of various ethnic and national backgrounds in the age of global capitalism, rapid industrialisation and urbanisation deepen local and particularistic responses as well as giving the individual, groups or nations a global perspective. Accordingly, this 'glocal' condition creates new perceptions of identity, and changes the world of meanings and symbols of the respective units (Featherstone, 1990: 14).

Before describing the particular aspects of this 'glocal' condition, let me briefly outline the principal dynamics of the question of identity and ethnicity. Our identity, be it individual, political, communal, ethnic or national, is shaped by *recognition*, non-*recognition* or mis-*recognition* of the 'others' (Taylor, 1994: 25). The genesis of the human mind develops in a dialogical sense, not in a monological sense. We can construct our identities only if we are able to experience others' reactions to our attitudes and behaviour. Unless we are defined by others, we cannot represent ourselves. Thus, it is impossible to build an identity without a dialogue with the 'other.' Here, 'the other,' as Baudrillard (1973: 174) states, is what allows us not to repeat ourselves forever.

Considering the perpetual encounters with the constitutive 'others,' identities, as Stuart Hall (1991b: 47) stated, "are never completed, never finished; they are always in process of formation." If we go further, we can argue that the condition of existence of every identity is the affirmation of a difference, the determination of an 'other' that is going to play the role of a 'constitutive outside.' Likewise, the construction of ethnic identity follows a similar path. Fredrik Barth (1969, 1994) has convincingly articulated the notion of ethnicity as mutable, arguing that ethnicity is the product of social ascriptions, a kind of labelling process engaged in by oneself and others. In the Barthian approach, ethnic identity is regarded as a feature of social organisation, rather than a nebulous expression of culture. Thus, one's ethnic identity is a composite of the view one has of oneself as well as the views held by others about one's ethnic identity. To put it differently, ethnic identity is the product of a dialogical and dialectical process involving internal and external opinions and processes, as well as the individual's self-identification and outsiders' ethnic designations – i.e. what *you* think your ethnicity is, versus what *they* think your ethnicity is (Nagel, 1994: 154). Ethnic boundaries, and thus identities, are explicitly socially constructed in relation to the 'Other.'

The advent of global capitalism, transnationalism and urbanisation has brought about a radical demographic change all over the world. Such an intensive demographic change that has accelerated after the World War II has, in fact, led to a kind of reverse invasion of the colonial-capitalist centre by its periphery. As Kevin Robins (1991: 25) put it "the periphery infiltrated the colonial core" in terms of culture, religion, language and ethnicity:

> [...] In a process of unequal cultural encounter, 'foreign' populations have been compelled to be the subjects and subalterns of Western Empire, while no less significantly, the west has come face to face with the 'alien' and 'exotic' culture of its 'Other.' Globalization, as it dissolves the barriers of distance, makes the encounter of colonial center and colonised periphery immediate and intense.

Since no group can now claim explicit superiority, each group can emphasise its own language, religion, and culture (ibid.: 170). Accordingly, ethnicity could openly and proudly be represented, vocalised and politicised. In this sense, the subjects of the age of globalism – in this case transnational communities – have constructed 'new ethnicities' as their new social identities. These new ethnicised social identities have become the principal characteristic of the modern 'glocal' condition. This 'glocal' condition, as Alexandra Ålund (1995) accurately has stated, is characterised by a parallelism between centrifugal and centripetal forces where processes of transnational compression are accompanied by processes of fragmentation.

The coexistence of the global and local in the form of 'glocal' results in the devaluation of authenticity, thus in the acceleration of the processes of cultural bricolage. This century has been mainly characterised by a drastic expansion of mobility, including tourism, migrant labour, immigration, modern diasporas, and urban sprawl. The cities all over the world have become stages on which heterogeneous populations interact with each other (Clifford, 1988: 13-14). Thus, the cultural authenticity partly ends in the urban world where different cultural baggages intermingle and become subject to bricolage. People belonging to such cultures of bricolage have had to 'translate' themselves to the newly emerging urban-global culture, and have had to live with more than one identity (Hall, 1993: 310).[5] Asad is an eloquent exponent of this state of cultural bricolage, or of what he calls *mélange*:

> In the vision of a fractured, fluid world, all human beings live in the same cultural predicament […]. Everyone is *dis*located; no one is rooted. Because there is no such thing as authenticity, borrowing and copying do not signify a lack (Asad, 1993: 9-10).

In a sense, authenticity is replaced with cultural bricolage in the era of late-modernity because the growing trend of 'global homogenisation' no longer allows national-cultural islands to exist. Thus, 'glocalised' identities are brought into open by the concomitant dynamics of local/global, traditional/translational and past/future.

Ethnic minority youth cultures are also subject to these processes of globalism and localism. In what follows, I will summarise the previous schools working on the youth cultures under the designation of 'subcultural theory' in order to see the differences of the contemporary minority youth cultures from the earlier ones. Thereafter, contemporary hip-hop youth culture will be briefly outlined to display the insufficiency of the subcultural theory in investigating the global-local youth cultures, and to expose the impact of global streams on local cultural forms.

Subcultural Theory

The concept of 'subculture' often refers to separateness by highlighting cultural contrast in terms of cultural clashes. The notion of 'subculture' was traditionally used as a convenient label to define some groups of people, who had something in common with each other and had a different way of life from the members of other social groups. The concept has its origins in research on American society. In the late 1940s, it came to be linked to the sociology of deviance. Studies of subculture, as I shall briefly touch upon in a while, pictured common people not only as highly differentiated, but as active and creative. Subcultures have usually been considered to be opposed to both the 'public' and the 'masses.' While the 'public' has been conceived as a body of rational individuals, responsible citizens who are able to form their own opinion and express it through officially recognised democratic channels, the 'mass' has often been portrayed as undifferentiated, irrational and politically manipulated.

The Chicago School of sociology, in which the tradition of subcultural studies has its roots, was interested in exploring the diversity of human behaviour in the American city. The notion of a mass society, on the other hand, was developed by critical theorists working in an entirely different scholarly tradition at the Frankfurt School (which was relocated at Columbia University in New York during the Second World War). These two academic legacies are to some extent fused in the subcultural studies in the Birmingham tradition of the 1970s, which focused on the relations between subcultures and media, commerce and mass culture.

The Chicago School of sociology concentrated on the investigation of human behaviour in an urban environment. Robert E. Park et al. (1925) portrayed the changing face of the modern city in relation to the division of labour, money, transportation, communication and social mobility. The subsequent members of the School dealt with the existing consequences of industrialisation and urbanisation. Cressey (1932) touched upon the social mobility of woman migrants; Milton M. Gordon (1947) studied the children of migrant ethnic groups; and

Howard Becker (1997/1963) worked with the jazz musicians as another form of deviant 'subculture.' During the 1960s the perspective on society's various 'subcultures' began to shift from the negative notion of 'deviation' to the positive notion of 'cultural multitude,' as exhibited by Becker (ibid.) in explaining the cultural productivity of the 'deviant' jazz musicians. Jock Young (1971), influenced by both the Frankfurt School's Marxist visions of a mass society and the Chicago School's liberal-pluralist studies of 'subcultures,' alternately considered 'subcultures' resistant and subordinate, politically hopeful and spectacularly impotent.[6] Young's main contribution to the theory of 'subcultures' was the way he defined 'leisure': leisure is purportedly non-alienated activity, which is undertaken by individual to win personal space. In fact, Jock Young's work acts as a bridge between the distinct theoretical and political agendas of the work associated with the Chicago School and those of the later Birmingham School.

The Centre for Contemporary Cultural Studies at Birmingham University (CCCS) was established in 1964, and profoundly shaped the theories of 'subculture' for the next two decades. Researchers turned their attention precisely to the category of 'youth.' Their analyses were influenced by the work of a number of British Marxist critiques – Raymond Williams, T. H. Thomson and Richard Hoggart, but also by continental theorists such as Louis Althusser, Antonio Gramsci and Roland Barthes. The primary aim of the Birmingham theorists was to locate youth subcultures in relation to three broader cultural structures, the working class or 'parent culture,' 'dominant' culture, and mass culture. Analysts at the CCCS emphasised the expressive culture of youth that is subject to the market forces. Culture of the post war youth was shaped by the affluence of the consumer market, the rise of mass culture, mass communication, telecommunication, education facilities, and the arrival of the whole range of distinctive styles in dress and rock-music (Clarke et al., 1975).

The analysts at the Birmingham School defined 'subcultures' as 'subsets – smaller, mere localised and differentiated structures within one of the larger cultural networks' (Clarke et al., 1975: 13). Subculture is both distinct from, and overlaps with, the culture of which it is a part. The school always dealt with working-class youth 'subcultures;' and their subcultural status was linked to their class subordination. Changes in leisure activities as well as commercialism fostered a 'generational consciousness' for working-class youth in a way that unbalanced their class- and family-based identity. 'Generational consciousness' is likely to be strong among those youngsters who are upwardly and outwardly mobile. It involves that young persons value the 'dominant' culture, and sacrifice the 'parent' culture (Clarke et al., 1975: 51). Working-class youth, having generational consciousness, affirm the 'dominant culture' while protesting it. In this sense, the theorists sharply differentiate working-class youth cultures from middle-class ones. Middle-class cultures – such as the hippie movement, student protests and drop-out 'subcultures' – attempt to transform the dominant culture as in new patterns of living, of family life, or work, because they spring from the social space of the dominant culture, which shapes the structure. The working-class youth cultures, on the other hand, affirm the dominant culture while they criticise the 'parent' culture from which they originate.

The key aspect of the agenda for the CCCS was a kind of symptom of class-in-decline. The main hypothesis was: when working-class communities have been undergoing change and displacement, and when the 'parent' culture is no longer cohesive, working-class youth responds by becoming 'subcultural.' Phil Cohen (1972) claimed that youth attempts to replace a lost sense of working-class 'community' with subcultural 'territory' – a shift which is symptomatic of the relocation of youthful expression to the field of leisure rather than work. In his work, where he explained the post war British youth living in the East End of London, Cohen (1972: 26) defines 'subculture' as:

A compromise solution to two contradictory needs: the need to create and express autonomy and difference from parents and, by extension, their culture and the need to maintain the security of existing ego defences and the parental identifications which support them.

Although they may win space, 'subcultures,' thus, play an essentially conservative role. Their conservative role is furthermore strengthened because they fail to bring about a major structural change and fail to provide the youth with career prospects. Subsequently, John Clarke, Stuart Hall, Tony Jefferson and Brian Roberts, in their theoretical introduction to *Resistance Through Rituals* (1975), carried the notion of 'subcultures' further, acknowledging the increasing role of 'affluence' and leisure in youth activity while insisting on youth's continuing location in class-based categories. To explain this dynamic relation between leisure and class, they returned to Antonio Gramsci, drawing on his notion of hegemony – a term that describes the means by which the ruling classes secure their authority over subordinate classes, not by coercion but by obtaining the latter's consent. This is done through on-going processes of negotiation and regulation between ruling and subaltern classes. The subaltern classes operate by winning space back and issuing challenges. The working-class 'subcultures,' thus, consistently win space from the dominant culture (Clarke et al., 1975: 42). Clarke et al., thus, emphasise 'resistance' more than Cohen, giving subcultures a more creative kind of agency. Yet, these analysts agree with Cohen's narrative of failure in a wider context: working-class youth's 'resistance' is acted out in the 'limited' field of leisure, rather than in the work place.

In contrast to most of the researchers at the CCCS, Angela McRobbie (1991/1978) has offered a very different perspective on youth subcultures, looking at the way subcultural analysis had tended more or less to equate subcultural youth with boys and to ignore the role of girls altogether. Dick Hebdige, on the other hand, reshaped the main focus of the school. His spectacular work, *Subculture: The Meaning of Style* (1979) offers a genealogy that is less bound up with class than the other researchers at the CCCS. Indeed, in his book priority is given to ethnicity rather than class. Subcultural style is always culturally syncretic – for instance *Ska* borrows from both reggae and the Caribbean traditions. To explain this syncretic process, he borrowed Claude Levi-Strauss' concept of *bricolage* – a term that I shall also very often cite in my work. Hebdige saw punks as *bricoleurs par excellence*, using dislocation as a form of 'refusal.'

The legacy of the CCCS was also seen in the subsequent works of Stuart Hall (1988, 1991, 1992, 1997) and Paul Gilroy (1987, 1993, and 1995). My theoretical framework is partly indebted to the works of both the Chicago and Birmingham theorists. Yet, in my work I seek to go beyond the approach of subcultural theory. As Chris Waters (1981) argued, subcultural theory seems to reify separate homogenous and oppositional cultural groups and regards 'cultures' as static entities. As pointed out before, from my point of view there are no static entities called 'cultures,' there are, instead, 'constitutive social processes, creating specific and distinctive ways of life' (Williams, 1977: 19). Furthermore, subcultural theory does not seem to be applicable for the study of contemporary minority youth cultures, which are, to a high degree, subject to transnational streams. Minority youth cultures such as hip-hop are based on a bricolage of styles, discourses, signs, symbols, meanings and myths that travel throughout the world. They emerge in a time of impurity and blending. The term subculture is insufficient to explore cultural forms of minority youth, whose identity formation processes are subject to a more complex set of dynamics rather than that of majority youth. Subsequently, I will explore the major landmarks of the formation of one of the minority youth cultures, i.e., hip-hop. Hip-Hop youth culture will be scrutinised in line with its origins and its impact on a remarkable number of working-class Berlin-Turkish youths that have been practising structural outsiderism.

Outsiderism: Ethnic Minority Hip-Hop Youth Culture

Today, youngsters live in a time of crisis, a time of exceptional damage and danger. Since the 1970s, deindustrialisation, post-Fordism, consumerism, economic restructuring and resurgence of racism and xenophobia have created fundamentally new realities for young people. Our discussions of minority youth cultures are incomplete if we fail to locate them within the racialised and ethnicisized social crisis of our time; but our understanding of that crisis is also incomplete if we cannot distance ourselves from the nostalgia of 1960s and if we fail to understand what young people are trying to express through their dance, dress, speech and visual imagery (Lipsitz, 1994: 18).

Unwanted as workers, underfunded as students, undermined as citizens, and wanted only by the police and the courts, minority youth recently seem to be subject to a state of structural outsiderism. Structural outsiderism can create minority youth cultures that offer the youngsters an identity and a sense of belonging in a harsh world. Modern cities tend to be fragmented into patchwork diasporic homelands such as Kreuzberg, Southall and Rinkeby. Despite the cultural stigma surrounding them, such minority youth cultures and diasporic homelands offer intimacy and security. It is the feeling of being subordinate outsiders that creates toughness, gangs and rap groups within ethnic minority youth as a form of reaction. Protest and opposition are simultaneously created in these occasions. The formation of gangs, rap groups, conflict, symbolic disputes and violence reflects the new poverty, civil insecurity and homelessness in society. The cultural markers of protest and opposition are frequently cosmopolitan in nature. Global hip-hop youth culture, which is inspired by the Bronx, Harlem and the NBA (National Basketball League), is an instance of such cosmopolitan minority youth cultures. Hip-Hop trousers, Rasta hair, new linguistic expressions with a strong black-American accent, and a permanent 'cool' posture "are scattered around the symbolically loaded 'dramaturgy' to provide roots but also to build barriers" against the life-worlds of dominant ethnic majority and migrant parents (Ålund, 1996: 27). These cultural markers serve to unite divided young people in one life style that symbolises protest and counter-culture. They attempt to create space for themselves by their peculiar music sound, noisy cars, expanding graffiti boundaries, rebellious dressing style, and symbols. All these cultural markers urge the youngsters to form an alternative family network in the street and youth centres. These relations formed in opposition to the outside world give potency to the youths to form a peculiar diasporic cultural identity on the parameters of 'authenticity,' transculturalism and transnationalism.

In Berlin, as in many other big cities of Western Europe, new cultures transcending frontiers, cultural amalgamations and transethnic urban social movements have taken successive forms. Kreuzberg is illustrative in this sense. Young people, in general, are socially conscious and critical of the increasing discrimination, segregation, exclusion and racism in society. Consciousness of a shared position of subordination in society is expressed via the words of rap music, graffiti on the city walls, paintings and drawings in a way that branches out into new and growing social movements against racism and enforced ethnic boundaries. These new syncretic forms of expressive minority youth cultures expose a social movement of urban youth that already has a distinct political ideology. Gilroy (1987) defines this movement in the British context as an utopian extension of the boundaries of politics, a powerful cultural formation, and an alternative public sphere which may offer a significant alternative to the misery of hard drugs and the radical powerlessness of inner urban life.

Hip-Hop youth culture, which is an amalgamation of rap, break-dance and graffiti, was first created throughout the 1970s by predominantly black and Latino dancers, musicians and graffiti artists in New York. Rap as a musical form started to appear on recordings from the late 1970s and drew on the Caribbean vocalising associated with Jamaican sound systems, African rhythm and blues and soul styles. These were later connected to fragments of Euro-disco music. Rap was created out of a series of musical exchanges across the Atlantic, forged together with the techniques of scratching and mixing, using turntables, mixers and drum machines. It was formed initially out of specific conditions within the Bronx area of New York City. Following blues, jazz and reggae, the ghetto became central to the emergence of rap. Unlike reggae artists, who were responding to the experience of immigration, rap in the USA was formed out of the experience of urban segregation. Rap, thus, emerges as the cultural form of resistance against social exclusion in the age of deindustrialisation. In other words, rap has become the music of the tense present for those who do not have a past to celebrate or a future to rely on.

Two different rap schools dominate the American rap scene: West Coast and East Coast. The East Coast rap refers to the non-commercial rap made in New York by the emergent artists, many of whom are women, Chicano, Korean and Samoan. The orientation of the lyrics is more significant than the rhythm and melody; and what is crucial is the message and the narrative of the artists. Contrarily, the West Coast rap is more commercial; and rhythm is more important than lyrics. Some scholars, in their exploration of hip-hop youth culture in the USA, neglect the East Coast rap tradition due to the focus on a very partial and commercial L.A. pop-rap scene (Brennan, 1994; Cross, 1993). Afrika Bambaataa, DJ Kool Herc and Grandmaster Flash are some examples of the East Coast rap. Ice-T, Tone Loc, Ice Cube and Easy-E are the examples of the West Coast rap.

New York City is the source of the global hip-hop youth culture. Just before the gangs of the Bronx disintegrated in the summer of 1972, there had been an explosion of writing on the walls of the Bronx. Early pioneers included Taki, Super-Kool and Lee. This was the beginning of the social practice we now know as graffiti. There had always been writing on walls, but the figurative and written type of graffiti of the dispossessed black and Chicano youth created a new form of art in the Bronx. In 1973 Kool Herc began to formulate what later became known as hip-hop by playing James Brown, doing shout-outs from the microphone, and screaming 'Rock the house.' He called his dancers B-boys. These 'break' (B-) dancers battled on the floor to see who could bust the most outrageous moves. They would dance solo or in crews. Breaking advanced very quickly into an astonishing combination of gymnastics, jazz and kung fu moves all held together by a pacing to the beat that marked out the territory of the breaker. Grandmaster Flash and Afrika Bambaataa who were in competition with Kool Herc also made major contributions to the hip-hop culture (Cross, 1993).

In the early 1980s, the intervention of Hollywood transformed the local Black & Hispanic American hip-hop youth culture into a global youth culture. The movies such as *Flashdance, Breakin,' Wild Style* and *Breakin and Entering* brought the new dance to the world. Accordingly, the meaning of the black and Chicano origin hip-hop youth culture was stripped away by means of mass media, modern technology and the entertainment/music industry. Although a great size of world youth population was attracted by this new youth culture, it was the minority youths that were largely fascinated by the message and content of the hip-hop culture. This new cultural form was attractive for the working-class ethnic minority youths that have been subject to structural outsiderism, exclusion, segregation, racism and xenophobia in their countries of settlement, because it was providing them with a great opportunity to articulate their social and cultural identities. Rap turned out to be an efficient informal way of articulation of identity for the ethnic minority youths in an environment where they could not express themselves formally through media.

As an exceptional global youth culture that emerged through contemporary transnational means of communications with a particularist local focus, hip-hop has also introduced an opportunity to the ethnic minority youths in the West to express their ethnicity and 'authentic' (parental) cultures (Ålund and Schierup, 1991; Ålund, 1996; Sansone, 1995). The daily life of the descendants of migrants depends very much on the management of ethnicity. Their ethnicity implies a great deal of self-reliance, skills in the presentation of self in different circumstances and a degree of integration in, and familiarity with, German majority society. In fact, their use of traditions requires both detachments from the parental culture and a particular form of ethnic allegiance. Through the agency of hip-hop and the rap lyrics, Berlin-Turkish youths, for instance, are capable of celebrating their Turkishness and diasporic positionings, as I shall specifically explain in the coming chapters.

Since the rappers are the major producers of the hip-hop culture, they seem to have a great impact on the construction of cultural identity of the minority youths. As 'organic intellectuals' and 'contemporary minstrels' of their own ethnic communities, they can transform 'common-sense' knowledge of oppression into a new critical awareness that is attentive to ethnic, class and sexual contradictions (Decker, 1992: 80; Negus, 1996: 105-113). As I shall later point out in drawing up the framework of the deployment of the parental culture, the Turkish rappers in Berlin also verbalise a 'double diasporic consciousness.' The working-class youth groups I worked with were highly attracted by Turkish *arabesk* music and hip-hop. *Arabesk* is a hybrid form of urban music, which appeared in Turkey in the late sixties as a reflection of their parents' first experience of immigration in the homeland. It narrates and musicalises the troublesome experience of dislocation, dispersion and longing for home. Hip-Hop, contrarily, reflects the experiences of migration and urban segregation in the diaspora. On that account, as arabesk music taste manifesting the continuation of parental culture represents one side of the 'double diasporic consciousness' of these youngsters, hip-hop represents the other side (see Chapter 6).

The study of modern diasporic consciousness has recently become a crucial aspect within the field of cultural and ethnic studies. In this work, I perceive the diaspora communities becoming more active, rational social agents making decisions, developing ethnic strategies and transnational networks to survive and to maximise their gains in their country of settlement. The Turkish diaspora in Western Europe, particularly in Germany, constitutes an illustrative sample in terms of the processes of identity and ethnic strategy formation of the modern diaspora communities. It is evident that the Turkish diaspora in West Europe with its three million members constitutes a transmigratory feature by which immigrants forge and sustain multi-stranded social relations that link together their societies of origin and settlement. The Turkish diaspora can no longer be exclusively defined as the foreign workers who have been driven away from their homeland as a necessity of the global capitalism; rather they should be seen as having become political and social actors in their new countries of residence.

* * *

To recapitulate, this chapter has been primarily concerned with the redefinition of notions of culture and minority youth culture. It was stated that there have been two dominant understandings of culture:

holistic and *syncretic*. While the holistic notion of culture perceives transnational migrants and their descendants as 'victims of displacement,' conversely the syncretic notion sees them as *'bricoleurs'* and active social agents. Subsequently, it was expounded that the study of ethnic minority youth cultures should consist of the analysis of global cultural flows, which shape the identity formation processes of the displaced individuals. Accordingly, the question of identity has been outlined as a matter of politics and process, but not of essence and inheritance.

This chapter has also explored the theories of youth culture and 'subculture,' which were put forward by the Chicago School of sociology and CCCS at Birmingham University. This chapter has claimed that these two schools, which have studied youth cultures through the notions of 'deviation' (by the Chicago theorists), class parameters and generational conflict (by the Birmingham theorists), have serious pitfalls. The theories of 'subcultures' have been found insufficient to study ethnic minority youth cultures. This is why my work attempts to go beyond the limits of these theories, combining the concepts of ethnicity, cultural bricolage, globalism and diasporic consciousness. To do so, Berlin-Turkish hip-hop youth culture will be thoroughly explored in the following chapters.

It is evident that the immigrants and their descendants take actions, make decisions, form political, religious, ethnic organisations, constitute discourses, and develop subjectivities and identities embedded in networks of relationships that connect them simultaneously to both their country of origin and settlement. Accordingly, in the next chapter I shall scrutinise the political participation strategies employed by the Turkish population in Berlin since the beginning of the migratory process in the 1960s. The mapping-out of these strategies will be reflecting on all of the Turkish communities in order to be able to locate the working-class minority youth culture within a broader framework. In this context, I will also suggest the notion of 'diasporic youth' as an alternative term to those problematic conceptualisations on Turkish-origin youth in Germany such as 'immigrant youth' and 'foreign youth.'

CHAPTER 1

Notes

1 This is a process that was undertaken somewhat earlier in the United Kingdom. For further information, see Clarke et al. (1975) and Hebdige (1979).
2 Although Faist (1991) has a Barthian perspective, he paradoxically refers to the 'second generation' Turks as migrants. Similarly, Thomas Tertilt (1996) also has the same tendency to place the children of immigrants in the category of migrants.
3 For a very brief summary of the various theories of globalisation, see Leslie Sklair (1993: 7-10) where he classifies the theories of globalism in three types: (a) world-system-model by Immanuel Wallerstein; (b) globalisation of culture model by *Theory, Culture and Society* group (TCS); and (c) global system model by himself.
4 Deterritorialization is one of the main parameters of the modern world, which implies the transparency of territories for some transnational actors such as modern diasporas, transnational corporations, money, and global communications networks (Appadurai, 1990: 295-310; Friedman, 1994: 210).
5 Although all cultures without any exception are subject to a bricolage quality, the juxtapositions of elements and practices in transnational migrant cultures are more drastic than those in relatively more established cultures.
6 In his work Young (1971: 134) concludes that 'it was not the drug per se, but the reason why the drug was taken determined whether there would be an adverse social reaction to its consumption. The crucial yardstick in this respect is the ethos of productivity [a point which I will return in the coming sections]. If a drug either stepped up work efficiency or aided relaxation after work it was approved of; if it was used for purely hedonistic ends it was condemned.'

Chapter 2

Constructing Modern Diasporas

This chapter sets out to provide us with a theoretical context to understand the way in which the diasporic identity is constructed and articulated by the Berlin-Turkish hip-hop youth. In doing so, my aim is not to reinscribe the ideology of cultural difference by locating the descendants of Turkish migrants as Berlin-Turks in a continuous space between Germany and Turkey. Neither am I attempting to exoticise these youths in their cultural space by pinning their identity on a kind of essence. What I want to do is to demonstrate that the whole question of identity is a matter of politics and process rather than of inheritance. In order to reveal a fuller view of the diasporic consciousness displayed by the working-class Berlin-Turkish hip-hop youth, I shall explore the nature of ethnicity as an expression of collective identity within the Berlin-Turkish population. Therefore, I will firstly examine how the Berlin-Turkish population has historically employed ethnicity as a survival strategy during the process of negotiation with majority society. Secondly, I will scrutinise the notion of diaspora under the guidance of contemporary scholars who offer various interpretations of the concept. Finally, I will contemplate the cultural identity of the Berlin-Turkish youths in the light of, and in relation to, the notion of diaspora.

The Changing Face of Ethnic Group Political Strategies

Contemporary labour-ethnic minorities in Europe can no longer be simply considered temporary migrant communities who live with the 'myth of return' or the passive victims of global capitalism. They have rather become permanent sojourners, active social agents and decision-makers in their destination countries. The strategies and organisations developed by the migrants and their descendants in their countries of settlement may spring from various material and political sources. These sources are namely the racial and exclusionary immigration policies of the country of settlement, the repressive political regime of their country of origin, their homeland's relations with other countries, the changing streams in world politics, inter-diaspora-relations and class interests. These factors, which are strengthened by global interconnectedness, have recently become the main determinants of the politics of identity undertaken by ethnic minorities in the West.

As these factors are applied to the Berlin-Turks, it becomes apparent that both internal and external factors have impelled them to construct some ethnic-based political participation strategies and identities. There is enough evidence that Turkish labour migrants in Europe have developed two various political participation strategies depending on the nature of problems they have encountered in time: a *migrant strategy* and a *minority strategy*. Both strategies have been principally formed along ethnic lines due to the institutional and political context of Germany since the first recruitment treaty in 1961.

In what follows, after a brief history of recruitment and migratory process in the Federal Republic of Germany (FRG), I shall examine how these political strategies have been constructed and articulated by the Berlin-Turkish migrants along ethnic lines. Subsequently, I shall introduce the notion of diasporic identity as a form of ethnic consciousness, which is peculiar to the working-class Turkish hip-hop youth in Berlin.

The Migratory Process

Migration into post war Germany started as labour recruitment to mitigate shortages in specific industries. Between 1955 and 1968, the FRG concluded intergovernmental contracts with eight Mediterranean countries: first Italy (1955), then Spain and Greece (1960), Turkey (1961 and 1964), Morocco (1963), Portugal (1964), Tunisia (1965) and Yugoslavia (1968). The German Federal Labour Office (*Bundesanstalt für Arbeit* – BA) set up recruitment offices in the countries concerned. Employers seeking workers had to apply to the BA and pay a fee. The BA then selected suitable workers, tested their work skills, gave them medical check-ups and screened police and political records.[1] Migrants were recruited at first for agriculture and construction, later by all branches of industry, where they generally had low-skilled manual jobs (Castles and Kosack, 1973). Guest-worker programmes were designed to solve immediate labour shortages in Germany by recruiting workers on temporary, short-term residence and work permits (Castles et al., 1984). The Turkish population in the FRG rose from 6,700 in 1961 to 605,000 in 1973 (Table 1).

Table 1: Germany's Non-German Population and Turkish Minority

Year	Non-German Population	%	Turkish Minority	%
1961	686,200	1.2	6,700	1.0
1970	2,600,600	4.3	249,400	16.5
1973	3,966,200	6.4	605,000	15.2
1977	3,948,300	6.4	508,000	12.9
1987	4,240,500	6.9	1,453,700	34.3
1989	4,845,900	7.7	1,612,600	33.3
1990[a]	5,342,500	8.4	1,675,900	32.0
1991[b]	5,882,300	7.3	1,779,600	30.3
1992	6,495,800	8.0	1,854,900	28.6
1993	6,878,100	8.5	1,918,400	27.9
1994	6,990,510	8.6	1,965,577	28.1

a) Data from 1961-1990 for the 'old' *Länder*;
b) Data from 1991 for the 'old' and 'new' *Länder*.
Sources: *Statistisches Jahrbuch für die Bundesrepublik Deutschland 1992, 1994, and 1995*

In the early stages of the migration, Turkish migrants were mainly men between the ages of 20 and 39, relatively skilled and educated in comparison to the average working population in Turkey, and from the economically more developed regions of the country (Abadan-Unat, 1976; Abadan-Unat and Kemiksiz, 1986; Martin, 1991). The ratio of rural migrants at this stage was just 17.2 percent. In the second half of the 1960s, recruitment consisted of rural workers (Gökdere, 1978). Berlin was relatively late in recruiting Turkish workers. Since the textile and electronics sectors demanded cheap female labour, it was conversely the women who first migrated to Berlin in 1964.

Turkish workers who migrated to Berlin by 1973 were primarily from the eastern provinces and from economically less-developed regions of Turkey.

As shown in the Table 1, there has been a continual increase in the non-German population through the post-war-period. The exceptions are the figures for 1977, which can be explained because the entry of non-European Community workers was banned in November 1973 by the German government due to the oil crisis, the consequent economic stagnation and political considerations. Since 1973, the composition of the Turkish migrant population has tended to become a more general population migration in the form of family reunification and political asylum rather than mainly labour migration.

The Formation of Ethnic-Based Political Strategies

Der Spiegel (14 April 1997), a prominent liberal weekly magazine, denounced the 'foreigners' in the country as 'dangerously alien' and as the cause of the failure of the 'multicultural society.' In the magazine, Turkish youths in Germany were presented as 'criminals,' 'fundamentalists,' 'nationalist' and 'traumatic.' A similar trend to the media coverage of the Turks in Germany has also recently been exhibited in the academia. Wilhelm Heitmeyer (1997), who was referred to in the *Der Spiegel* article, has become a polemical name after the publication of his book on the German-Turkish youth, *Verlockender Fundamentalismus (Enticing Fundamentalism)*. In his book, he concluded that it is the Turks who are not tempted to integrate and to incorporate themselves into the system. His main criterion in declaring the self-isolationist tendency of the Turkish-origin youths was their contentment to live with Islam and Turkishness. What was missing in both works was the underestimation of the structural constraints of Germany, which has remarkably shaped the survival strategies of migrants and their descendants. Such an approach, which does not consider the impact of the institutional structure of the receiving country on immigrant political mobilisation, is quite essentialist and exclusionist.

Why do migrants withdraw from 'host-society' political life? Patrick R. Ireland (1994) has drawn our attention to the legal conditions and political institutions of the receiving counties in mapping out the nature of immigrant political mobilisation. He has stated that "certain immigrant communities have withdrawn voluntarily from host-society political life in the face of institutional indifference and hostility" (1994: 8). Ireland has formulated the 'institutional channeling theory' as an alternative to the class and race/ethnicity theories to understand immigrant political strategies. Accordingly, he claims that the reason behind migrant groups' organising themselves politically along ethnic lines is primarily because 'host-society' institutions have nurtured ethnicity through their policies and practices. Similarly, Turkish migrants have hitherto organised themselves politically in Germany along ethnic lines because the institutional context in which they have been has primarily made them to do so.

The primary constituent of the German institutional context to which the immigrants are subject, is the laws of citizenship which frame the legal status of minorities. The Federal Republic of Germany (FRG) constitution, the Basic Law (*Grundgesetz*), recognises two categories of rights: *general* and *reserved*. General rights apply to all individuals in the FRG and include freedom of expression, liberty of person, and freedom of conscience (Art. 2, 3, 4 and 5). Reserved rights are restricted to German citizens, and include the right of peaceable assembly, freedom of movement, freedom of association, and freedom of occupation (Art. 8, 9, 11 and 12). The Basic Law does not prescribe how citizenship is recognised or conferred, but the criteria are based first and foremost on ethnic nationality. The rules governing the acquisition of citizenship are defined by the Basic Law Article 116, the preamble to the Basic Law, and the 1913 Imperial and State Citizenship Law (*Reichs- und Staatsangehörigkeitsgesetz*), and provide that citizenship is passed by descent from parent to child.[2] Article 116 of the Basic Law reads as follows:

(1) A German within the meaning of this Basic Law, unless otherwise regulated by law, is a person who possesses German citizenship, or who has been received in the territory of the German Reich as of 31 December 1937 as a refugee or expellee of German stock or as the spouse or descendant of such a person.

(2) Former German citizens who, between 30 January 1933 and 8 May 1945, were deprived of their citizenship on political, racial, or religious grounds, and their descendants, shall be granted citizenship on application.

The Imperial Naturalisation Law of 1913 was designed to make the acquisition of German citizenship difficult for aliens out of fear that the *Reich* was being invaded by immigrants from the East, especially Poles and Jews. At the same time, the law sharply reduced the barriers to the repatriation of ethnic Germans (*Aussiedler*) from outside the *Reich* (Brubaker, 1992: 114-119; Klusmeyer, 1993: 84; Marshall, 1992).

The claim to naturalisation has always been difficult for the non-EU 'foreigners' in the FRG, and has required repudiation of the citizenship of the country of origin. The non-EU 'foreigners' are denied the right to dual citizenship; even the children of migrants born and raised in Germany could not automatically receive the rights of citizenship.[3] The 'foreigners' who are willing to renounce their previous citizenship can be naturalised only after they have been living in Germany for at least fifteen years. In contrast, the *Volksdeutschen* (ethnic Germans defined by the Article 116 of the Basic Law) – primarily Poles and Russians who can improve German ancestry – have a constitutional right to naturalisation.

However, the German government recently established two mechanisms that, for the first time, provide migrants with the right to claim citizenship. According to the new *Ausländergesetz* (1991) and the *Gesetz zur Änderung asylverfahrens-, ausländer- und staatsangehörigkeitsrechtlicher Vorschriften* (1993), two groups of *Ausländer* have been legally entitled to naturalisation (paragraphs 85 and 86 of the *Ausländergesetz*). Paragraph 85 declares that 'foreigners' between the ages of 16 and 23, who have been resident in Germany for more than eight years, attended a school in Germany for at least six years and who have not been convicted of serious offences, have the right to be naturalised. On the other hand, paragraph 86 introduces that those 'migrants,' who have been resident in Germany for at least 15 years and possess a residence permit, have the right to naturalisation. The absence of a conviction of a serious criminal offence and financial independence of the applicant are also primarily crucial for the acquisition of citizenship according to this paragraph.[4] Besides, the new citizenship law, which was put into force since the 1st of January 2000, makes it possible for the children of immigrants to acquire dual citizenship up until the age of 23. The age of 23 is the threshold for the youngsters to decide on either German or Turkish citizenship.[5]

Non-European Union immigrants, or resident aliens, mostly have been given what Marshall (1950) defined as social and civil rights, but not political rights. The immigrants built a very real political presence in Germany where their political participation in the system was not legally allowed. The legal barriers denying political participation provided a ground for the Turkish immigrants in Germany to organise themselves politically along collective ethnic lines. As a response to the German insistence on the exclusionary *'Ausländerstatus,'* Turkish migrant communities have tended to develop strong ethnic structures and maintain ethnic boundaries.[6] The lack of political participation and representation in the receiving country made them direct their political activity towards their country of origin. In fact, this home-oriented participation has received encouragement from Turkey that has set up networks of consular services and other official organisations (religious, educational and commercial). Homeland opposition parties and movements have also forged an organisational presence in Germany.

This early form of political participation that was home-oriented has crosscut with the *migrant strategy*, the framework of which I shall discuss below. In the later stages of the migratory process, the legal position of the immigrants with regard to residence and political rights has remained provisional. They have been given the same rights as Germans in the unions and in workplace co-determination under the law (*Betriebsverfassungsgesetz*), but they are still excluded from all other forms of formal participation or personal influence in political decision-making process. This is the stage when the Turkish immigrants have been systematically marginalised by the state. As a response to this 'ethnic minorisation' they started forming their own associations along ethnic lines – a point which I shall again explore in the following section.

In addition to the constitutional barriers, the absence of a general immigration policy has also compelled the Turkish immigrants in Germany to *isolate* themselves in ethnic enclaves from the dominant society.[7] From its inception to the present, the Federal Republic's official policy has been that "Germany is not a country of immigration." Lacking a general immigration policy, the *Bundestag* (Federal Parliament) issued the *Ausländergesetz* (Foreigners Law) in 1965. This law did not give foreigners a right to residence, merely stating that "a residence permit may be granted, if it does not harm the interests of the Federal Republic of Germany." This term is a key phrase in policies regarding migrants. In the 1960s and early 1970s it was not only the granting of political rights to foreign immigrants, which was certainly not seen as being in the interests of the German Federal Republic, also the law of 1965 specifically excluded them from other civil rights:

Foreigners enjoy all basic rights; except the basic rights of assembly, freedom of association, freedom of movement and free choice of occupation, place of work and place of education, and protection from extradition abroad (*Allgemeine Verwaltungsvorschrift zur Ausführung des Ausländergesetzes*, § 6).

Thus, the German state established a system of 'institutional discrimination,' through which temporary guest workers could be recruited, controlled and sent away, 'as the interests of capital dictated' (Castles, 1985: 523). The main concern of the first stage of the *Ausländerpolitik* between 1965 and 1973 was economic considerations. The second stage of the law was shaped by concerns of increasing social problems and political tensions. The early policy was impracticable, not only because of the various international agreements granting rights of family reunification, to which Germany was a party, but also because many firms found that rotation led to problems of labour fluctuation and high training costs (ibid.). Accordingly, in November 1973 the entry of further labour force from non-EC countries was banned, and family reunion permitted. Afterwards, the Federal Labour Office decreed that work permits for migrant workers were not to be renewed if West German workers were thought to be available for the job concerned. This meant that in some cases the migrant workers were forced to leave their jobs and return home.

The third stage of the *Ausländerpolitik* started when the CDU (Christlich Demokratische Union – Christian Democratic Party) came into power in 1983. By the early 1980s the 'foreigners problem' had become a major issue in West German politics. While in power, the SPD (Sozialdemokratische Partei Deutschlands – Social Democratic Party) had moved towards increasingly restrictive policies on migrant rights. On the other hand, the CDU was proposing to implement stricter policies for the control of foreigners and encouragement of repatriation. A CDU resolution in the Federal Parliament in 1981 stated: "The role of the Federal Republic of Germany as a national unitary state and as part of a divided nation does not permit the commencement of an irreversible development to a multiethnic state" (Castles, 1985: 528). Consequently, Chancellor Helmut Kohl's government in coalition with CSU (Christlich Soziale Union – Christian

Social Party) and FDP (Freie Demokratische Partei – Free Democratic Party) radicalised the *Ausländerpolitik*, aiming for the restriction of further immigration and encouragement of repatriation. By 'integration,' the conservative government meant that those foreigners who were unable to adapt themselves to the German norms, values and laws were to be deported to allow those remaining to be assimilated. In addition to the so-called 'integration' the government restricted the entry of further immigrants, spouses and dependent children of immigrants by applying new quotas. Finally, the government encouraged repatriation with a decree between October 30, 1983 and June 30, 1984 by offering premiums of 10,500 DM plus 1,500 DM per dependent child if they left the country immediately. The government also 'guaranteed' the reintegration of repatriating children to the new conditions in Turkey by subsidising some adaptation schools and providing German teachers in these schools.[8]

The alteration of the ethnic strategies amongst the Berlin-Turks has considerably been bounded to the transformation of the *Ausländerpolitik* in Berlin as well as to the ethnically defined citizenship laws. The periodisation of the *Ausländerpolitik* in Berlin is slightly different from the rest of the Federal Republic of Germany. Thomas Schwartz (1992: 121-138) provides an overview of three phases of *Ausländerpolitik* in Berlin. In the first phase (late 1960s and early 1970s), when the wall was constructed, the law was characterised mainly in terms of addressing problems of urban planning. Accordingly, demographic and employment factors became the key concerns of policy makers, and 'integration' was considered a structural concern. Later, in the second phase of the *Ausländerpolitik* (1980s), 'representative politics' (*Beauftragtenpolitik*) emerged as the central orientation of Berlin government. Berlin was the first Land in the Federal Republic to establish an office of *Ausländerbeauftragte* (Commissioner for Foreigners' Affairs). The office was originally envisioned as a liaison between local government and the various ethnic organisations. The last phase is the one, which was introduced by the Red-Green coalition in 1998. This phase, which is in a sense peculiar to Berlin, has been dominated by concepts of anti-racism and multiculturalism – a point to which I shall return shortly. These phases of *Ausländerpolitik* have shaped the form of political participation of those Turkish migrants who lack legal political rights. In the following section, after pointing out the three phases of *Ausländerpolitik*, I will elaborate the main landmarks of the ethnic strategies developed by Berlin-Turkish communities in relation to the *Ausländerpolitik*.

Migrant Strategy

The first generation of migrants, who conceived themselves as temporary, arrived in their country of residence by leaving their families behind a painful experience. The nature of the migration to the West from Turkey is mostly chain migration. This type of migration has played a major role in the incorporation of kin and fellow villagers into the migration stream. Chain migration in Berlin has two aspects. The first aspect is the in-coming spouses and children who joined the process of migration with the family reunification in 1973 and onwards. The second aspect of chain migration is the dense in-coming of migrants from disaster areas in Turkey, in a way that led to high representation of people from the Varto/Erzurum and Gediz/Kütahya areas (earthquakes) as well as Konya and Isparta (floods) (Gitmez and Wilpert, 1987: 93).

Chain migration makes migrants' family relations or local community relations both in the country of origin and in the country of immigration more vital and instrumental. When the migrants arrive in the receiving country their kin and former neighbours give them shelter, advice and support. Their previous social group status and class, lack of language, the exclusionist incorporation regimes as well as the segregationist housing policies of the receiving countries make them stick together and develop solidarity by means of informal local networks. Their desperate will to return has made them invest at home rather than in Berlin. The migrant strategy is formed in their own local neighbourhood, in which they stick together, isolated from the rest of the society. Most socialising has been carried out with other Turks, preferably *hemsehris* (fellow-villagers, *Landsmannschaften*), in private homes, mosques, public restaurants, and coffee houses (the exclusive domain of men), and on structured occasions such as the large parties frequently held in rented halls to celebrate engagements, weddings and circumcisions (Mandel, 1990: 155). It is the development of social networks, based on kinship or common area of origin and the need for mutual help in the new environment, that made possible the construction of migrant strategy (Castles and Miller, 1993: 25).

The first generation migrants, who were recruited by Germany on the basis of *Gastarbeiter* (guest worker) system, have called themselves *gurbetçi*. The *gurbetçi* is the one who lives in a state of *gurbet*. *Gurbet* is an Arabic word which derives from *garaba*, to go away, to depart, to be absent, to go to a foreign country, to emigrate, to be away from one's homeland, to live as a foreigner in a country. It is important to note that *gurbet* does not necessarily refer to a foreign country; one can perfectly be in *gurbet* in one's own country: the state of *gurbet* covers, for instance, Turkish migrants living in Berlin as well as those living in Istanbul. The *gurbetçis* feel that their primary identification is with the village where they were born rather than the city. The emergent literature and music genres produced by Turkish artists in Western Europe draw upon a long tradition of exile and *gurbet* experiences (Çaglar, 1994; Mandel, 1990). The term *gurbetçi* dominated first generation German-Turks' discourse. Defining themselves as *gurbetçi*, Turkish migrants raised the points, which prevented Germany from becoming a homeland for them. A feeling of security, trust, behavioural confidence, certainty, assurance and finding social recognition are the dominant needs that the notion of *Heimat* fulfils. Germany could not meet these needs of the first generation immigrants. The discourse of *gurbetçi* in alliance with the 'will to return,' in this case, has become an essential survival strategy for the migrants in the process of quest for home.

The *Gurbetçis* used to mystify the homeland in their arts, literature and musical genres as a place to which they would return some day. It would be misleading to abstract them from their attachments to their traditional past and continuous process of migration in exploring their migrant identity. In their expressive culture they have tended to romanticise the past, and continuously sought the Turkey of the times they left behind in the 60s and 70s. The first generation migrants still keep the same discourse in their daily lives. Most of them are twice-migrants – an experience which they express as '*gurbetin gurbeti*' (exile of exile). Although such a 'double migrancy' discourse is still partly alive for most of the first generation migrants, it is subject to change. It is because, the migrants have started to understand that the 'will to return' was nothing but a myth, and that they were treated as strangers in both their country of residence and homeland. In Germany, they have been simply called as *Ausländer* (foreigner), and in Turkey as *Almanci* (German like).[9]

The migrant strategy was constructed sometime during the first decade of the migration wave in the sixties when the socialisation process of migrants was based on a non-associational community formation, ethnic enclave, *hemsehri* bonding, and a *Gastarbeiter* ideology. In this very early period of migration, the primary concern of migrants was to earn money and return to Turkey. In this stage, Turkish workers were demographically more homogenous, densely accommodated in *Wohnheims* (dormitory-like hotels) and were not very visible in the receiving society. In such conditions they need not form associations to become socialised and politicised. Yet there were some informal Turkish worker associations prior to the family reunification in mid 1970s. They were followed by the growth of religious and politically conservative associations in the 1970s. Until around 1981 it was possible to categorise the majority of Turkish associations within one of the two extreme poles of Turkish society. They were either affiliated with one of the Turkish worker associations attached to a centre-left political party in Turkey, or they were more religiously organised, some aligned with the extreme right parties (Gitmez and Wilpert, 1987: 107). It was in the early 1980s that Turkish migrants started to form ethnic and political associations.[10] It was a time when issues of 'integration' were highly discussed in Germany and became present in the *Ausländerpolitik*, and also a time when a new policy of 'assimilation or return' was put into force by the government of Helmut Kohl in Germany.

Minority Strategy

In 1983 the federal parliament passed a law encouraging *Ausländer* (foreigners) to leave Germany, and paying them to do so. However, since the beginning of the 1980s many German cities, especially Berlin, also established official institutions (*Ausländerbeauftragte*) for working with minorities of foreign origin. In this second stage of *Ausländerpolitik*, integration and/or assimilation became the major concern of the Federal Republic (Schwartz, 1992; Vertovec, 1996a). Since the early 1980s, the government of Helmut Kohl reflected the rising tide of rightist sentiments, putting into practice an *Ausländerpolitik* based on the restriction of all forms of new immigration, and a policy of 'assimilation or return' for all the 'foreigners' present in the country (Vertovec, 1996a: 384). At this stage of the *Ausländerpolitik*, the orientations of Turkish formal associations reached a turning point in Berlin. Those ethnic organisations, which were established at this stage, were highly oriented towards Germany. The rise of numerous ethnic associations was not only due to the rightist *Ausländerpolitik* radicalising between 'assimilation' and 'return,' but also to the exclusionary laws of national belonging,[11] rise of racist attacks, institutional racism, structural outsiderism, family reunification, growing consciousness of long-term settlement, upward social mobilisation, and to the widespread control of political movements in Turkey after the advent of the military regime in 1980. Accordingly all these aspects enforced the formation of ethnic and political associations amongst the Turkish population in Germany to come to terms with the problems emerging in both the countries of reception and origin.

Despite the existence of a modern welfare state which provides the most basic social services in terms of health, education and social security, Turks found it necessary and opportune to set up their own services to mediate between individuals and German institutions. Turks may have previously accepted German advocates; recently, "they are finding their own voice, their own advocates, and their own understanding of what it means and what should mean to be of Turkish-origin in German society" (Horrocks and Kolinsky, 1996: xx). The emergence of ethnic communities with their own institutions such as ethnic associations, cultural associations, youth clubs, *cafés*, agencies, and professions[12] give rise to the birth of a new ethnic-based political strategy, i.e. a *minority strategy*. The permanent settlement brings about the necessity of a long-live strategy rather than the migrant strategy, in order, not only to maintain culture, but more importantly to cope with disadvantage, to improve life chances against political exclusion and socio-economic marginalisation, and to provide protection from racism (Castles and Miller, 1993: 114).

Depending upon the integration policies of the receiving country, the formation of ethnic minority organisations might spring from various material reasons. Ethnic minorities may be seen as social groups which are the result of both 'other'-definition and 'self'-definition. On the one hand, the ethnic minorities are defined by dominant social groups in regard to their perceived phenotypical or cultural characteristics, which lead to the imposition of specific economic, social or legal situations. On the other hand, their members generally share a self-definition or ethnic identity based on ideas of common origins, history, culture, experience and values (ibid.: 28). Thus, the

CHAPTER 2

construction of ethnic minority is highly related to the political structure of the receiving society. As Castles and Miller (ibid.: 26) state,

> At one extreme, openness to settlement, granting of citizenship and gradual acceptance of cultural diversity may allow the formation of ethnic communities, which can be seen as part of a multicultural society. At the other extreme, denial of the reality of settlement, refusal of citizenship and rights to settlers, and rejection of cultural diversity may lead to formation of ethnic minorities, whose presence is widely regarded as undesirable and divisive. In the first case, the immigrants and their descendants are seen as an integral part of a society, which is willing to reshape its culture and identity. In the second, immigrants are excluded and marginalised, so that they live on the fringes of a society, which is determined to preserve myths of a static culture and a homogenous identity.

The experience of discrimination and racism in western European countries forced immigrants to constitute their own *communities* and to define their group boundaries in cultural terms (ibid.: 28). This is the new form of racism "which differs from the vulgar and compromised racism of biological differences" (Ålund, 1994: 63). The 'new racism' continues to focus on simplified and reified cultural differences, and it does not claim that different cultures have different values, but that they are different and remain so (Barker, 1981). The ideological pillar of new racism is the holistic understanding of culture, which does not encourage the cultures to mix and construct a bricolage. The rationale behind the holistic notion of culture, which leads to new racism, is that the dominant national identities could become uncertain. The formation of community in response to the racialisation process, in return, reinforces fears of separatism and ethnic enclaves on the part of the majority society, leading to the furtherance of exclusionary practices and racism.

These conditions have set certain parameters for the life of a Turkish minority in Berlin and the socialisation of the following generations. The internal social structure of Turkish population in Berlin presents additional contingencies which contribute to the perception and evaluation of world views and collective, ethnic and national identities (Gitmez and Wilpert, 1987: 91). The prominent advocate of ethnic minority strategy in Berlin is a conservative ethnic association, *Türkische Gemeinde zu Berlin* (TGB, Turkish Community of Berlin)

(Gitmez and Wilpert, 1987: 115; Özcan, 1994: 319). TGB attempts to eradicate the use of the label 'migrant,' and to be officially perceived as an ethnic minority in the long run like the Danish ethnic minority in Schleswig-Holstein and the *Sorben* ethnic minority in southern Brandenburg.[13] Acceptance as a minority implies that the residency, and not nationality, matters. It also implies that cultural diversity is not perceived as a danger but condoned as a social reality (Horrocks and Kolinsky, 1996: xiii).

Their attempt to go beyond the perception of being 'migrant' demonstrates the sharp discursive transition they have had after the former migrant strategy. The notion of 'migrant' has very negative connotations for the TGB members. Firstly, as Mustafa Çakmakoglu, the former head of TGB, put it, those 'who betray Turkey' qualify as migrants. Here, the former category of 'those who betray Turkey' is a political categorisation; it contains left wing and Islamic-universalist immigrants. TGB has a Turkish-Islamise ideology, which gives priority to Turkishness. Hence, those who underestimate Turkishness are considered 'traitors.' By subtracting themselves from this notion, the members of TGB attempt to differentiate themselves from those 'traitors.' Secondly, their refusal of the notion of 'migrant' is related to the term's negative historical connotations within the Turkish context. Migrants (*göçmen* and/or *muhacir*) in Turkey are those Balkan-Turks, Afghans and Kurds who migrated to Turkey. These migrants have usually been considered by the Turkish people to be competing for the scarce resources of Turkey with themselves. That is why the TGB members do not want to enjoy such an undesirable label.

Moreover, it is evident that a minority status can provide them with substantial cultural and religious rights such as acquiring bilingual education and gaining financial support from the Federal government for their mosques, schools and other cultural projects. To be perceived as an ethnic minority by the German constitution, the members of the concerned group should be German citizens. For this purpose, TGB tries to convince Turks not to neglect gaining German citizenship. Their minority strategy derives from their practical expectations from such a political category. As Abdul Janmohamed and David Lloyd (1990: 9) remind us, their discourse indicates that

Becoming minor is not a question of essence (as the stereotypes of minorities in dominant ideology would want us to believe) but a question of position: a subject position that in the final analysis can be defined only in 'political' terms that is, in terms of the effects of economic exploitation, political disenfranchisement, social manipulation, and ideological domination on the cultural formation of minority subjects and discourses [...].

Minority strategy develops within a binary relation with majority society. In this binary relation, the minority attempts to negate the prior hegemonic negation of itself by the majority society in a way that reaffirms its minor location. The collective nature of all minority discourses derives from the fact that "minority individuals are always treated and forced to experience themselves generically" in many fields of social life such as in the literary and/or political system (ibid.: 10). The literary system in Germany is an excellent example to illustrate the way in which a 'foreigner,' say a 'Turkish' novelist, expresses his/her feelings and emotions generically as a member of Turkish minority, not as a member of the German literary system. Aras Ören, Yüksel Pazarkaya, Zafer Senocak, Emine Sevgi Özdamar and Zehra Çirak are some of the Turkish-origin literary figures in Germany, writing from the margin. These novelists and poets are considered to belong to the so-called *Gastarbeiterliteratur* (guestworker literature) or *Ausländerliteratur* (foreigners' literature) sphere (Suhr, 1989; Teraoka, 1990). These literary figures are expected to reflect the problems of their own communities, and regarded as the spokespeople of the speechless by the dominant culture.

Most of these Turkish-origin literary figures such as Aras Ören and Zehra Çirak reject the label of 'Turkish' novelist/poet, because they "emphasise universal human values rather than cultural, national, or even class differences; [they are] global in scope rather than local in focus and concern; and they attempt to be unifying rather than oppositional" (Teraoka, 1990: 304).[14] As someone coerced into a negative, generic subject-position, the migrant individual is forced to respond by transforming that position into a positive, collective one. In our example it is the Turkish-origin literary figures that are forced to become the spokespeople of a Turkish minority.

The ethnic formation of minorities is not solely a product of ethnic groups' rational choice to come to terms with the discriminatory and racist polities of the receiving country. It is also evident that ethnic minorities can be formed 'from above' by the state itself as a result of the exclusionary political system. Immigrant workers in Germany are, on the one hand, integrated into the social system, but on the other hand not admitted to the political platform. This is due to the concept of the '*jus sanguinis*', which is expressed in the Article 116 of the German Basic Law, reserving citizenship to ethnic Germans based on blood. As non-citizens, 'foreigners' do not have the right to political rights. They cannot themselves struggle for their interests in the political system and have to find 'deputising majority speakers' (Radtke, 1994: 33). When the constitutional restrictions for migrants' political participation are combined with the contemporary local polities of 'multiculturalism' in Berlin, migrants are strongly encouraged into 'ethnic minorisation' by the state itself (Rath, 1993). As Radtke (1993: 36) reminds us, it is partly the official discourse of 'multiculturalism' that has induced migrant groups in Germany to form homogeneous communities around religious and traditional symbols, not only to protect a cultural identity in an unfriendly and sometimes racist environment, but also to present themselves in the way that the majority wanted to see them.

The construction of ethnic-based political strategies is strictly dependent on the policies implemented by the government of the receiving society. As I have tried to explain, those varying governmental policies concerning the 'foreign' immigrants – no matter if they were formed by the conservatives or social democrats – have contributed to the othering and minorisation of Turkish population in the FRG. Aras Ören, Turkish novelist and poet, warns of the dangers inherent in the acceptance of otherness and cultural difference:

[I am afraid that while] the conservatives lock us into our cultural ghetto by preserving the culture we brought with us as it is and by denying that there can be symbiosis or development, [...] the progressives try to drive us back into that same ghetto because, filled with enthusiasm, by the originality and exoticism of our culture, they champion it so fervently that they are even afraid it might disappear, be absorbed by German culture (Quoted in Suhr, 1989: 102).

The former political participation strategies, which have been developed by the Turkish migrants along ethnic lines, were both based on binary relation between the migrants and the majority society. The first strategy, migrant strategy, was characterised by a 'will to return.' It was a response to the early German recruitment politics, which was built on the notion of *Gastarbeiter* (guestworker). On the other hand, the minority strategy was a response to the culturalisation and minorisation of the Turkish population by the German institutional structuring.[15]

Diaspora Strategy

The first generation immigrants as a set of survival strategies have primarily developed these two ethnic-based political strategies. Conversely, their descendants who were born and raised in Germany have followed different patterns, depending on their class, gender and social status. Those who live in Kotbusser Tor, Kreuzberg, where I conducted my research, having grown up in an ethnic enclave have carried the norms and traditions of their parents in themselves as well as receiving those of the majority society and international society. Additionally, they also employed ethnicity, religion and culture for the construction and articulation of their identities. They have acquired a cultural identity, which springs from parental, dominant and global cultures. This cultural identity can be defined as *diasporic*. Diasporic consciousness refers to individuals' awareness of a range of decentered, multi-location attachments, of being simultaneously 'home away from home' or 'here and there' (Vertovec, 1997: 100).

The enhancement of telecommunications and the ease of travel made possible the emergence of alternate cultural forms and multiple identities for the diasporic youth. Above all, these transnational networks helped the descendants of the immigrants to dissolve the 'inevitable' binary relation between minority and majority. The following section will be an attempt to expose the main parameters of the modern notion of diaspora by referring to some scholars, and also to demonstrate the two inter-related main approaches on diaspora, as Vertovec (1997) put it: 'diaspora as a form of consciousness' and 'diaspora as a mode of cultural production.' Thus, it attempts to provide a theoretical ground for the understanding of the diasporic cultural identity of the working-class Turkish male hip-hop youth in Kreuzberg.

Diaspora Revisited

Recently, the notion of diaspora has been extensively used by a wide range of scholars aiming to contribute to the definition of transnational migrants. The new trend of diaspora studies defines the diasporas as exemplary communities of the transnational moment. The term 'diaspora' is derived from the Greek verb *sperio* (to sow, to scatter) and the preposition *dia* (through, apart). For Greeks, the term referred to migration and colonisation, whereas for Jews, Africans, Palestinians and Armenians the same term acquired more unfortunate, brutal and traumatic dispersion through scattering (Cohen, 1997: ix). Yet, the contemporary notion of diaspora is not limited only with Jewish, Greek, Palestinian and Armenian dispersive experiences; rather it describes a larger domain that includes words like immigrant, expatriate, refugee, guest worker, exile community and ethnic community (Tölölian, 1991: 5). The primary difference between the old and modern form of diasporas lies in their changing will to go back to the 'Holy Land,' or homeland. In this sense, the old diasporas resemble the story of *Ulysses* while the new ones have been like that of *Abraham*.[16] After the Trojan War, Ulysses encountered many problems on the way back to Ithaca. Although he had many obstacles during his journey, he was determined to go back home. Conversely, the experience of the modern labour diasporas resembles the Prophet Abraham's biblical journey. In the first part of the Bible, it is written that Abraham, upon the request of God, had to journey with his people to find a new home in the unknown and he never went back to the place he left behind.

The classification of Robin Cohen is quite influential in mapping out the differences between modern and old diasporas. His historical explanation of diaspora goes back to the Biblical Jewish diaspora, which was based on a forced dispersion experience. He has a clear picture of old and new diasporas, which he separates on the basis of the genesis of global economy. Old diasporas are twofold: a) forced diasporas such as Jewish and Armenian, b) colonising diasporas such as Greek and British. On the other hand, the modern diasporas are threefold: a) trading diasporas like Jewish and Lebanese; b) business diasporas such as British; and c) labour diasporas such as Irish, Indian, Chinese, Sikh and Turkish. The main driving force behind the construction of modern labour diasporas is the global economic needs, which bring about an extensive immigration from periphery to the global and regional centres.

William Safran, in his study of "Diasporas in Modern Societies: Myths of Homelands and Return," draws up the general framework of

an ideal type of diaspora. He defines diaspora as 'expatriate minority communities'
(1) that are dispersed from an original centre to at least two peripheral places;
(2) that maintain a memory, vision, or myth about their original homeland;
(3) that believe they are not fully accepted by their host country;
(4) that see the ancestral home as a place of eventual return, when the time is right;
(5) that are committed to the maintenance and restoration of this homeland; and
(6) of which the group's consciousness and solidarity are importantly defined by this continuing relationship with the homeland (Safran, 1991: 83-84).

Safran's ideal type of 'centred' diaspora, oriented by continuous cultural connections to a source and by a teleology of 'return,' is inapplicable to the recent experiences of diaspora like African/American, Caribbean/British, South Asian/British, Turkish/German and/or Algerian/French. These histories of displacement fall into a category of what Clifford calls 'quasi diasporas.' Similarly, Turkish diaspora (like the South Asian diaspora) "is not so much oriented to roots in a specific place and a desire for return as around an ability to recreate a culture in diverse locations. Such a state of diaspora falls outside the strict definition of diaspora" (Clifford, 1994: 306).

Clifford also states that the old version of 'centred' diaspora which has been formed around a teleology of return is getting looser because of the global social changes that mainly derive from de-colonisation, immigration, and globalisation. He avoids the old notion of diaspora to scrutinise and enlighten the modern diasporas because,

The transnational connections linking diasporas need not be articulated primarily through a real or symbolic homeland – at least not to the degree that Safran implies. Decentred, lateral connections may be as important as those formed around a teleology of origin/return. *And a shared, ongoing history of displacement, suffering, adaptation, or resistance may be as important as the projection of a specific origin* (Clifford, 1994: 306; emphasis mine).

Thus, Clifford suggests that some groups can become identified as more or less diasporic, having only two, or three, or four of the six basic features of Safran's ideal type of diaspora.

The changing nature of space and time in the age of globalism facilitates the emergence of diasporic consciousness. Globalisation emerging as the rise of communications, transportation, migration, modern diasporas, de-monopolisation of national legal systems, new international division of labour, and global culture, empowers the minorities against the hegemony of nation-state, and breaks up the conventional power relations between majority and minority. The modern "communicative circuitry has enabled dispersed populations to converse, interact and even symbolise significant elements of their social and cultural lives" (Gilroy, 1994: 211). For instance, the Turkish TV programmes are easily received in Europe by the Turkish diaspora. The official TRT International and some other private channels and newspapers spread the official ideology of the Turkish nation-state through the diaspora.

Thus, Turkish official ideology that has recently become more hegemonic and nationalist has a very important role on the construction of Turkish diaspora nationalism at the imaginary level which gives a special emphasis on Turkishness.[17] For instance, during the intervention of the Turkish Armed Forces into the Northern Iraq in the winter of 1996 to prevent the logistic settlement of the Kurdistan Workers Party (*PKK*) in the region, the Turkish TV channels organised an international campaign to collect money for the Turkish Armed Forces. In Germany, a big amount of money has been collected from the Turkish people. This is evidence of the transnational exploitation of the masses by the nation-state, and of the power of the ideology of nationalism. This change in the homeland's orientation to the diaspora is a part of the *realpolitik* because the homeland governments tend to exploit diaspora sentiments for their purposes (Safran, 1991: 93).

These changes in the global network, international politics, and internal politics have played an important role in the making of diaspora consciousness. The diaspora consciousness seems to be supplementing minority strategy by means of these global transformations. As Clifford (1994: 310-311) rightfully states, transnational connections with homeland, other members of diaspora in various geographies, and/or with a world-political force (such as Islam) break the binary relation of minority communities with majority societies as well as giving added weight to claims against an oppressive national hegemony. Through the agency of these connections, diasporic subjects have the chance to create a home away from the homeland, a home which is surrounded by rhythms, figures and images of the homeland provided by TV, video cassettes, tapes, radio, and by the local network they developed in time.

The diaspora consciousness requires the idea of dwelling *here* in the country of residence and a connection *there* in the homeland. The modern diasporas are no longer immigrant communities; they are rather sojourners. Diasporic discourses, as Clifford (1994: 311) states, reflect the sense of being part of an ongoing transnational network that includes the homeland, not as something left behind, but as a place of attachment in a 'contrapuntal modernity.' Clifford borrows the term 'contrapuntal' from Edward Said who has used the term to characterise one of the positive aspects of conditions of exile:

[…] For an exile, habits of life, expression or activity in the new environment inevitably occurs against the memory of these things in another environment. Thus, both the new and the old environments are vivid, actual, occurring together contrapuntally (quoted in Clifford, ibid.: 329).

Diasporic subject constructs his/her cultural identity in a dialogue between the past and the future, 'there' and 'here,' local and global, and heritage ad politics. The particular experiences of diaspora bring back the memories of the counterparts of those experiences that were once undertaken in the homeland. Memorising those experiences, on the one hand, reinforces the habits of life; on the other, reminds the diasporic subject the condition of dispersal or diaspora.

The contemporary diaspora discourses are developed on two paramount dimensions: *universalism* and *particularism*. The universalist axis refers us to the model of diasporic transnationalism, in the form of 'third space' (Bhabha, 1990), or 'process of heterogenesis' (Guattari, 1989), or 'third culture' (Featherstone, 1990) – a point to which I shall shortly return in the following chapters. The universalist dimension, which contains the use of all the aspects of globalism and transnationalism, refers to that the diasporic consciousness constitutes a post-national identity. The members of the post-national diasporic communities can escape the power of the nation-state to inform their sense of collective identity. In this new space it is possible to evade the politics of polarity and emerge as 'the others of our selves' (Bhabha, 1988: 22). This is the cultural space where the quest for knowing and othering the Other becomes irrelevant, and cultures merge together in a way that leads to the construction of syncretic cultural forms.

On the other hand, the particularist axis presents the model of cultural essentialism, or diasporic nationalism. The process of home-seeking, as Clifford offers, might result with the existence of a kind of diaspora nationalism, which is, in itself, critical to the majority nationalism, and an anti-nationalist nationalism (Clifford, 1994: 307). The nature of diaspora nationalism is cultural, which is based on alienation, and celebration of the past and authenticity. For migrants as well as for anybody else, fear of the present leads to mystification of the past (Berger, 1972: 11) in a way that constructs 'imaginary homelands' as Salman Rushdie (1991: 9) has pointed out in his work *Imaginary Homelands*:

It is my present that is foreign, and [...] the past is home, albeit a lost home in a lost city in the mists of lost time [...] [Thus,], we will, in short, create fictions, not actual cities or villages, but invisible ones, imaginary homelands.

As Clifford rightly states, those migrant and/or minority groups who are alienated by the system, and swept up in a destiny dominated by the capitalist West, no longer invent local futures. What is different about them remains tied to traditional pasts (Clifford, 1988: 5). Remaking the past, or recovering the past, serves at least a dual purpose for the diasporic communities. Firstly, it is a way of coming to terms with the present without being seen to criticise the existing status quo. The 'glorious' past is, here, handled by the diasporic subject as a strategic tool absorbing the destructiveness of the present which is defined with exclusion, structural outsiderism, poverty, racism and institutional discrimination. Secondly, it also helps to recuperate a sense of the self not dependent on criteria handed down by others – the past is what the diasporic subjects can claim as their own (Ganguly, 1992: 40).

Although, the main driving forces behind the construction of diasporic consciousness are compression of time and space in the form of globalisation, and the internal institutional context to which the minority community is subject in the country of settlement, homeland government's orientation towards the diaspora communities is quite determinant too. The changing nature of the orientation of the Turkish government to the Turks in West Europe has an influential impact on the construction of a kind of diasporic consciousness within the Turkish communities. The official attempts of the Turkish government to form a Turkish lobby in Germany make the Turkish communities that have various political and ideological standpoints, compete with each other for the claim to be the mere representative of the Turkish minority. These ethnic organisations which are in search for recognition by both the country of residence and homeland, tend to improve their orientation to the homeland, and to work for the political and economic interests of the homeland. Thus, such a transnational political network leads the Turkish minority organisations to play more on the axis of Turkishness as a result of the hegemonic ideology of the Turkish nation-state. Here, it should be stated that, while the official lobbying activities attempt to contribute to the creation of a diasporic consciousness on the one hand, they deepen the ideological cleavages between the extremely heterogeneous Turkish communities on the other. For instance, the competition between *Türkische Gemeinde zu Berlin* (TGB, Turkish Community of Berlin) and *Türkischer Bund in Berlin-Brandenburg* (TBB, Turkish Association of Berlin-Brandenburg) to conduct the lobbying activities, expands the divisions between the groups.

Therefore, the notion of 'diaspora' (with lower case 'd') should be considered a theoretical concept that meets the contemporary needs of the study of ethnicity and nationalism in a broader transnational level. The term 'diaspora' might also be useful as an intermediate concept between the local and the global, transcending the national perspectives which often limit transnational cultural studies (Gillespie, 1996: 6). The term 'Diaspora' (with a capital 'D') was once a concept referring to the traumatic dispersion of the Jews and the Armenians from their historical homelands throughout many lands. The connotations of the term were usually negative as they were associated with forced displacement, victimisation, alienation, and loss. Now, the term 'diaspora' is often used by the scholars as a beneficial term to practically describe any community that is transnational.

Contemplating the modern diasporic situations as the unsurprising feature of globalisation (particularly involving the advance of telecommunications and the ease of travel), Vertovec (1997, 1996b) states that there are three different approaches to the notion of modern diaspora, put forward by contemporary scholars. In sum, the first standpoint regards diaspora as a *social form* (Boyarin and Boyarin, 1993; Safran, 1991). Diaspora as a social form refers to the transnational communities whose social, economic and political networks cross the borders of nation-states. The second approach conceives diaspora as a *type of consciousness*, which emerges by means of transnational networks (Clifford, 1994, 1992; Hall, 1994, 1991; Bhabha, 1990; Gilroy, 1993, 1987; Cohen, 1997; Vertovec, 1997, 1996b). This approach departs from W.E.B. Du Bois' notion of 'double consciousness,' and refers to individuals' awareness of being simultaneously 'home away from home' or 'here and there.' And the last but not the least, is the understanding, which regards diaspora as a *mode of cultural construction and expression* (Gilroy, 1987, 1993, 1994; Hall, 1994). This approach emphasises the flow of constructed styles and identities among diasporic people. Subsequently, I shall provide a theoretical framework for the exploration of the construction and articulation of the diasporic cultural identity of the working-class Turkish hip-hop youth in Berlin.

Diasporic Consciousness

The labour migration into Europe is mainly a post war phenomenon resulting in the permanent settlement of millions of people away from their country of origin. After a few decades these peoples who used to be merely temporary workers, and treated so, have become sojourners, and constructed homes away from their homelands. The centring of ethnic minorities around an axis of origin, ethnicity and religion leads to the construction of a modern diasporic cultural identity which leans on both inheritance and politics. Diasporic cultural identity becomes the major politics of identity for the descendants of migrants who were born and raised in the country of residence. The gap between the institutional-societal treatment of the new generations and their own identification that they exhibit with the presentational or expressive forms of representation in the country of residence brings about the 'problem of identity.' The quest for identity for these new generations results with the employment and maintenance of ethnicity and religion as a source of identity. The self-identification of second/third generation Berlin-Turks is predominantly shaped by the symbolic ethnic and religious connotations.

The working-class Turkish hip-hop youngsters construct a form of diasporic cultural identity by means of global culture which transcend the boundaries of territorial nation-state. In this way, diaspora is described as involving the production and reproduction of social and cultural phenomena on a transnational axis (Vertovec, 1996b; Clifford, 1994; Appadurai, 1990; Hannerz, 1996). The diasporic identity constructed by ethnic minority youths has been a 'valuable component of the critique of absolutist political sensibilities' within nation-state (Gilroy, 1994: 210). As I will explain below, the construction of such a diasporic cultural identity has connections with the production and articulation of culture on a transnational level. This is evident in the production and reproduction of forms which are sometimes called 'syncretic,' 'bricolage,' 'creolized,' 'translated,' 'crossover,' 'cut'n' mix,' 'hybrid,' 'alternate' or 'melange.' Hall's metaphorical insights regarding diaspora, ethnicity and identity draw up the framework of the existing modern diaspora identities:

[...] diaspora does not refer us to those scattered tribes whose identity can only be secured in relation to some sacred homeland to which they must at all costs return, even if it means pushing other people into the sea. This is the old, the imperialising, the hegemonising, form of ethnicity. We have seen the fate of the people of Palestine at the hands of this backward-looking conception of diaspora – and the complicity of the West with it. The diaspora experience as I intend it here is defined, not by essence or purity, but by the recognition of a necessary heterogeneity and diversity; by a conception of 'identity' which lives with and through, not despite, difference; by *hybridity*. Diaspora identities are those, which are constantly producing and reproducing themselves anew, through transformation and difference (Hall, 1994: 235).

Hall explicitly distances himself from the old 'imperialising,' 'backward' notion of diaspora, and celebrates the modern notion that hosts hybridity and creolization. The production of such 'hybrid' cultural phenomena and 'new ethnicities' is especially to be found among diasporic youth whose primary socialisation has taken place with the cross-currents of differing cultural fields (Vertovec, 1996b: 29).

The construction of diasporic cultural identity derives from cultures and histories in negotiation, collision and dialogue. Diasporic identity is a disaggregated identity, and it disrupts the very categories of identity because it is not national, not genealogical, not religious, but all of these in dialectical tension with one another (Boyarin and

Boyarin, 1993: 721). Thus, the existence of the diaspora idea invites us to see the formation of cultural bricolage within the boundaries of the contested domains between the local and the global, between binary oppositions, between 'here' and 'there,' and between past and present. This permanent state of 'double consciousness' takes the diasporic subject beyond the modern nation-state and its institutional order. The main determinants giving a diasporic character to these cultures are, for Clifford (1994: 306), the obstacles, openings, antagonisms, connections that the respective group has experienced, and the transnational links facilitated by globalised communication and transport.

Transnational connections constitute what Clifford calls a 'multi-local diaspora culture' amongst the multiple communities of dispersed immigrant population (Clifford, 1994: 304). By the multi-locale diaspora culture, we do not mean a specific geographical boundary, but cultural boundary, which is linked with the homeland culture. Those dispersed people, once separated from homeland by geographical distance and political barriers, increasingly find themselves in 'border relations' with the homeland and their fellow diasporic 'mates' by means of modern technologies of transportation, communication and labour migration. The means of transportation, telephones, faxes, Internet, TV, radio, tape and videocassettes, and mobile job markets reduce distances and facilitate two-way traffic between diasporic subjects and homeland. Today, it is much easier to live in two worlds than it was two decades ago.

Most sociological studies have broadly described German-Turkish youth in terms of stereotypical notions like 'identity crisis,' 'in-betweenness,' 'lost generation,' 'split identities' and 'disoriented children' (Abadan-Unat, 1976, 1985; Kagitçibasi, 1987; Mushabe, 1985; Önder, 1996). German-Turkish youth were predominantly problematised in the Turkish scholarship. This is the rationale behind opening adaptation schools for the returnee children in Turkey with the co-operation of Turkish and German governments. This problem-oriented image drawn by many scholars is full of contradictions, and lacks sufficient empirical data. The 'second generation' (German: *die zweite Generation*; Turkish: *ikinci kusak*), often described in melodramatic terms as 'caught between two cultures but part of neither,' constructs its identity in a social field where they successfully negotiate various cultures (Mandel, 1990: 155). German-Turkish youngsters, like the other diasporic youths, tend to form a *bricolage* of cultures and identities, while at the same time keeping to their ethnic and cultural 'roots.' Thus, diasporic cultural identity should be mapped out within the co-ordinates of global (diaspora) and local (national-regional). These are as Hall comments "cultures of hybridity which have renounced the dream or ambition of rediscovering any kind of 'lost' cultural purity, or ethnic absolutism. They are irrevocably translated" (Hall, 1992: 310).

Turkish youth experience a permanent tension between homelessness and home in a way that leads to the construction of more meaningful, complex and multiple identities. Diasporic cultural identity of Turkish youth springs from their constant quest for home. For the modern diasporic subject, home is the place to which they cannot return. It is this perpetual dream of return, but not the act of return, which shapes the modern diasporic cultural identity. Should the condition of multiple identities, which is situated by the diasporic youth, be treated as the indication of their state of 'in-betweenness'? Or, should it be conceived as representing the 'third space,' or 'third culture'? This is the essential question, which I have tried to answer in my work. In the following chapters, I shall, from time to time, return to this question and elaborate upon the diasporic cultural identity of Turkish hip-hop youth living in Kreuzberg.

* * *

To recapitulate, this chapter has portrayed the transmission of the ethnic-based political strategies, which the Berlin-Turks developed since the beginning of the migratory process. These strategies have been outlined as *migrant strategy* and *minority strategy*. The change in the political strategies of the immigrants has been primarily presented as subject to the social, political, and economic relations between receiving society and ethnic minority. Then, it has been stated that, the more the ethnic minorities suffer from racism, exclusion, segregation, and majority nationalism, the more they tend to have associations with the homeland, co-ethnics, or with a world-political force such as Islam. Secondly, it was stated that this change is also a product of the globalisation, which appears as an individual consciousness of the global situation. Thus, the ethnic communities who are dispersed away from homeland acquire the chance to feel strong attachments, at symbolic level, to their homelands and co-ethnics by means of modern technology. Thirdly, it was argued that the homeland government's changing orientation to the expatriates has become a very determinant factor in the changing face of the ethnic-based political strategies. Accordingly, it was concluded that they always tend to exploit the immigrants' sentiments for their own purposes.

It should also be stated that there are no clear-cut boundaries between the strategies outlined above, they are rather overlapping. Diasporic consciousness has been introduced in this chapter as the contemporary form of ethnic consciousness. Diasporic identity is initiated by the expanding networks of communication and transportation. The Berlin-Turks tend to develop more transnational attachments with their homelands. By doing so, they transcend the obligatory binarism between themselves and the German nation-state. They rather prefer being attached to their 'imaginary homelands.' As Cohen (1996: 516) has stated, modern diasporic identities are mostly constructed on an imaginary axis:

[D]iasporas can be constituted by acts of the imagination [...] In the age of cyberspace, a diaspora can, to some degree, be held together or re-created through the mind, through cultural artefacts and through a shared imagination.

In the following chapters, the construction and articulation of the diasporic consciousness of the working-class Berlin-Turkish hip-hop youth and the formation of this complex diasporic culture will cover a wider space. By doing so, I will demonstrate that the whole question of diasporic identity is a matter of politics and process rather than of essence and inheritance. Accordingly, the following chapter will scrutinise the formation of a diasporic space in a multicultural setting. The delineation of the diasporic space shaped by the Turkish migrants in Kreuzberg will help us understand the nature of the urban landscape housing the working-class Turkish hip-hop youth.

Notes

1   The story of migration from the 'developing' countries to the FRG was successfully exhibited by John Berger et al. (1975) in the book, *The Seventh Man*. The photographs in the book taken during the journey from home to Germany can partly express the difficulties, which the immigrants had to experience during the migration. The photos taken during the medical check-ups, for

instance, evidently prove how degrading was the way the selection of the workers was conducted by the 'experts' of the recruiting country.
2 Until 1974, the father determined a child's nationality, but now either parent is sufficient.
3 It is common for Turkish applicants to reapply immediately after their German naturalisation for their temporarily-lost Turkish citizenship. Turkey allows dual citizenship once the military service of the applicant has been resolved.
4 For further information about the new German citizenship laws and regulations, see Brandt (1996).
5 For further information on the new citizenship laws and the related parliamenterian discussions see, Innenausschuß des Deutschen Bundestages (1999).
6 This strong ethnic boundary construction is what Rex (1994: 2) calls 'differential incorporation.'
7 Fredrik Barth (1969) has defined such withdrawal from the majority society as 'isolation.'
8 There are five adaptation schools in Turkey as such: one in Ankara, one in Izmir and three in Istanbul. These secondary and high schools are subject to the curriculum of the Ministry of National Education in Turkey. The schools are called *Alman Anadolu Lisesi* (German Anatolian Grammar School) where the medium of education is German. These schools were formed under the joint Cultural Treaty signed between Turkish and German governments in 1984. By this treaty it was agreed that the German government would contribute to finance the education of the returnee children and to provide 90 German teachers. In the first year of their arrival in Turkey, the students are placed in a prep-school where there are only returnees. Here, they are given intensive courses on Turkish language and literature, Turkish history, and Turkish geography. The following year they are placed in mixed classrooms with the local students. The rationale behind the mixed classroom programme is to assimilate them to the Turkish culture and way of life more easily. For a detailed information about the reintegration of the returnees, see Abadan-Unat (1988).
9 *Almanci* literally means German-like which bears witness to a combination of difference, lack of acceptance, and rejection.
10 For a detailed explanation about the history of Turkish ethnic

associations in Berlin and Germany, see Özcan (1994), Seidel-Pielen (1995) and Gitmez and Wilpert (1987).
11 For a detailed information about the laws of belonging in Germany, see Senders (1996) and Klusmeyer (1992).
12 For a detailed map of these associations, see *TBB Türkçe Danisma Yerleri Kilavuzu*.
13 Danish and *Sorben* ethnic groups enjoy minority status in Germany with accompanying language and cultural rights.
14 For further information on '*Gastarbeiterliteratur,*' see also Horrocks and Kolinsky (1996) and Gürsoy-Tezcan (1992).
15 It should be stated that ethnic strategies developed by Kurds and *Alevi*s have different dynamics and need further inquiry. However, *Alevi*s and their ethnic structuring will be explored in the following chapter.
16 The analogy of Ulysses and Abraham belongs to Emmanuel Levinas (1986: 348; 1987: 91). In explaining the attempt of conventional philosophy to seek the knowledge about the 'Other,' Levinas stated that the history of philosophy has been like the story of Ulysses who 'through all his wanderings only returns to his native island' (1986: 348). He preferred the story of Abraham to that of Ulysses. Conventional philosophy has always sought to return to familiar ground of 'being,' 'truth' and 'the same;' Levinas' endeavour was to take it elsewhere. He proposed that philosophy should accept that we do not, can not and should not know the Other, rather than seeking knowledge of it.
17 For a detailed map of Turkish TV channels and the spread of Turkish official ideology, see Aksoy and Robins (1997).

Chapter 3

Kreuzberg 36:

A Diasporic Space in Multicultural Berlin

Turkish migrants in Kreuzberg have constructed a social space of their own – a diasporic space where they have developed a web of social institutions, norms and values. This diasporic space has provided the Turkish population with a ground to acquire a set of positive and resistant articulations of identity in a country such as Germany that previously had an exclusionist ideology towards the immigrants. Resistance to exclusion in the Turkish diaspora context can take the form of distinct national and religious aspirations. I do not want to claim that diasporic cultural politics are somehow free of nationalist, religious and chauvinist agendas, but one should also remember that, as Clifford (1994: 307) has put it, such discourses are usually weapons used by relatively weak groups.

In modern diaspora experience that is facilitated by transnational circuit of communications and transportation, identities are constructed in a way that bends together both global and local, roots and routes, inheritance and politics, past and present. As I pointed out in the former chapters, modern diasporic identity is formed and articulated in both particularist and universalist axes. Kreuzberg 36, as a typical example of diasporic space, gives the individual the sense of simultaneously being 'here' (diaspora) and 'there' (homeland). What are the main constitutive entanglements turning this urban space into a diasporic space? What are the components of the particularist dimension of the modern diasporic identity? To what extent do the transnational Turkish media contribute to the construction of a distinct diasporic consciousness? What kind of discourses do the major Turkish ethnic organisations articulate to partake in the social and political life in multicultural Berlin? What kind of multicultural institutions have

CHAPTER 3

emerged in Berlin to incorporate the ethnic minorities into the mainstream? And how do the Turkish ethnic associations respond to the dominant discourse of multiculturalism? Accordingly, this chapter will primarily aim to answer these essential questions as well as to expound the principal features of Kreuzberg 36 as constituting a diasporic urban space for Turkish migrants.

A Turkish Ethnic Enclave

Kreuzberg is a densely populated area located in the centre of Berlin. It is full of various social and cultural undercurrents. On the one hand, it is the ever-lasting dream of many left wing, or liberal, Germans to buy a flat by the picturesque *Landwehrkanal* that crosscuts Kreuzberg;[1] on the other hand, it has been the main quarter of the working-class cultures throughout history. Kreuzberg has always been defined as a working-class area since the mid 17th century. It provided immigrants, guestworkers (*Gastarbeiter*) and asylum-seekers with shelter. In the seventeenth century, French Protestant refugees (Huguenots) found asylum there. In the nineteenth century, indigent, landless immigrants from Silesia, Pomerania, and eastern Prussia came in for the search of work. At the turn of the last century, the district served as home to industrial workshops and small factories, as well as to the workers employed in them (Mandel, 1996: 149; Knödler-Bunte, 1987: 219-238). Until the division of Germany in the aftermath of the World War II, Kreuzberg was situated adjacent to the district of *Mitte* that houses many historical monuments and the bureaucratic settlement of the Second Reich, Weimar Republic and Third Reich. After the division, it has become the very periphery of the West Berlin, hosting the '*Gastarbeiter*' from Turkey, Greece, Lebanon and Portugal. Reunification has brought a new outlook to the district. Recently, it is becoming one of the new centres of the expanding metropolitan city of Berlin. In this section, I will explore the social-cultural geography of Kreuzberg, but only with a limitation to Kreuzberg 36 and Kotbusser Tor where I conducted most of my field research.

The topography of the ethnic minorities in Kreuzberg has entirely changed since the reunification in 1991 (Table 2). For instance, the positioning of the Turkish minority has undergone a drastic shift. While the '*Gastarbeiter*,' who are predominantly Turkish and Kurdish, were previously dwelling in the south-eastern periphery of West Berlin, they have suddenly found themselves in the centre of the city with the reunification. Kreuzberg 36 resembles a kind of *'Kleines* Istanbul' (Little Istanbul), which is surrounded by the images, signs, rhythms, music, foods, shops, banks, traditional *cafés*, and major political issues of Turkey: a Turkish diaspora. Beyond that, in many senses, it resembles a cultural island within the urban landscape. With the ethnic minorities, working-class groups, left wing political groupings, anarchists and marginal youth, Kreuzberg represents a permanent state of *festivity*. It is literally a multi-cultural neighbourhood.

Table 2: Demographic Structure of Kreuzberg, 25.07.1996

Country of Origin	Population	Percent
Turkey	28,913	18.70
Ex-Yugoslavia	3,211	2.06
Poland	1,681	1.07
Greece	1,497	0.95
Italy	995	0.64
Croatia	1,320	0.85
Ex-Soviet Union	538	0.52
Iran	620	0.34
Bosnia-Herzegovina	1,611	1.04
Lebanon	740	0.47
Others	10,864	7.02
Germans in Total	102,553	66.34
Kreuzberg in Total	**154,543**	**100.00**

Source: Statistisches Landesamt, Einwohnerregister

Kreuzberg is surrounded by the districts of Neukölln in the south, Schöneberg in the west, Tiergarten in the north, and Mitte in the east. Traffic connections to Kreuzberg have extensively increased in time. Traffic has gradually been diverted towards Kreuzberg after the reunification in order to provide an efficient link between the east and west. As the youngsters express, Kreuzberg is no more a peripheral district where the children used to freely play in the streets without traffic. Now, it is a central place where there is constantly a traffic jam.

CHAPTER 3

The metro is the main form of public transportation. U1 and U15 are the regular trains connecting Kreuzberg to the rest of Berlin. The metro railway crosscuts the district through the bridges built just after World War I. There are also regular public busses passing through Kotbusser Tor such as No. 129 and No. 141.

For the Turkish population, Kreuzberg, or Berlin, is better connected to Turkey than to the other cities of Germany. Kreuzberg is full of Turkish travel agencies offering both regular and charter flights to various cities in Turkey such as Istanbul, Ankara, Izmir, Trabzon, Antalya and Adana. *Onur Air, Pak Tur, Pegasus Air, Öger Tur, Turkish Airlines,* and *Türk Tur* are some of these agencies. Sometimes, it is possible to find a return ticket to Istanbul with a price of 250 DM (approximately £ 100). This price may well rise to 800 DM in the summer vacation periods. Since the internal war commenced in the country once called Yugoslavia, these agencies have also provided ferryboat tickets to people who want to travel to Turkey by their own private cars. The boats generally depart from the Italian harbours in the Adriatic and arrive at the Turkish harbours in the Aegean Sea. As far as domestic transport is concerned for the Berlin-Turks, Kreuzberg is not efficiently connected to the other parts of Germany. It is almost out of question for them to travel by German Railway because it is not easily affordable, or by cheaper travel alternatives such as coaches and *Mitfahrzentralen*.[2] Turkish migrants, from time to time, visit their friends and/or relatives who live in the west. Almost all the members of the family join these kinds of visits; it is like a reaffirmation of family rituals. As this is a kind of family ritual, they prefer driving to their destination using their own cars.

Berlin-Turks have multiple links with their country of origin. The growth of modern communication and transportation networks has given rise to the Berlin-Turks' orientation to Turkey. TV channels, video tapes, newspapers, Internet facilities and charter flights facilitate and increase the pace of the communication between Germany and the homeland. To give an example: a commercial in the window of a travel agency in *Kotbusser Damm* was advertising "Weekend Shopping in Istanbul: 395 DM, 3 Days + Hotel." These modern constituents of globalism allow the Turkish migrants to construct a local network, which is sustained by the images of homeland. At first glance, Kreuzberg is like a very condensed copy of Istanbul. Restaurants, banks, mosques, *cafés*, music shops, *döner kebab* kiosks, graffiti, tagging and billboards on the walls, dressing style of the residents, and the faces around the district, they were all reminiscent of the atmosphere of Istanbul. On the walls of Kreuzberg one can see all kinds of political graffiti from various groups, radical left to radical right. Also one can witness various political organisations' buildings standing side by side, although they are ideologically quite oppositional in their groupings. While playing *tavla* (backgammon) in one of the traditional Turkish *café*s in Kreuzberg occupied by the middle-aged and elderly males, I had the impression that I was in a time tunnel that took me back to the Turkey of the sixties. The clothing type of the men, the way they shave their moustache, and the way they speak reminded me of a very secular section of people raised by the young republic of Turkey. That was an unchanging view in Berlin since the beginning of the migration: a frozen moment, or a picture in time.

Turkish migrants have set up their own community networks in all respects. They not only have *döner kebab* kiosks and bakeries, but also many other special services such as dentists, accountants, printing houses, TV stations etc. The bilingual telephone guide is an indication of such a community network.[3] From catering to mechanics, from pet shops to doctors, the 190-pages of the Berlin Yellow Pages (*Altin Sayfalar*) provides a wide variety of services to the Turkish-origin residents of Berlin. Another indication of the community network is the Turkish Guide for Advisory Centres (*Türkçe Danisma Yerleri Kilavuzu*) that was published by the *Türkischer Bund in Berlin-Brandenburg* (Berlin-Brandenburg Turkish Community) in 1996.[4] The guide provides an extensive network of advisory centres where Turkish residents of Berlin could apply in case of necessity. From employment to housing, from anti-racist initiatives to sheltering for women, the guide aims to compensate for the lack of information for the Turkish migrants and their children.

'Kleines Istanbul' (Little Istanbul)

Most of my research took place around Kreuzberg 36 and *Kotbusser Tor*, which literally constitute the centre of the Turkish ethnic enclave in Kreuzberg. Thus, in this section, I will precisely concentrate on the social-cultural mapping out of this quarter rather than the other parts of Kreuzberg. A mix of late 19th century *Gründerzeit* houses and post war 'modern' buildings surrounds Kotbusser Tor.[5] Leaving the train at *Kotbusser Tor U-Bahn* station, the first thing that confronts one is a newsagent whose owner is Turkish. A journey then starts through the heart of Kreuzberg. At the *U-Bahn* exit to *Adalbertstraße*, is another Turkish store selling flowers. Stepping out on the *Adalbertstraße*, one faces the *Mevlana Camii* (mosque) on the right hand, and a Turkish open market on the left hand. *Mevlana Camii* is quite different from the classical mosques in that it does not have a minaret.[6] It is located just over the *Kaiser's* shopping centre, which is popular among the Turks due to its lower prices. *Mevlana Camii* is the factual centre of the *Berlin Milli Görüs Vakfi* (Berlin National Vision Foundation), which has organic connections with the *Refah Partisi* (Welfare Party) in Turkey.[7] On the left side is the open market selling food, vegetables and fruits, mostly imported from Turkey. Further on, a passageway under a building permits the *Adalbertstraße* to continue. This 'bridge' is called *Galata* in remembrance of the historical *Galata Köprüsü* (Bridge) in the old centre of Istanbul. Above the passage there are situated two 'traditional' Turkish *cafés*: the centre of the conservative *Türkische Gemeinde zu Berlin*, and the meeting point of the extreme left wing '*Emek, Baris ve Özgürlük Blogu*' (Labour, Peace and Freedom Block). This corner of Kreuzberg mirrors the diversified nature of the Turkish population. While the small *café* is the meeting point of the adult *Alevi* community, the big one is popular for men of every age. Under the passage there are two *döner kebab* kiosks (Imbiss), a Turkish bakery called *Misir Çarsisi*, and a Turkish bookstore. *Misir Çarsisi* literally refers to Egyptian Bazaar. The name again springs from the historical *Misir Çarsisi*, which is located near the *Galata Köprüsü* in Istanbul.

Another stimulating phenomenon was previously represented by the posters and billboards stuck onto each leg of the *Galata* Bridge. Most of the posters were political slogans from the far right to the far left. The left wing slogans mostly denounced the illegitimacy of the political order in Turkey which bans the existence of Marxist, Leninist and Maoist organisations, which remained silent about the 'massacre' of the *Alevi*s, and which had no peaceful alternative solutions to the Kurdish question. On the other hand, the right wing slogans consisted mainly of the messages of the Turkish Grey Wolfs and religious groups. Sometimes, some concert and festival posters might have been seen here as well, e.g. 'Live Music: Trio from Istanbul at *Kestane Bar*,' or 'Concert: Baris Manço and *Cartel* at Tempodrom.' Lately, the

Kreuzberg Municipality renovated the Galata Bridge: the form of the legs was so restyled that it is no longer possible to stick any poster on. In doing so, the Municipality aims to ban the announcement of those political messages.

Walking along through *Adalbertstraße*, one comes across many *döner kebab* kiosks, travel agencies, groceries, bakeries, banks, glassware stores, and music stores; they are all Turkish. The classical Berlin buildings facing each other around an inner courtyard surround the street. In Kreuzberg, a particular form of building structure was erected to serve the working and living needs. This multi-layered, structurally dense and complex configuration was known as the *Hinterhaus* (back/rear house, or building), designed around a series of *Hinterhöfe* (back/rear courtyards). This living/working arrangement distinctly delimited a highly stratified social ordering, in brick and mortar, of classes and functions. The rear buildings, unlike those in front, were built of plain brick, lacked direct access to the street and sunlight, had no private toilets, and were invariably noisy and crowded (Mandel, 1996: 149).[8] The courtyards are the playground of children and the meeting place of youngsters when the youth centres are closed.

Adalbertstraße previously used to terminate at the Berlin Wall in the northern part. The street is cut across by three streets, i.e. *Oranienstraße, Naunynstraße* and *Waldemarstraße*. The first, *Oranienstraße*, is a quite popular place both for German and Turkish youngsters. On the left side of the street many modern *cafés* run by Kurds and Turks may be found. The customers of these *cafés* are very mixed, which is not the norm in Berlin generally. On the right side of the street, there are many German stores selling books, trendy clothes, tapes and CDs for the German rockers, hip-hop fans, and techno youngsters. Sometimes, in this corner of the street, a few multicultural carnivals and festivals are organised by either *Haus der Kulturen der Welt*, or *SFB4 Radio Multikulti*. These carnivals have recently reached extensive populations. The latest one in the Summer of the year 2000 had almost half-a-million people all around Germany. In these organisations, Turkish music groups also perform their pieces, such as the rappers *Islamic Force* and *Azize-A*. In such *festivals*, it is common to see some Turkish faces around, interacting with Germans, but most Turks prefer watching the *festival* through the windows of their houses facing the street.

The second street cutting across *Adalbertstraße* is *Naunynstraße* where the *Naunyn Ritze* youth centre is located. Opposite the youth centre is *Ballhaus* where some small size concerts and theatre plays are put on stage. This street is mainly occupied by the residents themselves. They are mostly Turkish and Kurdish *Alevis* from Erzincan and Erzurum. The third street is *Waldemarstraße*, which is also composed of Turkish and Kurdish residents. On the right part of the street is a kindergarten in which there is one Turkish youth worker. The kindergarten, *Çivili Park*, is combined to *Naunyn Ritze*. Next to *Çivili Park*, is *Bethanien* that is a monumental building with yellow bricks. The building, which resembles a Middle Ages feudal castle, used to be a hospital, but is now composed of various sections providing public services for the Kreuzberg people. The *Bethanien* consists of a Casino, a *Künstlerhaus* (art school), a Turkish language library called *Namik Kemal Kütübhanesi*, a music school, and a print house. The library is quite essential for the Turkish residents. There are daily papers, magazines and quite new scientific and literary books from Turkey in the library.

Taking the other exit at the tube-station, one arrives at *Kotbusser Damm* and *Reichenberger Straße*, which are parallel to each other and cut across by the *Landwehrkanal*. Kotbusser Damm is also surrounded by houses, a Turkish bank, Turkish stores and offices. Orient Bazaar is the most popular of the stores. It faces the *U-Bahn* station. It consists of a *bakkal* (Turkish mini market), a bakery, a music store, a jewellery store and an *Imbiss* (small kiosk). Kotbusser Damm leads to *Neukölln*, which is a neighbouring district where there is also a dense Turkish population (Table 3). Further on, the *Maybachufer* cuts across the *Kotbusser Damm* just after the bridge on the canal. There is an open Turkish market in this street on Fridays. It is very similar to its equivalents in Turkey. The sellers advertise their mostly Turkish goods through various screams. There is a large variety of goods in the market from vegetable to sea foods, and from glassware to clothing. Right across the open market in the *Kotbusser Damm*, there is a Turkish shopping centre opened in August 2000. On the other hand, *Reichenberger Straße* is dominated by the residents whose ethnic origins are Turkish, Kurdish, German, Lebanese and Portuguese. Unlike *Naunynstraße*, it is an ethnically mixed neighbourhood. *Chip*, which is the other youth centre where I conducted my research, is located in this street.

Table 3: Turkish Population in Berlin District, 30.06.1996

District	Population	District	Population
Mitte	440	Tempelhof	4,752
Tiergarten	8,623	Neukölln	26,904
Wedding	24,332	Treptow	361
Prenzlauer Berg	523	Köpenick	158
Friedrichshain	527	Lichtenberg	304
Kreuzberg	28,913	Weißensee	76
Charlottenburg	7,547	Pankow	340
Spandau	8,829	Reinickendorf	6,499
Wilmersdorf	2,176	Marzahn	175
Zehlendorf	845	Hohenschönhausen	106
Schöneberg	12,051	Hellersdorf	106
Steglitz	3,087	**Total**	**137,674**

Source: *Statistisches Landesamt, Einwohnerregister*

The social-cultural mapping out of Kreuzberg 36 is very similar to that of some other townscape examples which exemplify a different kind of diasporic space such as Southall, London (Baumann, 1996), Rinkeby, Stockholm (Ålund, 1991, 1996), and 32nd Street, Chicago (Horowitz, 1983). Diasporic characteristics of a particular townscape mainly spring from the way cultures are reified by its sojourners. Diasporic communities tend to reify culture at the same time as making and remaking it. Departing from the critical judgements of the youngsters about, for instance, the way their parents dress up, one could conclude that there is a strong 'cultural conservatism' amongst the first generation migrants living in Kreuzberg. Knowing both modern Turkey and Kreuzberg, the youngsters imply that some people are still living a life of twenty years ago. Looking at the dresses of the people going to the Friday Turkish bazaar in Kotbusser Tor, it is highly possible to see many women wearing very colourful eastern Anatolian clothes including traditional scarf, or black veil, and *shalvar* (baggy trousers); or else to see many men wearing religious robes with full sleeves, long skirts and turban.

For many in the Turkish diaspora, the cultural baggage brought from home is an absolutely vital element in the negotiation of identity, but it comprises a renovated set of practices and discourses, too. Reification of culture serves as a social strategy for the diasporic individual. There is no doubt that Turkish migrants are better off in Germany compared to their pre-immigrant social-economic status in Turkey. Representing pre-immigrant lifestyles as in their dressing styles and recollecting the hardships of the past as in their daily discourses, immigrants tend to justify their act of immigration as the right option. By reifying culture, maintaining pre-immigrant social networks (*hemsehri* bonds) and familial connections, those immigrants attempt to adopt themselves in the diasporic context where they find themselves alone and without the traditional support systems they were brought up with.

As stated before culture is a continuous process of change, whereas the first generation immigrants transform it into a heritage in the diaspora. In other words, as Baumann states in Southall (London) example (1996: 192), for diasporic communities cultural processes become transformed into cultural heritage, that could be reified in order to enculturate the young generations and to construct a cultural fortress of their own in relation to that of the majority culture. The process of cultural reification among the first generation Turkish migrants is also strengthened by the Turkish media. What follows in the next section is the impact of the Turkish media on the construction of a distinct Turkish diasporic identity, which partly invests on the preservation of culture as a heritage.

Interconnectedness in Space

For at least a decade, the presence of Turkish language mass media in Germany, and particularly in Berlin, has become so salient that the Berlin Commissioner for Foreigners' Affairs, Barbara John, even spoke of the dangers of '3T': easy access to Turkish language *television*, cheaper costs in *telecommunication*, and long-distance *travel* (Faist, 2000a). The Commissioner raised her concerns that the permanent spread of transportation and communication facilities between diaspora and homeland contribute to hinder the integration of immigrants in Germany. As seen from the statement of the Berlin Commissioner, the volume of the Turkish language media has reached an extensive level. The development of tele-communication technology has made the reception of almost all the Turkish TV channels and newspapers in Berlin possible. Turkish media in Berlin have achieved a remarkable cultural hegemony throughout the Turkish diaspora. To understand this one has to examine the rising interest of the Turkish media industry in the Turkish population living in diaspora. The major Turkish TV channels have had their own European units making special programmes for Turks living in Europe. TRT International (state channel) is the first of these channels. Then come Euro Show, Euro Star, Euro D, Euro ATV, TGRT, Kanal 7, HBB and Satel. All these TV channels apart from the TRT International can be received via satellite antennas. TRT Int is already available on cable (Table 4).

Table 4: Turkish TV Channels in Germany and the Rate of Audience

Turkish TV Channels	Percent
TRT-INT	47.0
Euroshow	22.0
HBB	0.5
Eurostar	7.0
ATV	2.0
TGRT	1.0
Kanal 6	0.5
Others	20.0

Source: Türkiye Arastirmalar Merkezi – Zentrum für Türkeistudien, Bonn 1995

The programme spectrum of all these channels may differ greatly from each other. TRT Int tends mainly to give equal weight to entertainment, education, magazine, movies and news. Since it is a state owned channel, it tries to promote the 'indispensable unity of the Turkish nation' by arranging, for instance, money campaigns for the Turkish armed forces fighting in the South Eastern part of Turkey. There are also many programmes concentrating on the problems of the European Turks. This channel can also be widely received in Turkey. Thus, in a way, it also informs the Turkish audience about the happenings of the European-Turks, mainly that of the German-Turks, whilst connecting the modern diasporic Turkish communities to the homeland.

Euro Show, Euro D, Euro Star and Euro HBB are private channels making secular based programmes. The majority of the programmes are composed of old Turkish movies, American movies, comedy programmes, dramas, Turkish and European pop charts, sport programmes, reality-shows and news. On the other hand TGRT and Kanal 7 are the religious based TV channels. Besides the actual programmes, these channels give priority to the dramas and movies with religious motives. Traditional Turkish folk music programmes are also a part of the policy of these two channels. Satel is another channel giving the Turkish and European pop charts. It is the favourite channel of the Turkish youngsters who have satellite antennae.

Apart from these satellite channels, there are a few more local Turkish TV channels in Berlin. TD1 is one of them. Turkish video movies, local news and sport programmes are the major components of the programme. It also provides news and some dramas from Turkey, previously copied from Turkish channels. There are also some other channels, which can be watched on the *Offener Kanal* (Open Channel) and *Spree Kanal*. They are both free channels to rent. *Aypa* TV, TFD (*Türkisches Fernsehen in Deutschland*), *Alcanlar* TV, *Ehli Beyit* TV are some of these TV associations.[9] Recently, there is also a new radio channel broadcasting 24-hour in Turkish: *Radio Metropol 94.8*. This channel was founded in the year 2000, and has a wide variety of programms ranging from local and international news to Turkish music.

Most of the major Turkish newspapers are also printed in Germany to be distributed in Germany as well as in the rest of Europe. *Hürriyet, Milliyet, Sabah, Cumhuriyet* and *Evrensel* are some of the Turkish papers printed in Germany. There are also many other sports and magazine papers from Turkey. Although the content of the papers is extremely limited in terms of the news about the homeland, they offer a wide range of news about Turkish diasporic communities in Europe. *Hürriyet* has its own Berlin supplement each Wednesday, providing community news (Table 5).[10]

Cultural hegemony of the Turkish media partly shapes the 'habitats of meaning' of the diasporic subject living in the West.[11] Turkish media mostly attempt to provide a stream of programmes, which is considered to suit the 'habitats of meaning' of the diasporic subject. For instance, the German-Turks are perceived by the Turkish media industry as a group of people who resist cultural change. This percep-

Table 5: Turkish Newspapers Printed in Germany[12]

Newspaper	First Publishing Date	Tirage (pcs) in 1995	Tirage (pcs) in 1997
Hürriyet	1971	107,634	107,000
Milliyet	1972	25,000	16,000
Sabah	1996	-	25,000
Türkiye	1987	40,000	40,000
Cumhuriyet*	1995	-	5,000
Milli Gazete	1973	11,000	12,000
Zaman	1990	4,000	13,000
Tercüman	1972	19,000	-
Yeni Günaydin	1991	14,000	-
Özgür Gündem	1993	8,000	-
Emek-Evrensel*	1996	-	8,000
Dünya*	1991	2,500	2,500
Ordadogu	1996	-	3,000
Total		231,134	231,500

* Weekly newspaper
Source: *Zentrum für Türkeistudien, Bonn 1995 and 1997*

tion, for instance, is the main rationale behind the selection of the movies and dramas. A high number of the films on each channel are the old Turkish films, which were produced in the late sixties and seventies.[13] The performance of the old Turkish movies, which touch upon some traditional issues such as Anatolian feudalism, bloodfeuds, migration (*gurbet*), desperate romance and poverty, reinforces the reification of culture within the Turkish diaspora. As Michel Foucault noted such films attempt to 're-programme popular memory' to recover 'lost, unheard memories' which had been denied, or buried, by the dominant representations of the past experienced in the diaspora (Quoted in Morley and Robins, 1993: 10). Hence, identity is also a question of memory, and memories of home in particular (Morley and Robins, 1993: 10). Before the private TV channels were opened, it was the VCR industry, which used to provide the Turkish diaspora with those kinds of movies.[14]

Berlin-Turks, whose 'habitats of meaning' have been extensively nurtured by the Turkish media, have also a different sense of place within the diaspora. The Turkish media play a very crucial role in the formation of a more complex form of belonging for the Turkish diaspora. The media create, for the diasporic communities, a symbolic bond to the homeland, a symbolic bond to various diasporic Turkish communities in Europe, and conversely also persuade the diasporic subject to become a sojourner in the country of settlement. Feeding the ethnic flame of Turkishness and Turkish culture, the Turkish media tend to create a distinctive Turkish identity in diaspora. The construction of such a distinct identity is indeed quite relevant to what the discourse of multiculturalism aims to do in Berlin. In the coming section, I will elaborate some of the Turkish ethnic organisations in Berlin and their discourses prior to the institutions and dominant discourse of multiculturalism. Subsequently, I shall expose the impact of the official ideology of multiculturalism on the culturalisation and minorisation of the *Alevi* community in Berlin.

Major Turkish Ethnic Associations in Berlin

The conventional notion of diaspora presupposes the existence of a homogenous community that had been forced to leave the homeland. This relatively homogenous community tends to exclude the majority society rather than diffusing into it. In fact, it would be misleading to name the Turkish communities living in Germany as a homogenous diaspora. While there are some communities such as the religious groups of *Süleymancis, Nurcus* and *Kaplancis* that might suit the definition of old diasporas as a social category, most of the Turkish-origin sojourners in Germany contradict this old notion.[15] Turkish religious communities (*cemaat*) having fundamentalist beliefs are built around what Salman Rushdie (1990) calls 'the absolutism of the Pure.' "The apostles of purity," he argues, are always moved by the fear that "intermingling with a different culture will inevitably weaken and ruin their own." What they believe is that communicating with the 'unbelievers' does not strengthen their spiritual belief system. A seventy-year-old Turkish *Sunni hodja* (religious leader, teacher, or preacher) of the *Rufai* sect in the Mevlana Camii, hints at the rationale behind the construction of a Islamic diasporic identity:

We [Muslims] prefer the company of the believers (*mümin*s). It is not enough to be Muslim. Muslim means to surrender to the will of God, but surrendering does not prove that someone is a trustful believer who has faith in God. There are three strata in an Islamic community: *Avam* (ordinary people), *Has* (Faithful people) and *Hasin Hasi* (most faithful people). The Holy Book, *Koran*, says we must stick together with the believers to strengthen our faith in God, and to progress spiritually against the material world. Thus, we tend to distance ourselves from the *Avam*. It gives us spiritual inspiration to be together with the trustful believers (Personal interview, 25 January 1996).

The Islamic man whom I talked to was a retired carpenter, and was not able to speak German at all, although he had come to Germany almost twenty-five years ago. His main concern has always been to keep the Islamic purity without intermingling with the majority society, most of whom he called unbelievers. The interview was accompanied by a German researcher friend of mine for whom I was doing simultaneous translation. In the end of the interview, the *hoca* fulfilled his mission by inviting my friend to convert to Islam (*irshad*). Like many other Turkish *Sunni*s his main intention is to remain in Europe until the last European Christian has been converted to Islam.

The elite of those religious groups had to immigrate to Germany after the 1960 military *coup d'état* in Turkey. The practice of migration has gained a mystical meaning for these religious groups. They constructed a resemblance between their experience and that of the prophet Mohammed. The prophet migrated from Mecca to Medina in order to be able to free his Islamic community from the oppression of the non-believers. It is believed that the experience of migration (*hijra*) gave the believers the chance to test their faith in God. Thus, by doing so, the Muslim immigrants believe that the act of migration has strengthened their faith (Atacan, 1993: 57). These groups have formed their own cultural and religious islands in Germany. What they form is a kind of relatively homogenous Islamic Diaspora (with a capital 'D').[16]

These separate religious groupings resemble archipelago islands, which do not have surface connections to each other. They spring from various schools in Islam and always have different interpretations of the holy book Koran, but their common denominator is their relation to the receiving Christian society. They prefer sticking together within their own closed religious communities and distance themselves from the Christian society. Although most of the religious communities are loyal to the universal Islamic binarism between *Dar'ul Islam*

(Land of Islam) and *Dar'ul Harb* (Land of War), they are not able to free themselves from their particularist and national understanding of the Islamic religion. For instance, religious Turkish communities do not consider the Indian-origin *Wahabbis* a valid form of Islam.

The conflict between various Islamic schools prevents the existence of a homogenous Islamic Diaspora: it is extremely diversified. Some of the groups have an universalist vision of Islam that is, to a certain extent, independent of nationalist connotations. *Süleymancis, Nurcus* and *Kaplancis* are the Islamic sects (*tarikat*) having a relatively universalist discourse. They attempt to disconnect themselves both from the country of origin and settlement. On the other hand, some other groupings have a powerful orientation to Turkey in their understanding of Islam, e.g., *Avrupa Milli Görüs Teskilati*, AMGT (Association of National Vision in Europe).[17] AMGT has a wide network in Berlin as well as in Europe. The organisation has a modern youth cultural centre in Kreuzberg, where some of the Turkish youngsters go for leisure activities such as watching religious plays, playing billiards and watching cable TV. The group also opened an officially recognised public school in Kotbusser Tor, Kreuzberg in 1981. They run the school covertly, since they are still considered an illegal organisation. Recently they succeeded to get financial support for the school from the Berlin Senate. The School of Islamic Sciences consists of primary and secondary schools. German is the medium of education in the school, Turkish, Arabic and English are the other languages the students are supposed to learn. The organisation also covertly runs some Koran teaching courses in its own mosques.

All of these religious organisations are considered illegal in Germany. The only official religious organisation is *Diyanet Isleri Türk Islam Birligi*, DITIB (Turkish-Islam Union, Religious Affairs). DITIB is the official religious representative of the Turkish government. It has the biggest Islamic audience in Berlin. DITIB has a nationalist vision of Islam. It has a community school in Kreuzberg, where the students are taught Turkish history, Turkish geography, Turkish and Arabic. DITIB has thirteen mosques in Berlin out of almost fifty. In these mosques, Koran courses are conducted. Deriving from various sources of Islam, all these religious communities have separately constructed Islamic Diasporas as a social practice and category.[18]

Besides the religious-based ethnic associations, Turks have founded some other ethnic organisations in Berlin that are based on the ideological and political cleavages in Turkey. The first group of organisations can be gathered under the umbrella of the *Türkische Gemeinde zu Berlin* (TGB). The concept of *Türkische* here means ethnic *Sunni*-Muslim-Turk, so it excludes other Anatolian peoples like Kurds, *Alevis*, Circassians and Assurians. These groups have a conservative, nationalist and religious basis, and have attachments to the right-wing political parties in Turkey such as the True Path Party (*Dogruyol Partisi*, DYP), the Motherland Party (*Anavatan Partisi*, ANAP), the Virtue Party (*Fazilet Partisi*, FP), and the Nationalist Action Party (*Milliyetçi Hareket Partisi*, MHP). They also have connections with the conservative parties in Germany like CDU and CSU. Their preference for the conservative Christian parties stems from their traditional opposition to the left in Turkey, and from their political choices in the homeland. As an ethnic organisation they have two principal discourses, i.e. culture discourse and minority discourse.

These groups celebrate the authentic and mythical Turkish culture that they trace back to the very early ages in Central Asia in contrast to the relatively new German culture which can only be traced back two hundred years. The former head of TGB, Mustafa Çakmakoglu, for instance, underlines the cultural difference between Turkish and German societies:

We [Turks] have got a strong culture, which goes back two thousand years, whereas Germans have a two hundred-year culture. Their history consists of unification [in the nineteenth century], nationalism, enmity towards France, warfare, Marshall Plan and power. But we have culture (Personal interview, 2 February 1996).

By saying so, Çakmakoglu attempts to reify Turkish culture as a discrete unity. His use of the notion of culture resembles what Clive Harris (1997) calls CULT(ure). This holistic and essentialist notion of culture grants a privilege to cultural authenticity, which is a process of self-awareness arising from the discovery and recognition of traditional local-cultural formations in their own historical settings. His discourse also underlines the conventional differentiation between 'culture' and 'civilisation' in a way that celebrates the former.

TGB also claims to be the most important representative of the Turkish minority in Berlin before the other German and Turkish bodies. The largest Turkish ethnic-political grouping apart from TGB is *Türkischer Bund in Berlin-Brandenburg* (TBB). Some other groups of people have come together through their own nuclear organisations under the umbrella of the TBB. These nuclear organisations are, for instance, some specialised organisations like doctors, academics, students, students' parents, *Alevis* and some left-wing organisations etc. Here, the concept of *Türkische* literally refers to '*Türkiyeli*' (people from Turkey) in Turkish. It is an attempt to include both the left-wing and Kurdish-origin people that feel themselves in a kind of exile. Although they have a more universalist vision compared to the other Turkish communities, they also have a visible political orientation to the homeland. They run some political activities showing that these groups of people have become the sojourners and have interest in the internal politics of the receiving country. For instance, in the parliamentary elections in Berlin (October 1995) three Kurdish-origin Turkish citizens were elected for the Berlin Provincial Parliament (2 from the *Grünen* and 1 from the *PDS*), and 10 other Turkish citizens were elected to the municipality parliaments. These groups of organisations are also in favour of the acquisition of German citizenship for the Turkish citizens. Yet, the elite of the TBB is against the acquisition of an ethnic minority status in the German society because they believe that such a political shift would increase the xenophobic sentiment in Germany towards the Turks. So they are quite sceptical about the notion of ethnic minority.

Whatever their political orientation is towards the country of residence or to the homeland, it is very clear that each type of organisation tends to form interest groups that can mobilise Turkish minority in social, political and economic respects. The setting of the earlier Turkish migrant organisations in Berlin used to be defensive: in order to resist the feeling of exclusion and loneliness they constructed a local solidarity network. Whereas the contemporary ethnic organisations seek to promote the political participation of the Turks in a way that leads to a bridge formed between the majority and the minority. Thus, while these groups in contrast to the religious groups prefer interacting with the majority society, it is misleading to believe that these diversified groups constitute a homogenous Turkish diaspora.

All these organisations indicate that the diversified Turkish ethnic minority, apart from those segregationist religious groups, prefers incorporating into, and interacting with, the majority society. They tend to incorporate themselves into the political interest groups like political parties and labour unions. This is the indication of the construction of a *Gesellschaft* network, rather than a traditional *Gemeinschaft* network. The institutionalisation of the Turkish minority in the form of *Gesellschaft* can be observed in the economic sphere (free enterprise, investment in Germany), the political sphere (political organisations which are oriented to Germany, to Turkey, or to both), and the leisure time activities (music courses, family tea gardens, folklore courses). While the Turkish minority attempts to mobilise itself by means of interest groups formed to interact and negotiate with the German political institutions, Berlin administration has recently produced some multicultural organisations to answer the new incorporatist demands raised by the Turkish minority. Accordingly, I will now briefly explore these multicultural initiatives, and scrutinise the dominant discourse of multiculturalism in Berlin.

Institutional Multiculturalism in Berlin

Multiculturalism is one of the prevailing notions and/or institutions of the present time. Parekh defines multiculturalism as numerical plurality of cultures that is creating, guaranteeing, encouraging spaces within which different communities are able to grow up at their own pace. At the same time it means creating a public space in which these communities are able to interact, enrich the existing culture and create a new consensual culture in which they recognise reflections of their own identity. According to Parekh, "multiculturalism is possible, but only if communities feel confident enough to engage in a dialogue and where there is enough public space for them to interact with the dominant culture" (Parekh, in Parekh and Bhabha 1989: 27). One way of promoting this ideal is to provide forms and manifestations of ethnic diversity with greater public status and dignity.

In Western European context, for instance in Great Britain, Germany, the Netherlands and Sweden, the ideology of multiculturalism serves as a new way of public incorporation, which the modern nation-state has put into play *vis-à-vis* migrants and their descendants. The form of multiculturalism, which was put into words by Parekh remains to be an ideal. As I will demonstrate below, the dominant ideology of multiculturalism aims to imprison minority cultures in their distinct boundaries, even closing up the channels of dialogue between cultures.

Berlin is one of the world cities where there is an extensive infrastructure promoting multiculturalism in one way or another. Berlin has always been a world city, which has housed various cultures. There are some initiatives attempting to embody a pluralist and multicultural city in which all the constitutive components of Berlin could co-exist in harmony. Die *Ausländerbeauftragte des Senats* (Commissioner for Foreigners' Affairs), das *Haus der Kulturen der Welt* (House of the World Cultures), *SFB4 Radio Multikulti* and *Werkstatt der Kulturen* (Workshop of Cultures) are some of these multicultural initiatives.

Die Ausländerbeauftragte des Senats is an office that was founded in 1981 as a part of the Berlin Senate administration to co-ordinate policies in the areas of the health, family, housing, education, welfare and police departments, and to take care of the groups with particular problems.[19] Its primary function, though, is to act as a liaison agency between the local government and various ethnic associations established in the city. The other function of the office involves public relations including publishing a monthly, 100-page magazine (*Top-Berlin International: Ein Informationsforum*), and offering an extensive list of videos and publications on specific ethnic communities in Berlin,[20] legal procedures and material encouraging children's and youth activities, vocational guidance for youth and etc. Recently, the office has initiated a set of poster-billboard campaigns with slogans such as '*Miteinander leben in Berlin*' ('live together in Berlin') and '*Wir sind Berlin: wir sind Helle und Dunkle!*' ('We are Berlin: We are light and dark!') in order to be able to recapitulate the ideas and perceptions of the Berliners on the co-existence of differences (Vertovec, 1996a).

Haus der Kulturen der Welt serves as an exhibition venue, conference and seminar centre, concert and festival venue. It was built in 1957 as the Congress Hall (*Kongreßhalle*). In 1989, it was given a new name. It is the stage where the non-European cultures have been introduced to the Berliners by means of exhibitions, conferences, movies, concerts and festivals. It aims to strengthen the roots of multicultural Berlin. Since Turks and Kurds compose approximately more than one third of the minority population living in Berlin, recent developments in Turkey have always been on the agenda of the *Haus*. Islam is at the core of contemporary interest. Berlin is trying to understand the current revival of Islam through the prism of Turkey.

SFB4 Radio Multikulti was founded in September 1994 as the fourth station of *Sender Freies Berlin* (SFB), which is the local public broadcasting corporation. "The whole world is at the end of the scale: FM 106.8 Mhz" is the motto of the non-stop radio channel. It was initially planned to be a three-year-project financed by SFB and Federal Ministry of Employment and Social Services, whereas the radio is still broadcasting. It broadcasts ethnic music programmes in eighteen different mother tongues, including German as a foreign language (Vertovec, 1996a).[21] The channel broadcasts none of the western music forms. Turkish is one of the languages represented amongst the ethnic music samples. Turkish pop music, Turkish rap and Turkish art music cover the biggest space in the Turkish language programmes. The programmes are set up by three producers of Turkish-origin. Aras Ören, who is a popular novelist and has been living in Berlin since the sixties, is the supervisor of the Turkish programmes for the SFB. However, a recent public survey carried out among the Berlin-Turks indicates that 12 percent of the Turks are aware of Radio Multikulti, and only 4 percent of them regularly listen to it. The same survey also depicts that the radio could not be received well in Kreuzberg and Wedding (Meseth, 1996).

SFB4 also organises cultural carnivals and festivals in collaboration with *Haus der Kulturen* in Kreuzberg and in some other parts of Berlin. In these carnivals, all the 'ethnic' components of Berlin are represented with their music and folk dances. These carnivals and festivals might give us some clue about how the state attempts to represent the 'ethnics' to the 'dominant' culture. Carnival-type activities define 'ethnics' as possessing 'folk culture' and not the culture of distinction. It can also distract attention away from the central problem of structural inequalities in access to resources (Bottomley, 1987: 5).

Werkstatt der Kulturen was opened in October 1993 in the district of Neukölln where there is a large Turkish population. It has been designed as a *Begegnungszentrum* (encounter centre). It is financially supported by the *Ausländerbeauftragte* of the Berlin Senate and governed by a board of trustees elected every two years from local organisations. The *Werkstatt* attempts to promote understanding between the cultures of the area and to try new ways of togetherness (*Miteinander*), especially among youth. It promotes exhibitions and conferences; coordinates projects, training courses (photography, painting, ceramics, video-making and music-making) and seminars concerning matters surrounding expressive arts, inter-cultural dialogue, the plight of refugees, and violence against minorities in the city (Vertovec, 1996a).

Despite the existence of such strong multicultural initiatives in Berlin, it is quite doubtful to claim that the minorities living, for instance, in Kreuzberg or Wedding are widely aware of them. When asked, most members of the Turkish minority reply that they are not aware of the existence of these initiatives and their works. On the other hand, those who are aware of these initiatives, do not trust the 'multicultural' policies. What they believe is that, these kinds of initiatives are nothing but a 'face-saving' effort by the Berlin government. Yet, this does not mean that these initiatives do not have any impact on the ethnic minorities. Those diasporic subjects, who are attached to Turkish ethnic organisations in one way or another, are culturally being shaped by these initiatives. In what follows, this issue will be raised.

Essentialising and 'Othering the Other'

In fact, the representation of a wide variety of non-western cultures in the form of music, plastic arts and seminars is nothing but the reconfirmation of the categorisation of 'the west and the rest.' The rationale behind the representation of the cultural forms of those 'others' in these multicultural initiatives inevitably contributes to the broadening of differences between the so-called 'distinct cultures.' The ideology of multiculturalism tends to compartmentalise the cultures. It also assumes that cultures are internally consistent, unified and structured wholes attached to ethnic groups (Çaglar, 1994: 26). Essentialising the idea of culture as the property of an ethnic group, multiculturalism risks reifying cultures as separate entities by overemphasising their boundedness and mutual distinctness; it also risks overrating the internal homogeneity of cultures in terms that potentially legitimise repressive demands for communal conformity.

Furthermore, all these so-called multicultural institutions apparently embody a process of *culturalisation*. Culturalisation – a culture-related smoothing out of social inequality, social anomalies and discrimination – occupies a prominent place in the process of change currently affecting European society (Ålund, 1996; Ålund and Schierup, 1991). Social differentiation, segregation, institutional racism, discrimination and class differences are all reduced to, and legitimised in, culturalisation of differences. Thus, actual multiculturalism in both Germany and Europe happens to represent a form of integration of cultural diversity into a system of structural inequalities (Ålund and Schierup, 1991: 139).

This type of constructed multiculturalism in Berlin permits the supposedly 'distinct cultures' to express themselves in some public platforms such as *Haus der Kulturen der Welt*. Multiculturalist meta-narrative might, at first glance, seem to be a 'friend' as John Russon (1995: 524) stated. These multicultural platforms, in a way, sharpen the process of 'othering the other' in the imagery of self, or in other words, leads to a form of ethnic 'exotification.' Russon (1995: 524) explains that:

Now, it is fairly common gesture, in the name of pluralism, to insist that we treat others as others, and accept their ways as, perhaps, 'interesting,' 'private' to them, and especially not the same as ours. [T]his exotification which 'tolerates the other' is another product of the alienating gaze of the reflective ego, and it fails in two important ways. First, it makes the other a kind of lesser entity open to our patronising support, despite our complete rejection of its value as analysing other than the cute contingencies of someone else's culture; thus there is an inherent power relation here in which the other is made subordinate to our benevolence and superior reason. Second, it fails to acknowledge that, just as *our* program of tolerance has implications for the other – it contains that other in its view – so too does the ethnicity of the other contain us. Our so-called 'democratic' and pluralistic ideal is as much an ethnic expression as that of the other is an ethnicity [...].

Russon's remarks on 'tolerance' remind us of the way in which public and private spheres are highly differentiated by the ideology of multiculturalism. This ideology, as John Rex (1986, 1991) has described, involves nurturing commonality (shared laws, open economy and equal access to state provisions) in the former and ensuring freedom (maintain the traditions of ethnic minorities) in the latter. Russon, first, prompts us to think that multiculturalism tends to promote the confinement of cultures in their own private spheres with a limited interaction with other cultures. In other words, the distinctions between private and public, or between politics and culture "can relegate the contentious differences to a sphere that does not impinge on the political" (Taylor, 1994: 62).

The differentiation between public and private has always contributed to the reinforcement of dominant class or group's hegemony over the subaltern groups. The cultures that hardly interact with other cultures are tempted to become a static heritage. Thus, Russon, here, draws our attention to the point that the official discourse of multiculturalism contributes to the reification of cultures by the minority communities. Secondly, he underlines the issue of power relations between the dominant culture and the others. This is the clientelist side of the policy of multiculturalism – a point to which I shall return shortly. Clientelism tends to petrify the existing social conditions without making any change in the power relations between 'master' and 'disciple.'

Renato Rosaldo also raises what Russon attempts to criticise by the notion of 'tolerance' in a slightly different way. Searching the correlation between culture and power, Rosaldo (1989: 198-204) rightly claims that power and culture have a negative correlation. In saying so, he refers to the examples of the Philippines and Mexico. In the Philippines and Mexico, for instance, full citizens are those who have power and lack culture, whereas those most culturally endowed minorities, such as Negritos and Indians, lack full citizenship and power respectively. Thus, having power refers to being postcultural and vice versa: "the more power one has, the less culture one enjoys; and the more culture one has, the less power one yields. If *they* [minorities] have an explicit monopoly on authentic culture, *we* [majority] have an unspoken one on institutional power" (1989: 202).

Rosaldo takes the discussion further, and concludes that making the 'other' culturally visible results with the invisibility of the 'self.' Thus, the policy of multiculturalism attempts to dissolve the 'self' within the minority. Dissolution of the 'self' is also related to the celebration of *difference* by minorities because the notion of difference makes culture particularly visible to outside observers. Hence, not only the multiculturalist policies, but also minorities themselves contribute to the process of dissolution of the 'self' as well as of the institutional power within the minority. In the following section, as an attempt to illustrate this theoretical framework I will explore the construction and articulation of *Alevi* ethnicity and culture in Berlin, in relation to the dominant discourse of multiculturalism.

The Case of Manifest Alevism in 'Multicultural' Berlin

Alevism is a heterodox religious identity that is peculiar to Anatolia. It is practised by some Turkish and Kurdish segments of the Anatolian society. Turkish *Alevi*s used to concentrate in central Anatolia, with important pockets throughout the Aegean and Mediterranean coastal regions and the European part of Turkey. Kurdish *Alevi*s were concentrated in the north-western part of the Kurdish settlement zone between Turkish Kurdistan and the rest of the country. Both Turkish and Kurdish *Alevi*s have left their isolated villages for the big cities of Turkey and Europe since 1950s.

Alevism itself is the main source of identity for the *Alevi* youngsters. Previously, the *Alevi* youngsters of Turkish ethnic origin in Germany, used to identify themselves with their Turkishness. They used to carry Turkish ethnic symbols to express their ethnicity as a response to the rising racial attacks and discrimination in Germany: e.g. a Turkish flag on their belt buckles. Although most of the urban *Alevi*s have always had to dissimulate their identities due to the supremacy of the *Sunni* order in the public sphere (*Takiyye*), they continued with their rituals in their private spheres. Their children had to play with the *Sunni* children in the streets without giving out any clue, which might reveal their *Alevism*. In a way, they had to assimilate to the dominant ideology of *Sunni*-Turkism. And then what happened? Why did they suddenly need to express their *Alevi* identity publicly? While they were celebrating their Turkishness against the racial attacks, why did they turn to celebrating their *Alevism*?

*Alevi*s have started to radically declare their religious identity publicly after the recent tragic incidences in Turkey, like the massacre of 37 *Alevi* artists in Sivas (July, 1993) and of 15 *Alevi* people in a densely-*Alevi*-populated neighbourhood of Istanbul (*Gaziosmanpasa*, March 1995). When the *Alevi*-leftist-oriented *Pir Sultan Abdal* association organised a cultural festival in Sivas – a central Anatolian City that is historically divided between *Sunni*s and *Alevi*s – in July 1993, numerous prominent *Alevi*-origin artists and authors, including Aziz Nesin (not an *Alevi*), attended. The festival was picketed by a large group of violent right-wing demonstrators who were clearly keen on killing Aziz Nesin. The author, Aziz Nesin had previously provoked the anger of many *Sunni* Muslims by announcing his intention to publish a translation of Salman Rushdie's *Satanic Verses*. Throwing stones and burning rags through the windows of the hotel where the participants of the festival were staying, the demonstrators succeeded in setting fire to the hotel. Thirty-seven people were killed in this fire, due to the indifferent attitude of the police forces of the '*Sunni*' Turkish state. This was a very crucial incident leading to the radicalisation of the *Alevi* movement in relation to the sluggishness of the state apparatus.

Relations between *Alevi*s and the Turkish state reached even lower depths with clashes between the police and *Alevi* demonstrators in the *Gazi* neighbourhood of Istanbul in March 1995. *Gazi Mahallesi* is a ghetto that is dominated by *Alevi* residents. The hostilities started when an unknown gunman in a stolen taxi fired a number of shots against a group of men sitting in a *café*, killing one *Alevi*. Police were remarkably slow in taking action, and the rumour soon spread that the local police post might have been involved in the terrorist attacks. The day after, thousands of *Alevi* people from the Gazi neighbourhood went on to the streets to protest about the murder. The police and the demonstrators clashed, and the police killed fifteen Alevi demonstrators (Bruinessen, 1996b: 9-10). These incidences have opened a new era in *Alevi* revivalism both at home and in the diaspora.

Similarly, the diaspora context, to a certain degree, alleviates the already deep-set antagonisms, suspicion, and animosity between *Sunni* and *Alevi* youths. In fact, many *Sunni*s become still more hostile towards *Alevi*s. The unchecked politicisation of mosque-centred religious preaching that proliferates in Germany is often directed against 'infidel' and 'immoral' Germans, communists, and by extension, *Alevi*s (Mandel, 1996: 157). The separate *Sunni* and *Alevi* value systems and histories are, to a large extent, reproduced among the diasporic youth in a way that reflects different patterns of socialisation in each group. These different patterns of socialisation influence the overall future orientations of *Sunni* and *Alevi* youths towards Turkey and Germany (Mandel, 1990: 167).

Diasporic *Alevi* youngsters have experienced something different from their *Alevi* counterparts living back home. After those crucial incidents happened in Turkey, their Turkishness, which they used to celebrate in reaction to the notorious racist incidents in Mölln and Solingen, no longer offered a refuge for them. The homeland Turkey, which has become a land of repression and sorrow, has turned into a 'lost homeland' for *Alevi* youngsters. The orientation of the *Alevi* youngsters to homeland differs from that of the *Sunni* youngsters. While the *Sunni* youth may keep alive their orientation to the homeland, the *Alevi* youngsters may well be in search of homing in Berlin. Another aspect reminding them of the 'bitter' reality of homeland is the conditions of their counterparts in Turkey. Since the milieu they visit in the summer vacations is either in the ghettos of the big cities or in the small towns and/or villages, they have a restricted vision of youth in Turkey. What they describe, when asked, is mainly the working-class youth in the homeland. They suppose that all the youngsters in Turkey are suffering, and have to work all the time.

The incidents of *Sivas* and *Gazi Mahallesi* have become the pillars of the political *Alevi* revivalism both in and outside Turkey. They have recently founded some political-cultural organisations in Berlin and Germany. Anatolian *Alevis'* Cultural Centre (*Anadolu Alevileri Kültür Merkezi*, AAKM), Democratic *Alevis* Association (*Demokratik Aleviler Birligi*), *Ehl-i Beyt* Path (*Ehl-i Beyt Yolu*) are just some of those organisations established in Berlin. The AAKM is the most popular one of those *Alevi* organisations centred in Berlin. This organisation was founded in 1989. It is run by a committee of people and financed by the Berlin Senate and the *Alevi* population in Berlin. A mix of Zaza-Kurdish *Alevis* and Turkish *Alevis* constitutes the members of the AAKM.[22] The centre is located in Wedding that is another Turkish enclave in Berlin. There is a '*Cemevi*' in the centre. *Cemevi* literally means communion house where the co-religious people meet up and have their religious ceremonies. The religious ceremony is called *ayn-i cem* (Mass), which springs from the word *cemaat* (community).

The authentic style of the *cem* rituals taking place in the Anatolian *Alevi* villages are very small-size social and religious gatherings where the *Alevi* residents of the village meet up, worship and solve their mutual social problems in the presence of a holy communal guide. The spiritual guide is called *Dede*, or *pir*. The *Dede* is considered to be descending from holy lineage. They typically wander much of the year, travel from one group of his *talip* followers to the next, and lead *ayn-i cems*. In these mystic *ayn-i cems*, love of god, which is reflected on the human being, is celebrated. According to the teachings of *Alevism*, human being is the reflection of the beauty of God. Unlike the *Sunnis*, who turn towards the *Kaaba* during the pray, the *Alevis* face each other in a circular position. Human being is the *Kaaba* in the *Alevi* teaching. Facing the other refers to seeing the spiritual light of saintliness (*nur*), which is considered to be appearing on the other's face. Besides being the platform of worship, *Cem* is also the place where the public court (*halk meclisi*) is organised to solve communal and individual problems in a very democratic and egalitarian way. In the court, everybody has equal right to speak.

There are two other very important elements of the *Alevi* teaching. The first one is '*ser ver, sir verme!*', which literally means 'better die than give away a secret.' This element of *Alevism* is not only an ethical value. That is also a political manoeuvring that springs as a result of the need for *takiyye* (dissimulation). Another determinant of the *Alevi* matrix is '*eline, beline, diline sahip olmak*', which means 'to control one's hands, tongue and sexual needs.' This is the very ethical motto of the *Alevi* teaching that is inevitably taken in childhood.[23] *Alevism* has a strict set of social control norms and rules, which defines the framework of 'correct behaviour.' In case of violation of these rules, sect members might be penalised by exclusion from all group activities and payment of fines. No one could escape from the judgement at the major annual rites called *görgü* or *ayn-i cem* where the *Alevi* creed is renewed and reviewed, and serious offences are admitted publicly before the community. The *Dede*, in these communal gatherings, aims to maintain peace and harmony between sect members by helping them reconcile their differences. These rituals have always been carried out in closely-knit village units throughout history. After the migrations from rural to urban areas in Turkey and abroad, *Alevi* communities faced the danger of losing those rituals. Recently, new *Alevi* organisations have been set up in the urban spaces to provide the *Alevi* people with community services. By doing so, *Alevi*s tend to restructure their rituals and institutions in accordance with the urban needs.

Other activities conducted by the AAKM include the organisation of *sema* dance courses for the *Alevi* youth and public concerts. *Sema* dance is a ritual signifying the love of God. The audience dances *sema* in small mixed groups, an atmosphere of dignity and restraint prevails. Each dancer takes his or her place according to traditional choreography with an air of detached, deep concentration and without any suggestion of bodily contact. The *sema* dance is accompanied by an authentic Turkish musical instrument with strings, called *saz* or *baglama*. The *sema* courses have a social function besides being a cultural teaching. These courses attempt to get the children of the community away from the 'dangerous' streets, and to give them self-respect.

The Centre also organises public concerts for the *Alevi*s in Berlin. '*Alevi* Cultural Night' is one of those gatherings. This organisation is very illustrative for the purposes I want to scrutinise further. This is why it will be beneficial to expose the main features of this festival. The gathering was held on the 28th of September 1996 in the Berlin Erika-Hess-Stadion, Wedding. It was a huge event with approximately two thousand people in the audience. Most of the participants were *Alevi* folk singers who were invited from Turkey for this special occasion. They sang *Alevi* poems (*Degis*) from the Turkish folk poets (*halk sairi*). Amongst the guests were Barbara John (Commissioner for Foreigners' Affairs), Hans Nisblé (mayor of Wedding, SPD), Franz Schulz (mayor of Kreuzberg, *die Grünen*), Ismail Hakki Kosan (member of the Berlin Senate, *die Grünen*), the members of the *Türkische Bund*, and the Turkish and German media. The way the AAKM members represented themselves in the programme was very instructive. The speakers of the AAKM stressed the killings of the *Alevi*s in *Sivas* and *Gazi* neighbourhood. They reconfirmed, or reconstructed, the fact that these incidences have become two crucial landmarks of the *Alevi* mythology. Since this was a chance for the AAKM members to represent themselves in front of the high-ranking German politicians and media, they also stressed the difference between *Alevism* and *Shiism*.[24] They, in a sense, attempt to make a distinction between themselves and the orthodox version of *Shiism*.

The speeches of the German politicians were also very instructive in their own respects. Barbara John emphasised the pluralist structure of the city of Berlin, and the place of the *Alevi*s in this scene. She stated her willingness to see the *Alevi*s freely expressing their cultural identity in the public space. The dubious *culturalist discourse* raised by Barbara John tends to relegate social conflicts to the domain of culturalised iconography (Schierup, 1994: 38). Her discourse of multiculturalism raises three crucial aspects. Firstly, it reveals the negative correlation between culture and power in the context of minorities, which I previously touched upon (Rosaldo, 1989: 198-206). Secondly, *Alevi*s as well as many other minority groups such as Iranians, Kurds and Chinese are allowed by the institutional power to express their difference in the 'public sphere.' The expression of 'difference,' although, has the advantage of making culture particularly visible to outside observers, it posits a problem because such differences are not absolute. Thirdly, her discourse hints that the majority society might benefit from the appearance of *Alevi*s in the public space, because the *Alevi*s have developed a stronger subjectivity like many other minorities living in a permanent turmoil. Thus, she attempts to reproduce and strengthen the binary opposition of 'us' and 'them.'

Aminor group among the German liberals such as Barbara John and Hans Nisblé are aware of the differences between *Sunni*s and *Alevi*s. They are quick to appropriate the *Alevi*s for their own political project and to use them as an example of Turks who 'successfully integrate' (Mandel, 1996: 156). Similarly, Hans Nisblé attempted to place *Alevism* as a political balance of power against Islamic revivalism. In the concert, he called the German people to stand by the *Alevi*s against the challenge of 'radical Islam within' prevailing over Europe and Germany. Nisblé's speech was very illuminating in the sense that he was announcing a general view that is quite dominant in the western way of thinking. The favourable perception of *Alevism* by the German intelligentsia and media is, of course, highly related to the Western textual reading of the contemporary Turkey, which was, at that time, governed by a religious based coalition. This view conceives *Alevism* as a shield of secularist regime in Turkey against the radical Islam. Such an interpretation of *Alevism* has become the dominant paradigm both in Turkey and Europe. This paradigm inevitably contributes to the radicalisation of *Alevism* in political sense. Accordingly, the way *Alevi*s are defined by the German media and politicians also encourages *Alevi*s to form a community discourse.

It is not only the institutional power of multiculturalism encouraging *Alevi*s to develop a community discourse, but it is also the fact that, paraphrasing Hall (1992), speaking from margins sometimes could make more echo. It is evident that *Alevi* organisations tend to construct a community discourse by reifying some aspects of the *Alevi* culture. Mobilising many *Alevi*-origin people by those public concerts and mass ceremonies, for instance, provides, to use Gilroy's words, "important rituals, which allow its affiliates to recognise each other and celebrate their coming together" (Gilroy, 1987: 223). Thus, in diaspora, highly effective informal networks forge a community of a sort that has never existed at home, as it attempts to worship and celebrate in concert (Mandel, 1996: 161). Habitual adherence to the rituals, as Russon (1995: 514) rightly posits, allows us to recognise ourselves as an 'us,' as a 'we.' Borrowing the Hegelian terminology, the demand for self-consciousness is met in a dialogue of mutual recognition taking place in a collective process. Thus, there only remains a singular space for the individual at the margin to form his/her self-consciousness, i.e. the communal acts of mutual recognition. In this communal life, rituals and customs define who 'I' is. It is the *Alevi* communality offering the individual a ground to achieve self-consciousness.

As Mandel (1996: 162) has rightly put it, some *Alevi* groups in Germany have taken advantage of Western freedoms to adopt a more conservative, inward, communal orientation, unfettered by past political and social constraints. The highly politicised group of *Alevi Gençligi* (*Alevi* Youth) – a faction in the AAKM – is an illustrative example for this radicalism. In July 1996, there were many posters on the walls hung by the *Alevi* Youth to commemorate the massacre of the *Alevi* intellectuals in July 1993 in Sivas to the *Alevi* residents of Kreuzberg. Those posters, which were written in a '*Kanak Sprak*'[25] – a point to which I shall return shortly, were overtly interpreted as a challenge to the 'others' who were not *Alevi*.

The way the *Alevi*s are represented in the diaspora by themselves, politicians, and media does nothing but increase the cleavages and the polarisation among the Turkish minority in Berlin. Such a representation of *Alevi*sm also contributes to the reduction of social problems to essentialist ethnic and religious clashes. This polarisation within the Turkish community is also reflected in Turkey because these *Alevi* organizations have strong links with their equivalent partners and political organisations in Turkey. Thus, the rising cleavages and competition between the diversified Turkish groups is directly transferred to Turkey. This is how diaspora has an influential impact on the homeland political affairs. To illustrate the case, the AAKM had organised free flights for *Alevi*s to attend the opening ceremony of an *Alevi*-based political party (Democratic Peace Movement) in August 1996, in Ankara. It is an example of the impact of the diasporic subjects on the homeland politics.[26]

On the other hand, although the youngsters in *Naunyn Ritze* and *Chip* are quite distant from the political loading of religion, *Alevism* and *Sunni*sm have become the main determinants of the matrix of youth ethnicity (youthnicity). The *Alevi* youngsters in *Naunyn Ritze* rarely talk about the differentiation and conflicts between themselves and the *Sunni*s. On the other hand, the *Sunni* youngsters usually raise this conflict by saying that *Alevi* youngsters are discriminating against the *Sunni*s. The girls whom I interviewed in *Chip* were all *Sunni*s. They have *Alevi* friends from *Naunyn Ritze*. Although they sometimes meet these friends, they complain about the differentiation that the *Alevi* friends have made against their *Sunni* friends. They argue that their friends advance this differentiation to exclude them. In fact, it would not be surprising to hear exactly the same discourse from the *Alevi* youngsters *vis-à-vis* their *Sunni* friends. It seems quite normal for the *Alevi* youngsters to distance themselves from the *Sunni*s and to re-establish the boundaries after those incidences in Sivas and Gaziosmanpasa. Thus, they do not think that they are discriminating, whereas the *Sunni* youngsters, who have a majority consciousness and who have been raised by the official doctrine, cannot yet accept the fact that the *Alevi* minority is declaring its identity publicly by threatening the previously existing order.

Some graffiti samples that I saw nearby *Chip* in *Reichenberger Straße* were giving some essential clues about the conflicting temperament of the *Sunni* and *Alevi* youngsters in Kreuzberg. The first example of graffiti was

Alevileri S. K. M

that means "I fuck the *Alevi*s." 'S. K. M.' is a kind of hidden expression of 'fuck' in Turkish. Above the same graffiti, there was another example that was most probably written by the same person, saying

$$\begin{matrix} & C & \\ Bozkurt & & C \\ & C & \end{matrix}$$

that means 'Grey Wolf – three crescent.' Three crescents are the symbol of the extreme right wing grey wolves in Turkey. The nationalist Turkish mythology depicts that it is the grey wolf (*Bozkurt*) that accompanied and guided the Turkish nation all the way through the massive migration from Central Asia to Anatolia. The grey wolf is considered by the Turkish nationalists to be the mythological guide of the Turkish nation. These two examples of graffiti written on the same wall are quite complementary. It signifies that Turkish nationalist ideology excludes the *Alevi*s. The clash between the *Sunni*s and *Alevi*s has also been carried onto the symbolic level. As I shall point out in the coming chapters, ethnic symbols are extensively used by the Turkish youngsters as a constituent of their identity.

As far as the construction of ethnic-based political participation strategies (migrant strategy and minority strategy) is concerned, *Alevism* in the diaspora conveys a similar process to the other Turkish diasporic communities that I outlined in the previous chapter. Yet, *Alevism* nowadays corresponds to a further radicalised community discourse due to the recent incidences in Turkey. Investing in the cultural differences, this radical *Alevi* revivalism can be contemplated as one of the new social movements in the sense that Alain Touraine and Alberto Melucci mentioned earlier (Touraine, 1977; Melucci, 1989). The common denominator of contemporary social movements such as the peace movement and the ecology movement is that they are not directly involved in struggles focused on production and distribution of material goods and resources. Instead, they are increasingly concerned with debates about symbolic resources. Moreover, participation in these movements is no longer simply a means to an end but it is considered a goal in itself.

The contemporary metanarrative of multiculturalism has something to do with the transformation of the recent social movements. Multiculturalism tends to transform social conflicts into ethnic and religious ones. Radtke (1994: 32-37) points out that this transformation takes place under the hegemony of the state, which forms a kind of neo-clientelist system:

The clientele of the state are organizations, which have a clientele of individuals themselves. In both cases the dependency is reciprocal: The institutional or individual client will try to present himself as fitting into the programme of the patron; the patron will only continue to exist if he has the lasting support and trust of his clientele [...] The liberal model of competing interests ends up in patronage, lobbyism and paternalism [...] The effect of Multi-Culturalism in connection with clientelism is not ethnic mobilisation but self-ethnicisation of the minorities. As long as they do not have any political rights and as long as there is no policy of affirmative action, Multi-Culturalism inevitably ends up in folklorism. Minorities in Germany are kept away from the public sphere and invited by the legal system to form apolitical communities (*Gemeinschaften*) in the private sphere instead of interest groups [...] Multi-Culturalism translates the concept of plurality of interests into a concept of plurality of descents [...] Multi-Culturalism is only a reversal of ethnocentrism [...].

Thus, Radtke identifies the political practice of multiculturalism in Germany as clientelist and its effects as a 'folkloric' self-ethnicisation of minorities.

Accordingly, the AAKM can be interpreted as a clientele organisation fulfilling the requirements of the ideology of multiculturalism. As an obedient subject of the state, the AAKM, thus, reaffirms the hegemony of state whilst reifying *Alevi* culture and tradition. Furthermore, it seems to imprison the social reaction of a subordinated working-class group in a cultural cage that is offered by the state. Multiculturalist metanarrative gives a chance to the masses to represent, vocalise and narrate their own ethnicities and cultures freely without undergoing any change in the relations of production and distribution. The policy of multiculturalism gives 'space' to the minorities to express themselves, but not 'rights' such as political rights. In other words, as Gillian Bottomley (1987: 4) stated in the Australian context, multiculturalism has tended to obscure the primacy of economic and political structures in determining the limits of possibilities for migrants to Germany. They have concentrated on culture and have, in doing so, made the cultural field an important terrain of struggle.

Similarly, having restrictive regimes of incorporation for the migrants and 'foreigners,' Germany attempts to give the Turks a sense of belonging by means of multiculturalism. The ideology of multiculturalism provides the German government with a form of what Michel Foucault (1979) called *governmentality*. *Governmentality* refers to the practices characterising the form of supervision a state exercise over its subjects, their wealth, their misfortunes, their customs, their souls and their habits. Foucault's modern 'administrative state' is based on the idea of a 'society of regulation' differing from 'the state of justice' of the Middle Ages that was built on the idea of a 'society of laws' (Foucault, 1979: 21). According to Foucault the modern state regulates our bodies, souls, habits and thoughts by giving us a sense of *freedom*. In the modern societies freedom has become a fruitful resource for government. Accordingly, the policy of multiculturalism enables minority cultures to represent themselves 'freely.'

* * *

To summarise, Turkish migrants living in Kreuzberg have created a new home away from their homeland. This diasporic space reflects various snapshots, discourses, images, rhythms, narratives, social networks (*hemsehrilik*) and familial connections from the pre-immigrant life-worlds of the migrants. The formation of a diasporic space through images, sounds, symbols and traditions from the homeland has served the migrants as a 'fortress' protecting them against institutional discrimination, assimilation and racism. The presence of the networks of transnational communications and transportation connecting the diaspora to the homeland has also strengthened the construction of a diasporic identity. Thus, the diasporic identity that has been built by the migrants as a social strategy has been reshaped and reinforced through transnational networks extending the official ideology of Turkishness.

In this chapter, I also claimed that multiculturalism assumes that cultures are internally consistent, unified and structured wholes belonging to ethnic groups. Although having promised to include and incorporate ethnic minorities into the main stream, the contemporary ideology of multiculturalism has done nothing but excluding and imprisoning ethnic minorities in their own isolated cultural islands. Thus, it would be misleading to argue that multiculturalism serves as a policy of inclusion *vis-à-vis* ethnic minorities. Rather, the ideology of multiculturalism has led to the further minorisation and culturalisation of ethnic minorities in Berlin. Having been guided by multiculturalism, ethnic groups in Berlin such as *Alevis* have made attempts to invest in their 'authentic' rituals rather than intermingling with the other cultures. Correspondingly, these various cultures have created their own static and essentialist cults refusing to infuse with the others. Thus, multiculturalism, in fact, creates separate 'CULTures' that are distinguished from each other with distinct boundaries. This is a serious obstacle before the process of cultural bricolage as well as leading to cultural reification and essentialism. Therefore, it would not be a mistake to rename multiculturalism as 'multi-CULT-uralism,' which means the sum of distinct cultures, or actually of cults.

The major Turkish ethnic associations in the diaspora have developed a culture discourse that is based on the holistic notion of 'CULTure.' This demotic discourse of the ethnic minority associations, in fact, parallels the dominant discourse of multiculturalism aiming to locate the minority cultures within discrete and fixed boundaries (cf. Baumann, 1996). The policies of multiculturalism in Berlin have mainly encouraged the ethnic minorities to organise themselves along culture lines. The mobilisation of ethnic associations along culture lines has limited their prospects in undertaking political initiatives for any structural change. This chapter has also outlined the social, political, economic, ethnic and demographic structure of Kreuzberg 36 to provide us with a broader perspective in order to scrutinise the diasporic consciousness of the working-class Turkish hip-hop youth. The next chapter will examine the sense of place and 'homing' for the Turkish hip-hop youth in the diaspora.

Notes

1 Günther Grass (1981) has described Kreuzberg as an 'utopia' of ethnic admixture and internationalisation. In this sense, Kreuzberg has exotic connotations with its multi-ethnic demography in the imagery of left/liberal Germans.
2 *Mitfahrzentralen* are private travel agencies providing the customers with a service to travel by private automobiles to many different destinations, sharing the cost of petrol with the driver.
3 *Berlin-Brandenburg Is Rehberi: Altin Sayfalar* (Berlin: Karma Verlag & Werbeagentur, 1995).
4 *Türkçe Danisma Yerleri Klavuzu: Beratungsführer für Türkische Berliner/-Innen* (Berlin: Karma Verlag & Werbeagentur, 1996).
5 The urban renewal and housing rehabilitation projects in Kreuzberg have been carried out with massive public aid and a host of regulations and laws enforced by the offices of the Senate for Housing and Construction and the Senate for Social Affairs since the mid 1970s. All urban renewal and housing rehabilitation projects have been pursued in close cooperation with private property owners, the tenants, the State and other public and private non-profit development cooperatives (Holzner, 1982).
6 Considering the architectural unity and order, the local authorities have rarely permitted the foundation of a mosque with a minaret in Berlin. Also, the petitions of the neighbourhood are taken into consideration by the local government in evaluating the applications of the Islamic groups to construct a mosque. That is why, the Muslims are allowed to worship in converted mosques,

which are not supposed to change the original architectural style of the city. For the discussion about minaret in Berlin and Germany, see "Gebetsrufe? – Ja bitte!" *die Tageszeitung (Taz)* (7 January 1997); "Einübung in mehr Toleranz" *Taz* (6 March 1995); "Gurke des Tages: Moschee in Bobingen" *Taz* (4 December 1992); and "No Rest in the Ruhr" *Time* (24 February 1997).

7 The Welfare Party was banned in January 1998 by the Turkish Constitutional Court. The reason for closing the Party was the justification that it was based on religious ideology and that its fundamentalist activities and statements were against the secular republic. Immediately after the Welfare Party was closed, the Virtue Party was founded to inherit it.

8 The majority of apartments occupied by Turkish migrants used to be substandard. For instance, in the district of Kreuzberg as a whole, seventy-one percent of all housing units were constructed before 1918, twenty-eight percent had no bath, twenty-seven percent had neither bath nor toilet, and seventy-four percent had individual room stove heaters only. Through their insecure status in Germany most Turkish immigrants preferred to invest in Turkey rather than spending on housing in Berlin. As a result, they continued living in the cheapest, oldest and least desirable apartments. After the rehabilitation of the housing units in Kreuzberg, Turkish tenants could not, or did not want to, afford to pay the rising rents. Thus, some of them had to find cheaper places outside Kreuzberg. A big proportion of those rehabilitated housing units have attracted the liberal intellectual individuals or families of upper income levels who consider it chic to live in modern comfort amidst the charm of 19th century *Gründerzeit* housing such as the apartments by the *Landwehrkanal*, Spree river (Holzner, 1982). *Waldemarstraße* and *Naunynstraße*, on the other hand, have remained occupied by the immigrants from Turkey.

9 *Aypa* TV is a secular-based news channel, combining the news both from Turkey and Germany; TFD is a religious-based channel, representing the view of *Milli Görüs*; and *Alcanlar TV* and *Ehli Beyit* TV are *Alevi*-based channels, representing different views.

10 For further information about the reception of the Turkish language media in Germany see, Heinemann and Kamcili (2000).

CHAPTER 3

11 The notion of 'habitats of meaning' belongs to Ulf Hannerz (1996). Hannerz has developed the notion in relation to the co-existence of local and global at once. TV and print media have an important impact on the formation of our habitats of meaning. As some people may share much the same habitats of meaning in the global ecumene, some other people may have rather distinct and localised habitats of meaning.

12 *Yeni Günaydin* (liberal) and *Özgür Gündem* (left-wing) were shut down afterwards. *Sabah* and *Evrensel* have recently entered the market.

13 Before the hegemony of the American film industry prevailed over the world market, the Turkish film industry produced a vast amount of film until the early eighties.

14 J. Knight (1986) states that 80 percent of the German-Turks used to watch Turkish videos daily.

15 For further inquiry about *Süleymancis, Nurcus* and *Kaplancis*, see Schiffauer (1997).

16 Diaspora with capital 'D' implies the form of diaspora in which the community attempts to preserve its own 'distinctive' culture.

17 AMGT is an illegal political organisation in Germany. According to the figures of the *Verfassungsschutz-Bericht (1995)*, they have 3,000 members in Berlin. AMGT has a wide institutional network all around Europe. The organisation has organic links with the Islamic Welfare Party (*Refah Partisi*) in Turkey. For the origins of the Welfare Party, see Toprak (1981) and Çakir (1990).

18 For a detailed explanation on the religious organisations in Germany, see Trautner (2000). Trautner, in his work, rightfully claims that Islamic resurgence has rather a stuationalist and contextualist nature in Germany, rather than having an essentialist substance.

19 Barbara John – a member of the Christian Democratic Party – has held the office since its inception in 1981 through successive governments of Social Democrat – Alternative List coalition of 1989-1991 and the grand SPD-CDU coalition.

20 Most of the publications and videos are on Turks. Some of the other ethnic communities on which publications and videos have been prepared are Indians, Africans, Chinese, and Iranians.

21 These languages are as follows: Albanian, Arabic, Bosnian, Greek, Italian, Croatian, Kurdish, Macedonian, Persian, Polish,

22 Kurds are divided into two main tribes: *Zazas* and *Kirmanchis*. *Zaza*-Kurds are mostly from Dersim, Tunceli. Unlike the *Kirmanchis*, they are predominantly *Alevi*. *Kirmanchis* belong to the *Sunni* Islam, which is the 'official' religious school in Turkey. Although there is an overwhelming Kurdish nationalism blowing in Turkey and all around Europe, the *Zazas* have recently tended to identify themselves distinctively from the rest of the Kurds. Most of the *Zaza* populations in diaspora recently have a tendency to give priority to their *Alevi* identity rather than to their Kurdishness. Their identification of themselves might differ, depending on their political or religious orientations. The dominant ethnic identities that the Zazas employ in diasporic conditions are either *Alevi* or *Zaza*, or *Dersimli* (being from Dersim). Since the *Zazas* are mostly centrifugal Kurdish-*Alevi*s, they have got a peculiar history of their own. Dersim rebellion against the young Turkish Republic in the late 1930s is considered as an *Alevi* and Zaza uprising (Bruinessen, 1996a).

23 This parental teaching is what Bourdieu calls the 'ideology of virility' which adults tend to employ towards young generations as a way of keeping wisdom – and therefore – power for themselves (Bourdieu, 1993: 94).

24 *Alevism* is also known as Anatolian version of *Shiism*, but it is a much more hybrid form of belief consisting of many different rituals and religious undertones such as Sufism, Shamanism, Christianity, Judaism as well as Islam. For the heterodox nature of *Alevism* see, Ocak (2000).

25 '*Kanak Sprak*' is the creole language spoken and written by the working-class Berlin-Turkish youth.

26 Another example would be the religious based *Milli Görüs* association centred in Berlin transporting its own audience to Turkey to vote in the early general elections held in 1995. The flight was free of charge, and also the vote-goers were paid extra on top of their travel expenses.

Chapter 4

Identity and Homing of Diaspora

Kreuzberg as a Turkish ethnic enclave connotes a very particular set of images, signs, symbols, sounds and associations, which revolve around its reputation as '*Kleines* Istanbul' (Little Istanbul). As portrayed in the previous chapter, Kreuzberg has become a 'diasporic space' for the Turkish migrants who exhibit a cultural continuum between the homeland and the country of settlement. Kreuzberg, as a diasporic space, has a crucial impact on the identity formation of the Turkish youngsters. The way the youths construct their identities in the shifting boundaries of various life-worlds is imbued with the social, cultural and political landscape of this ethnic enclave. In this sense, this chapter, on the one hand, aims to investigate the main life-worlds of the working-class Turkish youths, shaping the process of their identity construction. In doing so, the multicultural competence, which they develop in the process of negotiating within and between these distinct social spaces, will be demonstrated. On the other hand, I will also briefly recite the multicultural discourse of the middle-class Turkish youth living outside Kreuzberg in order to build, by way of contrast, a broader view of the working-class youth.

Life-Worlds of the Working-Class Turkish Youth in Kreuzberg

The increasing autonomy of life-world forms, which goes beyond the boundaries of production, results in a higher level of individual differentiation in everyday life and in a release from traditional family ties. As Alberto Melucci (1989: 51) has stated, the consequences of such an autonomy may be as follows: increasing independence felt by individuals from family bonds; increased social mobility at both everyday life level and occupational level; and multiplication of cultural identities and life-styles. Turkish ethnic minority youth in Kreuzberg always shifts between the spaces of home, street, school and youth centre. There is always a clear-cut boundary between these social spaces produced by the diasporic youth. In this section, I will scrutinise the multiplication of cultural identities in these various highly gendered life-worlds and how the male diasporic youths manage to construct a syncretic form of culture by crossing various milieus and discrete life-worlds. These non-conscious acts of 'crossing' or cultural reproduction by the youngsters will be explicated by a set of examples on code-switching.

Life in the Youth Centre

Undoubtedly the youth centre occupies the biggest space in the lives of the youngsters. The youth centre serves as a refuge from the parental discipline for the minority youth and acts as a haven from the hostility of the 'outside world,' and as a place in which dignity, self-respect and recognition are internally defined. They live like 'brothers' and 'sisters' in the centre. The youngsters consider the centre a substitute 'family' environment where they congregate, cook, entertain, communicate and protect themselves against external challenges. There is always a hierarchy in this 'family' setting amongst the youngsters. The elders feel themselves responsible for the younger members; and the young ones respect the elders. To illustrate the situation of respect, when the younger members realise that a relatively older member of the group is arriving into the *café*, they stop making noise and become more respectful to each other. Rather than the German youth workers the youngsters respect better the 'elder brothers' whom they see as a part of 'their own community.' This respect from the youngsters springs from the hierarchical structure behind in-group relations.

The ethnic minority youths are stuck with a kind of 'language of fatalism' (Hebdige, 1987: 40), or to an *arabesk* way of life. The common lines, which they use to express their state of being, are '*Ahh ulan ahh!*' (deep sigh with an inner resistance), '*Acimasiz dünya!*' (Cruel world!), '*Bütün insanlar suçlu!*' (Human beings are all guilty), or '*Isyanlardayim!*' (I am fed up!). Most of the youngsters have no future prospect in their own eyes. They generally attend the vocational schools (*Berufsschulen*) to gain a degree, but they actually do not feel attached to those related occupations. Although most of the youngsters have job training such as mechanics, hairdressing, and building construction, they do not prefer carrying on the profession they had in the school.

Life in the Street

Street is another space where the youngsters form a different form of life-world. The streets of Kreuzberg 36, in a broader sense, witness the struggles of resistance, local political cultures, a particular articulation of a post-industrial political-economy and urban myths of gang violence. Street as a 'public space' is transformed into a 'private space' by the working-class youths. When the centre is closed, for instance before 15.00 o'clock, and during Sunday and Monday, the street becomes the favourite meeting space where the youths congregate and 'hang out.' Streets become essential for the working-class youths in terms of the 'production of space' in the sense that Henri Lefèbvre (1989) stated. Listening to music in their own sport-cars with high-decibel volume, having a chat with their own 'mates' on some particular street corners, speaking loudly, and staring at strangers are all the spatial practices of the youths. These practices are employed by the youths to produce their own social space and territory as opposed to the strangers and parental discipline.

Street, which is a safe habitat for the residents, might well be irritating for some others. The streets in the peripheral space, such as ethnic neighbourhood, have their own mythified stories. The streets of Kreuzberg have many such stories as such. Those streets have hosted many spontaneous riots and uprisings as well as many multicultural festivals. May Day in the year 1989 witnessed one of these riots in Kreuzberg.[1] Taner, one of the participants, narrated the incidences with nostalgic mimics:

> In the May Day we plundered almost everything we saw. We exploded. This social explosion might happen again. We were plundering the posh shopping centres and cars in the streets, even the Turkish pilgrims were plundering. Approximately ten shopping-centres were plundered by Turkish, German, Kurdish, drunk, pilgrim etc. It was like Los Angeles in 92, and Kadıköy in May Day 1996.[2] We were dancing while plundering. I was extremely happy that day, I was fighting against the system. These incidences happened mostly in Kreuz-

berg. It was like a 'revolution.' We were all together, Turk, Kurd, German, Fascist and Arab.

Taner's narrative gives us more clues about the character of the streets of Kreuzberg. The streets house some united battles of Turkish and German dwellers in the May Day uprisings as well as in some other spontaneous uprisings such as anti-racist demonstrations.[3]

Previously, the main occupants of the streets were the mythical gangsta groups like 36ers, 36 Boys and 36 Juniors in *Naunyn Ritze*. Taner, who is one of the founders of the 36ers, said that the gangsta group was providing the youngsters with an alternative sense of family: "My group was my family. We were all together with the younger ones like a family. For instance we did not let the little kids smoke, and we used to protect them." The youngsters roaming around the streets are aware of the fact that, someday, they might risk imprisonment through fighting, carrying guns and drug use. Since they have been living with this risk for so long in their ethnic enclave, it seems that they have internalised this risk. The experience of imprisonment turns out to be a source of *distinction* for the boys.[4] This *distinction* makes them feel 'cool.' It is as if the youngsters, who previously were jailed, affirm the meaning of the word 'cooler' in American slang: 'cooler' means jail, a place where someone cools down.

The youngsters see their elder friends, who spent some time in jail, as a role model. Bülent (20) was a new face in *Naunyn Ritze*. He was previously in jail due to the drug use and violence. For Bülent, the jail experience has ruined his life. He thought that he had nothing left to lose or to win. He has been in such a pessimistic state of mind. On the other hand, as a person who has had a jail experience, he was highly respected by the youngsters within *Naunyn Ritze*. Apart from the other elder 'brothers,' he was another symbol of authority in the centre. Although he was in despair for the prison experience, he had the tendency to use this experience as a distinction, or the symbolic capital, in his relation with the community youngsters.

Another source of *distinction* that the ethnic minority youths tend to have on the street is the mobile phone. Almost all the guys have a mobile phone, which is a symbol of masculinity. They have no money but they have 'handy' (mobile phone). It gives a 'cool' style to the youngsters. Sitting in a Turkish *café*, such as *Café 1001* in Charlottenburg, many mobile phones could be seen on the tables. It is as if the phones are in a symbolic battle on the table. Gülsen (16) explained that if she quits smoking, her elder brother promised to buy her a mobile phone.

Friendship is also a vital constituent of the life-world in street. Turkish youngsters express that after a certain age it becomes easier to communicate with the co-ethnics because the mimicry counts to a wider extent in the age of adolescence. It becomes difficult for them to have a silent communication with the Germans through mimics, and to have serious talks with them. They see it as a cultural difference between their German friends and themselves. Thus, they tend to give up 'hanging around' with the German friends. They imply that at this age they need mature and satisfactory talks with their friends, whereas their German 'mates' seem very childish to them. They cannot have a proper *'muhabbet'* (in-depth talk) with their German 'mates.' The difference between diasporic Turkish youths and their German 'mates' springs from the fact that they have a rather different mimicry and subjectivity. Raising the difference in mimicry as a reason of not getting on well with German 'mates' is, in fact, a way of representing difference in the process of identity construction. Bhabha's definition of mimicry is quite illuminating in finding out its importance for the identity formation and articulation:

Mimicry is at once resemblance and menace [...] In mimicry, the representation of identity and meaning is rearticulated along the axis of metonymy. As Lacan reminds us, mimicry is like camouflage, not a harmonisation of repression of difference, but a form of resemblance, that differs from or defends presence by displaying it in part, metonymically (Bhabha, 1994: 90).

Mimicry attempts to include some while excluding some others. What really matters in mimicry is the expression of resemblance with the co-ethnics as well as expressing difference from 'others.' The discourse of mimicry constructed by the Turkish youth is "a form of defensive warfare, which marks those moments of civil disobedience within the discipline of civility: signs of spectacular resistance" (Bhabha, 1994: 121). Raising mimicry as a difference provides minority youths with an instrumental ground, where they could develop a form of resistance against the dominant regimes of representation.

On the other hand, subjectivity is also an essential element of inter-ethnic friendships between Turkish and German youths. Migrants' children or grandchildren have a permanent negotiation between the world of youths and the world of grown-ups due to their particular subjectivity. For instance, being able to summarise or translate the key points of a news story engage in dialogue with adults, form opinions, take a stand on issues, and even challenge and attempt to change elders' views makes a young person feel 'grown-up' and encourages others to perceive them as such (Gillespie, 1996: 118).

Courtship is another constituent of the street life to be mentioned. Going out with a German girl is quite normal for the Turkish boys. In the *Naunyn Ritze* youth centre, there were some boys going out with German girls, and cohabitating with them. Nevertheless, both the Turkish boys and girls held a strong belief that the Turkish boys' relationships with German girls would not result in marriage. One of the Turkish girls stated "the reason why 'our' guys are going out with the German girls is just to *use* them and to do that thing, which they cannot do with the decent Turkish girls." Claire E. Alexander's classification of 'private women' and 'public women' in mapping out the modes of courtship of the male black Londoners (Alexander, 1996: 157-186) is also applicable to the working-class Turkish youth in Berlin. Turkish boys generally consider Turkish girls to be 'our' women. It is significant that when the boys encounter Turkish women in Kreuzberg, or in other districts of Berlin, they rarely enter into interaction with them. Having been contemplated as sexually inaccessible, at least for casual encounters, by the Turkish youth, the Turkish women have their own place in the private sphere of the Turkish boys, whereas the German women belong to the public space that is easily accessible. The association of the German women with the public space allies Turkish boys more closely to the power relations reflected in wider society.

The youngsters have also been used to living together with the presence of police in the street. They call the police officers '*amca*' that literally means 'uncle' in Turkish. Neco says, "we are so close to the police officers, so we consider them our relatives." The youngsters can easily recognise the civil police officers 'hanging out' or driving around in the street. Since there is drug traffic around *Kotbusser Tor* and the youth centre, the police always inspect the district. While the presence of police in the streets is tolerated by the youngsters, they are seriously disturbed by the police occupying their own space in the youth centre because the youth centre is considered somewhere safe from police interference.

Life in the School

School is also one space, which is quite distinct from the other social spaces in regard to the differentiation of the people with whom the youths interact. The youngsters who attend the high school always complain about their teachers. They believe that the reason behind their failure is the racist and discriminatory behaviours of their German teachers to whom they have to be subject. Be it male or female, never-ending discussions with the teachers are the common problem. They always tend to blame the teachers, but not themselves, for the failure they experience.

A remarkable amount of the youngsters were raised in Turkish classrooms where there were almost no Germans. The children of the migrants have been subject to certain regulations with regard to education. The official policy in most of the provinces of Germany requires that 'foreigners' in the classroom should not exceed 20 percent of any school class (in Berlin the quota could be extended up to 50 percent).[5] This regulation is considered to be one of the factors behind the presence of high numbers of Turkish children in *Sonderschule* (Table 6). *Sonderschule* is a different kind of primary school having special classes for children who are believed to have 'learning difficulties.' Most of the immigrants' children are asked to attend these schools because of their 'impotence' in German language. Depending on their success, the students of *Sonderschule* have a chance to switch to the other schools. Then, these students most likely encounter some other problems such as the incompatibility of the previous *Sonderschule* curriculum to the new curriculum. The hierarchical structure of the German educational system, in a way, tends to imprison the children of immigrants who are in rather disadvantageous position.[6]

Table 6: The Number of the German and Non-German Students in Kreuzberg

A. *Grundschulen*

Classes	German	Foreigner	Foreigner %
Class 1	803	866	52.9
Class 2	924	942	50.5

Class 3	856	892	51.6
Class 4	948	763	44.6
Class 5	815	752	48.0
Class 6	751	747	49.9

B. Hauptschulen

Classes	German	Foreigner	Foreigner %
Class 7	158	262	62.4
Class 8	159	270	63.0
Class 9	192	180	48.4
Class 10	151	198	56.7

C. Realschulen

Classes	German	Foreigner	Foreigner %
Class 7	64	74	53.6
Class 8	58	53	48.0
Class 9	61	69	53.1
Class 10	103	118	53.4

D. Gymnasien

Classes	German	Foreigner	Foreigner %
Class 7	191	59	23.6
Class 8	171	46	21.2
Class 9	154	41	21.0
Class 10	183	57	23.8

E. Gesamtschulen

Classes	German	Foreigner	Foreigner %
Class 7	289	189	39.5
Class 8	297	167	36.0
Class 9	263	210	44.4
Class 10	262	201	43.4

F. Sonderschulen

Classes	German	Foreigner	Foreigner %
Class 1,2	67	29	30.2
Class 3	36	17	32.1
Class 4	21	17	44.7
Class 5	14	12	46.2
Class 6	33	20	37.8
Class 7	20	16	44.4
Class 8	25	11	30.6
Class 9	16	--	--
Class 10	8	--	--

Source: Der Bezirksbürgermeister von Berlin-Kreuzberg, October 1996

German and middle-class Turkish families do not prefer sending their children to the primary and especially to the secondary schools in Kreuzberg, because they believe that children raised in these schools with the working-class migrants' children, become more violent and less academically able. Being raised in these classrooms, Turkish children often display a lack of confidence in their interaction with the majority society due to their inadequate German language and their deficient empathy with the Germans. The consequence of the lack of interaction could overtly be seen in the common playground of the Turkish and German children. The *Naunyn Ritze* youth centre has a park and playground for the children in *Waldemarstraße*. There is always a youth worker in the park, dealing with the children. What was striking for me was to see that Turkish and German children (6 to 12-year-old) hardly interacted in their games. Sometimes, this lack of interaction might also lead to violent acts between children. For instance, once the German children built a little wooden-house under the supervision of the Turkish youth worker in the children's play park of the *Naunyn Ritze* youth centre, then the Turkish children silently came to the park at night and destroyed it.

It seems that the official authorities are reluctant to do something in order to open the channels of communication and interaction between the children of the ethnic groups. In an interview, I asked Barbara John, Commissioner of Foreigners' Office, whether she was trying to change this picture. She said "we cannot force the people to do this or that; all we are trying to do is to convince the Turks to leave Kreuzberg to live in better conditions." The rationale behind this official discourse seems to be aiming to disseminate the Turkish enclave in Kreuzberg.[7]

Life in the Household

Family is another space where the youngsters live.[8] The general assumption within and outside the Turkish community concerning the nature of the Turkish family is that working-class Turkish families are relatively more crowded than their German equivalents. The number of the members of the families ranges from six to ten for the twenty youngsters whom I interviewed in *Naunyn Ritze* and *Chip*. Most mothers are either housewives or manual workers. On the other hand, most fathers are manual workers on either construction sites or assembly lines. Some parents have retired and a significant number are unemployed. The ones who are retired have the chance to switch between Turkey and Germany.

Discipline within the family is the primary aspect. Those youngsters, who are very relaxed and self-confident in the public space, suddenly turn out to be very silent and 'respectful' under the power of a father. Parents try to keep their children away from the streets and the youth centres. They believe that interacting with 'deviant' German and Turkish youth in the streets and youth centres will make their children disrespectful. Thus, they encourage their children to go to some community associations such as *Alevi* associations, *hemsehri* (fellow-villager) associations, community centres and/or mosques.

Another assumption about the Turkish family structure in Berlin is that the familial bonds within the Turkish community are more powerful than in German society. Although these bonds become weaker in comparison to working-class family culture in Turkey, the children are still expected to live with their parents until they get married. The parental culture is still quite influential in choosing a marriage partner. Parents still have their say in the selection of a spouse. The criteria of selection are usually very simple: the potential spouse should preferably be from the same ethnic and religious origin. For instance, a German spouse is not preferred unless s/he converts to Islam; and there is also a strong boundary between *Sunni*s and *Alevi*s in terms of marriage. Hitherto, arranged marriages from Turkey were quite widespread. The youngsters have recently come to terms with the ever-lasting wish of their parents to go for arranged marriages. Although I have no statistical data indicating the decreasing pace of arranged marriages from Turkey, the radically resisting statements of the youngsters were quite instructive in understanding the new trend. The girls are the ones who used to extensively suffer from arranged marriages. When their 'age of marriage' came, their parents used to arrange a marriage for them during the summer vacation (*izin*) spent in Turkey.

Another aspect worth mentioning in its relation to the familial life of the youngsters is represented by the conversations about the relatives, friends and immovable belongings back in Turkey. The family members talk either about relatives they miss or the immovable belongings they left behind or recently bought. Daily, by means of those in-family-conversations and collective memories, youngsters revisit living relatives; or they watch the videotape they previously recorded in a wedding ceremony in Turkey; or else they watch the videotape showing the summer cottage and/or house they bought in the previous visit to Turkey. Each of those ritualised practices signifies an imaginary journey back home for the youth in the diaspora.

No one, neither parent, nor teacher, nor youth worker has a complete knowledge about the youngsters' life worlds. The youths always switch between these different spaces. They should negotiate and compromise between various social-cultural scapes in order to find a way through. What they construct in these shifting spaces is a kind of cultural bricolage leading to the formation of a *Third Culture*. The *third culture*, to which I will shortly return in the following chapter, "is a bricolage in which elements from different cultural traditions, sources and social discourses are continuously intermingled with and juxtaposed to each other" (Çaglar, 1994: 33).

The production of the third culture by the Turkish diasporic youth is a production going beyond the conventional Hegelian and Marxist understandings of production. Stereotypically it is believed that working-class diasporic youths do not produce anything, they just 'hang around' and do nothing. This is a common opinion amongst parents, majority society, formal institutions and scholars. Such a stereotype is bound to the ideology of productivism. As Henri Lefèbvre (1989) has rightly posed, production does not necessarily require either product or labour. His notion of production is quite different from that of economism:

> [W]ords, dreams, texts and concepts produce labour on their own account; [...] This leaves us with a curious image of labour without labourers, products without production processes, or production without products, and works without creators (no 'subject' and no 'object' either) (Lefebvre, 1989: 72).

Turkish diasporic youth in Kreuzberg produces a web of social spaces composed of youth centre, street, school and household. This is a social space constituting a locus of communication by means of signs, symbols, images and objects, a locus of separations and a milieu of prohibitions (insiders-outsiders). Furthermore, this is a space giving rise to the production of a postcultural youth culture in the 'borderlands' of 'various cultures.' All these life-worlds are imbued with the diasporic space in Kreuzberg. In what follows I shall describe the major constituents employed by the working-class Turkish youths to construct a new home in Kreuzberg.

'Sicher in Kreuzberg': The Homing of Diaspora

Modern diaspora identities inscribe a homing desire while simultaneously creating syncretic cultures in the borderlands. The question of desiring home in diaspora is precisely linked to the processes of exclusion operating in the given circumstances. The discourse of home in the diaspora is an essential need to challenge the existing regimes of exclusion and subordination. In this sense, the youngsters refer to Kreuzberg as 'Little Istanbul.' As it was explained above, all the images, signs, symbols and objects in Kreuzberg contribute to the mystification of Istanbul and Turkey in the imagery of the Turkish minority. The use of familiar signs and symbols in the diaspora is, in fact, a quest for homing. All the youngsters without any exception use the word 'sicher' in explaining how they feel in Kreuzberg. The word 'sicher' literally means 'sure' and 'secure.' Being sure of what, and feeling secure against what? Kreuzberg is the new home for them, where they are always sure of their moves and positions.

Kreuzberg is literally a Turkish ethnic enclave providing Turkish migrants and their descendants with a web of solidarity, security and confinement. Yüksel (26) expressed how they rarely go outside

Kreuzberg, apart from those places where their schools are located. When they leave Kreuzberg, they have the feeling that they have gone outside their home:

If Kreuzberg did not exist, then Germany would be unbearable to live in for us. Here the water and the climate are awful. Nothing has taste here, but wherever I go outside Kreuzberg I am longing for, let's say, a woman going back home from shopping with a full bag in her hands. Kreuzberg is a habit.

Kreuzberg no longer marks an international frontier for the Turkish youth. They navigate between their worlds, not only when they make an annual vacation trip to Turkey (*izin*), but also "daily when they leave the Turkish inner sanctums of their cold-water flats, their Turkophone families and neighbours, their *Kleines*-Istanbul ghetto to enter the German speaking work world and marketplace, where the characteristic economic relations between *First* and *Third* worlds are linguistically, socially, and culturally reproduced" (Mandel, 1996: 151).

Kreuzberg is their very own living territory, they feel secure there and they do not have any feeling of alienation. It is the Germans from other districts, according to Neco (25), who feel alienated in Kreuzberg, not the Turks. No youngster feels attached either to Germany or Berlin, but they are attached to Kreuzberg. The youths identify themselves with Kreuzberg. Kreuzberg provides them with a sense of security, behavioural certainty, assurance and confidence as it previously did, and still does, to their immigrant parents (Çaglar, 1994: 53).

The feeling of being simultaneously 'home away from homeland' or 'here and there' reveals a form of 'double consciousness' and 'awareness of multilocality' in the imagery of the diasporic youth. The awareness of multilocality or 'double consciousness' becomes a crucial aspect of their identity formation and articulation. When the youngsters have been asked about where home was for them, they all hesitated to pose clear boundaries between Turkey and Kreuzberg. When I asked Ayhan (20) from *Naunyn Ritze* about his feelings on Kreuzberg, he said:

The moment when you asked the question, my hair stood on end. I love Kreuzberg. I feel myself secure here. Everything is normal here; the rest of Berlin is like a dead-land. On the one hand, it is making us suffer, on the other hand there is always someone here helping you. For instance I learned graffiti and break-dance here. It has brought some things to us as well as taking away some other things from us. It is cool. Seriously speaking, for me home is Kreuzberg. Home is where we live in. Some people might think that I have become conceited and that I am in vain, but here is my home. I have not been brought up in Turkey.

The youngsters are highly attached to their own local boundaries. Owning the district they live in, they place a boundary between themselves and the majority society. Their own street is a kind of protective wall for them; they hardly leave the street. Kreuzberg is a 'fortress,' which they and their parents have constructed in the span of time. The streets of Kreuzberg give the warmth of home to the youngsters. For instance, while their German 'mates' meet in each other's house to converse or to entertain, the Turkish youths prefer meeting in the street. When the centre is not open in the holidays, they meet in front of the youth centre.

Although they have strong local identifications, they may also vary in their identification depending on the context. Neco said: "When we are asked where we are from in Berlin, we say we are from Kreuzberg; but if the same question is asked to us outside Berlin we say we are from Berlin. We say we are from Berlin, because we know that Berlin always seems exotic to the other Germans. Berlin is Kreuzberg." By doing so, Neco and his 'mates' seem to be aware of their situational local identification, which prompts them to play with the images of the townscape in the imagery of outsiders.

"Berlin is Kreuzberg." This narration of Neco refers to the fact that the youngsters realise that Kreuzberg used to be previously conceived by the west Germans as the major exotic and enigmatic quarter of Berlin. Referring to this perception, Kreuzberg youngsters tend to have a strong pride with their own territory. Neco's narration about Kreuzberg seems to be complementary to what Yüksel (26) said:

Once upon a time, Kreuzberg was like a battlefield. Everything was falling apart here. Some of the families didn't even have a toilet of their own; they used to share the common toilet with the other families in the courtyard of the building. Some of the houses had neither electricity nor water. We grew up in such an environment. Everything has changed along with the reunification. Before the reunification, the West German tourists often used to visit Kreuzberg just to have a quick look without getting off the tourist bus. They were afraid of us. It was as if they were visiting a zoo, and the bus was like their cage protecting them from the dangerous animals. Then, when they got back home, they expressed their enthusiasm and happiness to their friends in visiting Kreuzberg.

Kreuzberg gives the youngsters a sense of security, not only because it is a space they were born into, but also because it is a place they can socially control. The social control of the living space is based on mainly ethnic and *hemsehri* (fellow villagers) bonds. *Hemsehrilik* is a network of solitary interpersonal relations based on regional ties. It is thought of as a primordial tie like kinship (Çaglar, 1994: 159). Although the *hemsehri* bonds have recently become weaker, they are still crucial instruments, which the youngsters play with. For Eyüp, a 22-year-old-boy in *Chip* youth centre, *hemsehrilik* is still a very important concept: "I automatically fancy my *hemsehris* from Aksaray (a middle Anatolian city). For instance, I don't like the people from Samsun and Konya, whereas my *hemsehris* are worthy for anything." Bagdagül, an 18-year-old-female from *Naunyn Ritze*, is also very sensitive about the issue of kinship and *hemsehrilik*: "*Hemsehrilik* is very important here. Almost all Kreuzberg belongs to *us*." Here, 'us' refers to the Turkish residents from Erzurum – a city in the eastern Anatolia. Then, she added that she did not bother about *hemsehrilik*. There is a contradiction in her narration. On the one hand, she is internalising the category of 'us,' on the other she posits a distinction between herself and the rest. In fact, she is aware that *hemsehrilik* is a crucial social capital for herself as well as for the rest of 'us.'

However, there are some aspects of this ethnic enclave that the youngsters dislike. These aspects are basically related to their privacy. Gossip is an important institution in the Turkish enclave of Kreuzberg. Almost all the residents know what is going on in Kreuzberg. Yüksel (manager of the rap group *Islamic Force*) has brought a yellow aluminium window from Turkey for his music store in *Adalbertstraße*, the very next day almost everybody in Kreuzberg heard the news, even found out how much it had cost Yüksel. He stated that the kiosk at the opposite side has already ordered the same aluminium from Istanbul just after he fixed his window.

The community culture of the neighbourhood also has a great impact on the gender relations as well as on the institution of gossip. Boys say, "Kreuzberg girls are our sisters." They can easily determine which girl is a stranger in their own district. They chase the 'stranger girls' in the streets and make insolent remarks to them without looking at their nationality. Elif, youth worker, described how she had some problems in the very first days when she started to work in the *Naunyn Ritze* youth centre. Firstly, she was chased by the youngsters in the street; and then the boys in the centre started to compete between themselves for her attention without knowing that she was a youth worker in the centre.

Gossip is also an influential instrument for the parents to keep their children under control. There is always a social control on both boys and girls, so that they must be careful in their relations with the other sex. The girls, for instance, are always afraid of getting caught by some familiar eyes when they 'hang around' with boys. They are concerned of being given the label of 'nasty girl.' Most of the girls in the centre also refrain from smoking in public, because they fear their elder brothers or parents. Thus, they tend to smoke secretly in the toilet, or outside the centre. Smoking at such an early age gives them a feeling of freedom. It is a symbol of freedom, which they consider against the authority of parental power and male dominance. The role of gossip is not also very different for the boys from the parental perspective. Ayhan (20) says,

If one of my relatives sees me hanging around with a German girl, then the next day everybody here and in Turkey hears this 'unacceptable' thing. They start making gossip about my family and me. They accuse my parents of not having been able to raise good children.

Ayhan's statement underlines the fact that gossip is a strong means of social control. As Marie Gillespie (1996: 154) stated, gossip that focuses on violations of moral codes, norms and values serves to reinforce them. Furthermore, gossip reinforces the boundaries between insiders and outsiders in the process of inter-ethnic relations as well as in that of intra-ethnic relations, i.e., German-Turkish and/or *Alevi-Sunni*. Thus, gossip strengthens the sense of living in a secure community space as opposed to the hegemonic culture, and also provides the subordinated masses living in the margin with a source of positive identity.

However, the youngsters are well aware of the limitations of Kreuzberg; feeling secure is not enough for the youngsters. From time to time, the youngsters express their willingness to move out. Kreuzberg indeed 'has a bad name,' as I have heard expressed in many conversations I had with the youngsters. Most of the youngsters have no thought about their future prospects. Yet, they are not content with their expectations. They complain about the stereotypical perception of Kreuzberg held among the German employers and school administrations. Devrim (17) made many job applications to do his obligatory praxis (*Praktikum*) as a student. He had no positive response: "Of course, they don't accept me, because I am from Kreuzberg. I will keep applying." Mehmet (18) is another youngster trying to study social pedagogy:

I am trying to be registered in one of these schools. I call them to get some information. In the beginning of the conversation, everything goes fine. I speak as good as the Germans without any accent. Then they start asking questions about my background to get informed. When I tell them my name and that I am living in Kreuzberg, suddenly the conversation changes. The person who is on the other side of the line hesitates for a while; it is like a silence for a second. Then he tries to find some excuses to explain to me that I am not eligible for their school. Kreuzberg has a bad reputation. I am not eligible for their school, simply because I am a Turk living in Kreuzberg.

These examples as well as some others, which have been described to me, indicate that a Kreuzberg address by itself is a handicap when looking for job. I have not been able to confirm this impression statistically, but I was convinced by those youngsters, who were hopelessly applying for jobs, that this impression has some truth in it.

The youngsters are also aware of the fact that moving out of Kreuzberg is very difficult. Mehmet (18) and his parents moved out for two years, and then came back again: "it was very difficult for us to live outside Kreuzberg. All my friends and relatives are living here. Here I feel much better although there are many obstacles to living here." Affirming the importance of close ties is the fact that many of those who can afford to move to a 'nicer' area do not. They stay and repair their homes, reasserting the image of the community as a good place to live. The expression of the wish for moving out, for social advancement, is predominantly a class issue. It is the class difference that makes some people express their wish to move out of this ethnic enclave more readily than the others are. Hikmet (30), a final year student of medicine, spoke of his intention to move out for the future of his children. Ferat's (18) father who has a university degree and a small-scale private enterprise also expresses his wish to move out for the future of his only son.

Kreuzberg is a diasporic space for the working-class Turkish youth. It gives the youngsters a complex sense of homing. On the one hand, as long as these youngsters are surrounded by the signs, music, rhythms and major issues of Turkey in the diaspora, they tend to have an 'imagined sense of belonging' to the homeland Turkey, which has been 'deferred' as a spiritual, cultural and political metaphor. On the other, they develop a strong sense of homing to the 'Turkified' Kreuzberg due to the same reason.

Middle-Class Turkish Youngsters and the Question of Identity

A good understanding of the social discourses of the working-class Turkish diasporic youth partly depends on the incorporation of the class aspect into the analysis. In this section, I will reflect upon the question of identity as it is expressed by a middle-class Turkish youth group living outside Kreuzberg. As I pointed out before, this is the group of youngsters who constituted the third group of the research, *BTBTM* youth. At the end of their group discussions, which they undertook within their own group under the supervision of Nurdan, they organised a youth festival (*Jugendfest*) where they presented their views on various issues such as xenophobia, racism, hostility in the media, generation conflicts, and specially the question of identity. The festival was held in one of the multicultural venues of Berlin, *Werkstatt der Kulturen*, on the 18th of May 1996. Barbara John, commissioner of Foreigners' Office, Ingrid Staumer, senator of cultural affairs, Hayrettin Erkmenoglu, Turkish counsellor in Berlin, German and Turkish media were in the audience.

The festival was primarily set up in order to present to the audience how 'multicultural' and cosmopolitan the Berlin-Turkish youth was. The sense of being '*multikulti*' in all the spheres of daily life is a crucial symbolic capital for these youngsters. Multiculturalism becomes a principal source of identity politics for them. The multicultural capital provides them with a sense of recognition by German society. This is the way they gain access into the mainstream culture. They extensively use the term '*multikulti*' in expressing their music taste, friendships, life styles, and their neighbourhood. In this sense, the selection of the folklore, dance and music performances for the festival was made to underline their multicultural image: a Jewish music group, an amateur German dance company called *'Multikulti'*, a Turkish folklore group, and a Kurdish folklore group. *BTBTM* youths were also very curious about not calling the festival as *'Türkische Jugendfest'*, because they were keen on showing their cosmopolitan and multicultural identity.

Besides the discourse of multiculturalism, which became apparent in the festival, another crucial point was displayed by the youngsters: the correlation between representation and the question of identity. These are the youngsters who are mostly represented in both German and Turkish media in Berlin. Berlin-Turks are proud of them, because these youngsters are the 'good' representatives of the Turks living in Berlin, and they are the ones who have been able to integrate into the German society 'without losing their Turkishness.' Germans are also proud of them because these youngsters represent 'how well' the German integration policies have been working.

It is evident that contemporary discussions on identity are partly related to the dominant regimes of representation in the media. It was striking for me to realise in the course of the research that it was the middle-class youth that attempted to draw attention to the 'question of identity' rather than the working-class Turkish youth. The working-class youths that are relatively away from the manipulation of media, seem to be quite content with their identity without problematising it. On the other hand, since the middle-class youths have been in a dialogical relation with the media, they tend to conceive the 'identity question' as granted. The way these youngsters raised the issue of identity was, in fact, a reflection of their representation in the media.

The question of identity is mostly problematised by the media in a way that influences the identity formation process of ethnic minority youth. The middle-class youths give response to their own representation in the media. What they discussed in the *Jugendfest* was not their own identity problems. What they did was, in fact, having a 'chatter about the chatter' about their identity. The chatter about their identity, which they chattered was the chatter, made up by the media. This is like the chatter about the sport that we chattered about, not the sport itself as a practice (Eco, 1986: 162-163).[9] Thus, we rather tend to discuss about what is represented to us by the media, but not about the event itself. In addition to their difference from the working-class youth in terms of their problematisation of the identity issue, the middle-class youngsters also have a different sense of place in the diaspora. Unlike the working-class Turkish youth, they do not feel any attachment to the places they are living in. They rather attach themselves to the *'multikulti'* city of Berlin. In what follows, I will shortly examine their sense of place and home in the diaspora.

Middle-Class Turkish Youth: Cosmopolitan Self and 'Heimat'

The middle-class Turkish youth has rather a cosmopolitan understanding of home. They mainly express that they long for Turkey when they are in Germany, and yearn for Germany when they are in Turkey. They rather feel an affinity with Berlin rather than with their neighbourhood and Germany. What strikes them in Berlin is its multicultural character. Multilocality is very influential in their identification of themselves as well. Gülten (17) expresses her feelings about home in such a way:

Home is where you are living, and where your friends are. For the time being, home is both Germany and Turkey for me, I do not want to define home actually. Home itself should attract you. I am still in search of home. Home should be something, which depends on your way of life. I miss Germany when I am in Turkey. Mine is something cosmopolitan, something which I will never be able to define: Both Turkish and German. We take the good parts of both. This is richness.

The middle-class youths all either have dual citizenship, or are in the process of gaining it. They see dual citizenship as being equal to the Germans, and having a cosmopolitan identity. For instance, if they have a problem with the police, they state that the police have a tolerant behaviour towards the Turks having German passport, and that "they can't ask you stupid questions like 'Where are your residence documents?'" This group of youngsters is much more mobile compared to the working-class youth. They sometimes prefer going to other countries for vacation such as the USA, Morocco, Spain and France. Another advantage of German citizenship appears in this case, i.e. there is no need for a visa to go to other European Union countries. However, some youngsters insist on not having German citizenship. Dilek (18) is one of them. She does not want to have German citizenship, she states:

[T]he Germans want to assimilate us. If I have German citizenship, then I will be doing what they want me to do. I don't want to. As a Turkish citizen who was born here, I must have the same rights as the German citizens. This is discrimination and racism, and I am fighting this. I am against a given identity. As long as they don't accept dual citizenship, I won't get the German citizenship.

Having a cosmopolitan identity, the middle-class youth, in fact, seeks social change in their country of settlement. On the other hand, the disadvantaged working-class youth, as Brake states, "is not anti the prevailing social order, but seeks a place within it" (Brake, 1980: 26). By raising the question of identity, the middle-class youths aim to negate the way they are presented by the German media, which homogenises the German-Turkish youth. In the context of Turkish diasporic youth, another crucial difference between the two youth cultures is that the form and style of the working-class youth culture is mediated by the local neighbourhood whilst that of the middle-class youth culture is mediated by the translocal class orientation. Apart from the fact that Berlin-Turkish youths have a multicultural competence, there is also another general aspect worth mentioning, i.e., their linguistic competence that enables them to switch codes, as they find appropriate.

Language and 'Code-Switching'

Berlin-Turkish youth, be it working-class or middle-class, undoubtedly manifests relationships of 'boundary transgression' by means of linguistic competence. Turkish youths have a peculiar language of their own. They speak a creole language. It is a mix of Turkish, German and American-English. This new form of city speech in the migrants' suburbs is a verbal celebration of ghetto multiculturalism, twisting German, Turkish and American slang in resistance to the official language. Leaving aside the American slang, which they pick up, from the movies and songs, they habitually switch between Turkish and German, and sometimes between three languages Turkish, Kurdish and German. Although imperfectly, the youngsters tend to use all these languages at once in order to express themselves. In linguistics, this is called code-switching. S. Poplack (1980: 588) defines code-switching as "the alternation of two [or more] languages within a single discourse, sentence, or constituent." Poplack states that there are three major types of switching: i. intra-sentential switching; ii. inter-sentential switching; and iii. tag-switching, or emblematic switching.

i. Intra-sentential switching: This type of switching includes the switches made within a sentence.
Example: Nezaman *Fahrprüfung* yapacaksin?
           (When are you going to get *the driving test?*)
This type of switching may well be made by all the youngsters from each segment of the community. It does not really require a full competence in both languages. This is the common switching type that the working-class Turkish youngsters mostly repeat.

ii. Inter-sentential switching: These types of switches occur between sentences. Each clause or sentence is uttered in one language or another. Proficiency in both languages is the precondition of this switching mode because major portions of the utterance must conform to the rules of both languages.
Example: Ben bir zamanlar çok kitap okurdum.
           Ab und zu hab' ich mal so'n Drang, was zu lesen.
           (Once upon a time I used to read a lot.
           Time to time I feel a desire to read something.)
The *BTBTM* youngsters, who were in the Gymnasium, were often repeating the inter-sentential switching in their mutual conversations. On the other hand, the working-class Turkish youths were not capable of switching inter-sentially as well as the others, since they had a lack of grammatical knowledge on Turkish and German.

iii. Tag-switching, or emblematic switching: This type involves the insertion of an exclamation. Poplack (1980) calls this type of switching 'emblematic switching' because it serves as an emblem of the bilingual character in a monolingual sentence. Emblematic switching is also quite common for any youngster.
Example: *Ich meine*, ben de kitap okumasini seviyorum.
           (*I mean*, I like reading too.)[10]

Sociolinguistically code-switching may well have some functions for the bilingual utterer. Rene Appel and Pieter Muysken (1987: 118) have pointed out the following functions of code-switching. Firstly it has referential function for the utterer to fill in the lexical gaps of one language. Since the speaker does not know the exact equivalent of a word, s/he consciously tends to switch to the other language. Secondly, it has directive function for the speaker to involve and/or to exclude a person from a part of the conversation. Thirdly, it may have an expressive function for the speaker to express her/his transcultural identity. Fourthly, it may have a phatic function for the utterer to emphasise something in his/her utterance by changing the speech-tone and the language. In the fifth place, code-switching may have a metalinguistic function for the speaker who wants to impress the others by showing his/her linguistic skills. Finally, it may also have a poetic function in switching puns and jokes.

Apart from these types of code-switching, the youth may make other mix-ups between Turkish and German due to the different grammatical character of the languages. Turkish language springs from the Ural-Altaic language family like Finnish, Hungarian, Mongolian and Korean languages. Turkish is from the Altaic group as Mongol and Korean. All these languages share three common features. These features are namely agglutination, vowel harmony and lack of grammatical gender. Turkish is a language without any article and with many suffixes. This is the reason why the Turkish youngsters tend to adopt German nouns without any article, and they sometimes add suffixes for case – and plural-marking.

Example a: Burada *Grundschule*den önce *Kindergarten*'e gitmek sart.
(It is obligatory here to attend *the Kindergarden* before *the primary school*.)
-den : Ablative case in Turkish
-e : Dative case in Turkish

Example b: Yasak yerlere grafiti yaptigin zaman *Ruhm*un oluyor.
(When you make graffiti on the illegal places, you get *fame*.)
-un : Genitive case in Turkish

Example c: En çok *Action-movie*leri seviyorum.
(I like the action-movies most.)

-ler : Plural marking +
-i : Accusative case in Turkish

They also sometimes mix verbs by paraphrasing with the Turkish verbs. They usually use the German infinitive verbs in combination with the Turkish auxiliary verbs of *yapmak* (to do, to make), *etmek* (e.g. *devam etmek*: to carry on), and *olmak* (to be).

Example a: Kimleri *einladen* etmek istiyorsun?
(Whom do you want to invite?)
Example b: Ceketini neden *abmachen* yapmiyorsun?
(Why don't you take off your jacket?)
Example c: Dün olanlari gördügüm zaman *überraschen* oldum.
(When I saw what happened yesterday, I got surprised.)

The language, which is used by the working-class Turkish youth, is basically called *Kanak Sprak*.[11] *Kanak sprak* should, in fact, be written as '*kanake sprache*' in German, but this is the way the Turkish youngsters vernacularise it like many other examples. They quite often spell the words in the way they are pronounced. The words that are written on the cover of the tape of rap group *Cartel* are quite illustrative in this sense. The group have written the Turkish vernaculars of the English and German words such as '*existira sipesiyal tenks*' instead of extra special thanks, '*ekistira gürüse*' instead of extra *Grüße* (greetings), '*Asiyatik Variyors*' instead of Asiatic Warriors, '*Getobilaster Tüm*' instead of Ghettoblaster Team, and '*Kiroyzberg 36*' instead of Kreuzberg 36.

* * *

To summarise, having to practice various life-worlds, the working-class Turkish youth in Kreuzberg acquires the competence to behave appropriately in a number of different arenas. There are linguistic, social and cultural boundaries between their life-worlds (youth centre, street, school and household). The youngsters always have to translate and negotiate within and between these rigidly defined boundaries. The way they behave in these life-worlds is imbued by the conditions of the diasporic space in which they have been living. As far as it constitutes a symbolic bridge and cultural continuum between the diaspora and the homeland, Kreuzberg, '*Kleines* Istanbul,' turns out to be the new home for the youngsters. Kreuzberg provides the working-class youth with a 'fortress' protecting them against the destabilising effects of racialisation, rising unemployment, misrepresentation and discrimination. To put it differently, Kreuzberg serves as a security valve for the youngsters to soften the firm strokes coming from the external world. The youngsters in Kreuzberg also develop a 'demotic' discourse against the dominant discourse of the majority society (cf. Baumann, 1996). Their multiculturalism developing in response to the dominant ideology of multiculturalism (a form of high-culture) springs from their own form of resistance.

This chapter has been concerned with the question of identity and how it is predominantly related to representation and dominant discourse. In this sense, it was noted how the middle-class Turkish youths are highly influenced by their representation in the media. The German media tend to represent the Turkish youth as a homogeneous group suffering an identity crisis while wedged between two cultures. The media problematise the process of identity construction and articulation by the Turkish youngsters. As depicted above, these youngsters, who are responsive to the media, take their representation in the media as a starting point to redefine their identity. Taking the 'identity crisis' as granted, the youngsters tend to 'chatter about the chatter about their identity.' It was also stated that the multicultural discourse of the middle-class youth was essentially shaped by their concern about integrating into the mainstream multiculturalism. This is why their discourse of multiculturalism that is defined in relation to the dominant discourse of multiculturalism is, by and large, different from that of the working-class Turkish youth. Thus, this chapter has provided a ground for the investigation of the working-class hip-hop youth culture in particular by portraying the cultural identity formation and articulation processes of the working-class minority youth has been portrayed in relation to that of the middle-class youth. The following chapter will elaborate the primary features of the expressive hip-hop culture among the Turkish youths living in Kreuzberg.

Notes

1 For further information about the 1989 May Day demonstrations, see "Steine in die Senatskosmetik," *Taz-Berlin* (2 May

1989); "DGB zählte 610.000 beim Tag der Arbeit," *Taz* (2 May 1989); and "In Kreuzberg kommandieren wir," *Der Spiegel* 47/1990.

2   In the May Day demonstrations of 1996, a youth was killed, many others were wounded and the underclass people living in the margins in Kadiköy, Istanbul plundered many shopping centres, banks, and offices. The riot was partly organised and partly spontaneous. To put it differently, spontaneity in this occasion was the metalanguage of the peripheral space and/or marginality.

3   Here, paraphrasing from Antonio Gramsci (1971: 198), it should be stated that 'spontaneity is the characteristic of the history of subaltern classes and indeed of their most marginal and peripheral elements.'

4   I am using the term *distinction* in the sense that Pierre Bourdieu used it. Bourdieu, in his work *Distinction* (1984), calls attention to how different kinds of capitals (social, cultural, symbolic and economic) have been put into play by members of each social class and group in order to create a difference or *distinction*.

5   Article 35a of the Berlin-Brandenburg Education Act required a 30 percent quota for the 'foreigner' students. If the number of foreign students exceeded the 30 percent quota, and then either this quota could be extended to 50 percent under the condition that all the foreigner students spoke fluent German, or the 'foreigner classrooms' could be formed. Article 35a was declared void in September 1995 through the initiatives of the Association of Berlin-Brandenburg Turkish Parents (ABBTP). According to the figures of the ABBTP, the percentage of the Turkish students who have been educated in the 'foreigner classrooms' in Berlin was 20 percent for the *Grundschule* and 50 percent for the *Hauptschule*. For further information, see *10 Jahre Elternarbeit 1985-1995: Eine Documentation des Türkischen Elternvereins in Berlin-Brandenburg e. V.*

6   According to the figures of the *Statistische Veröffentlichungen der Kultusministerkonferenz, Dokument* No. 119 (Dec. 1991), 55.8 percent of the foreigners in *Sonderschule* in Berlin was made up by the Turkish students (Table 6).

7   A regulation, which was issued in 1975, has already forbidden foreigners from taking up residence in some districts of Berlin.

These restrictive zoning laws, enforced by the *Ausländerpolizei* (Aliens Police), identify three quarters of the city – Kreuzberg, Wedding and Tiergarten – as off-limits to the last desirable foreigners (those from the Third World). These are the districts with the highest percentage of Turkish residents, with 21.2 percent, 17.6 percent, and 6.2 percent respectively. It seems that the zoning laws, regulating the whereabouts of foreigners, went successful because the Turkish population of some new districts such as Neukölln and Schöneberg has become more than that of Wedding and Tiergarten, with 19.5 percent and 8.7 percent respectively (Source: *Statistisches Landesamt, Einwohnerregister*, 30.6.1996). The further stage of this process also seems to be convincing the Turks to leave Kreuzberg and settle down in some other districts of Berlin.

8   Although I have had limited material on households, due to the nature of my research, the family, as a principal constituent of the diasporic space needs to be taken into consideration in order to understand the diasporic consciousness.

9   Umberto Eco attributes to the 'chatter about chatter about sport' in order to express the impact of the press on the interpretations which we consider as our own.

10 The examples for code-switching were taken from the unpublished paper of Hasim Anik and Fügen Sengün (1995).

11 '*Kanak Sprak*' is also the title of the book that has been written a Turkish writer, Feridun Zaimoglu (1995). In his book, he has edited many brief articles written by some Turkish youngsters in a wide variety from the rappers to the Islamic fundamentalists. He attempts to explore the street German used by the Turkish youth with their own vernaculars. He ironically calls the world of the young Turks '*Kanakistan.*'

Chapter 5

Cultural Identity of the Turkish Hip-Hop Youth in Kreuzberg 36

The previous chapter portrayed the prevalent life-worlds of the diasporic Turkish youth in order to demonstrate the major constituents of their identity formation processes. This chapter primarily sets out to delineate the process of cultural bricolage and the cultural sources that shape the processes of identity formation of the working-class Turkish hip-hop youth. Being subject to a kind of structural outsiderism, the working-class ethnic minority youths tend to celebrate their past and cultural authenticity. This tendency becomes apparent in their rising orientation to their homeland, religion and ethnicity, which thus become their main cultural sources. Secondly, I shall describe both the particularist and universalist constituents of the Turkish hip-hop youth culture in Kreuzberg. The particularist components of their leisure culture are *'âlem'* (meeting with friends), *düğüns* (wedding ceremony) and *arabesk* music, while the universalist ones are rap, graffiti, dance and 'cool' style. Turkish hip-hop youngsters tend to express themselves by means of these expressive forms of culture as they are seldom represented positively in the German media. In mapping out the main framework of the cultural identity formation process and leisure culture of these youngsters, I shall demonstrate the multicultural competence of ethnic minority youths.

Cultural Sources of Identity Formation Process Among the Turkish Youth

As it was outlined in Chapter 1, the modern individual has recently become subject to the simultaneous interplay of the global and the local (*glocal*). In the age of *glocalism*, individuals and groups tend to form new identities by going back to basics. In this process of cultural identity formation, 'authentic' culture, ethnicity and what is related to the homeland become an important source of identity politics. Next, I shall examine these sources in order to display the particularist elements of the cultural identity of the Turkish hip-hop youth.

Orientation to Homeland

Orientation to the homeland can be perceived as one of the primary sources of identity for the diasporic youth. The diasporic youth tends to see Turkey as a shelter to protect themselves from their exclusion and ghettoisation in the public sphere, and to feel a sense of belonging. The symbolic bridge between the country of settlement and the homeland is built by means of regular summer vacations (*izin*), by listening to pop and rap music originating both in Germany and Turkey, and by an interest in famous football players like Tayfun playing in European level teams like *Fenerbahçe*. All three are examples of how the advancement of the means of transnational communications and transportation multiplies the diasporic communities' orientation to their homelands.

Orientation to the homeland is a never-ending issue for the Turkish communities in Berlin. Although there is a broad typology of different communities among the Turkish minority, orientation to the homeland is practically identical within almost all the communities. An obvious example is religious groups, who form various kinds of diasporic communities separated by strong boundaries from German society. These groups survive with the cultural and religious baggage they brought from Turkey, and prefer not to interact with the majority society. However, nationalist groups and left-wing secular groups, too, although they prefer interacting with the majority society, are also largely oriented to homeland affairs such as Turkey's internal politics and economic situation, which are often discussed in the traditional Turkish *cafés*, meeting places and leisure time activities.

The mythified summer vacations (*izin*) remain the main aspect of orientation to the homeland. The annual journey to Turkey has always been a great source of amusement for the youngsters. Previously, the rationale behind the *izin*s was mainly to visit relatives. Nowadays, the vacations have mainly become a journey to the land of sun and beaches. Before the Yugoslavian war, driving by car all the way through

Eastern Europe from Germany to Turkey was the most convenient way of travel. Most of the youngsters now talk about those days with nostalgia: The fun they used to have on the way with all the other family members and relatives; the enthusiastic impatience to arrive at the Turkish border, Kapikule; leaving the land of 'oppression' and 'discipline' behind; and living the journey with a feeling of 'full freedom.' Now, the children of those days have grown up, and they prefer going to Turkey with their own friends by plane as quickly as possible. The dreamy journeys of the past have only remained in the pictures taken during travels, in the nostalgic thoughts and conversations within the family.

Music is another primary aspect of the youngsters' orientation to Turkey. The rapidly growing market of pop music in Turkey has also influenced the young generation of Turkish pop-music singers in Germany. Recently, the music market in Turkey has become a significant career opportunity for a large number of pop and rap music singers in the Turkish diaspora. Accordingly, many Turkish-origin singers returned to settle in Turkey in order to have a share in the Turkish music market.[1] For instance, *Cartel*, a German-Turkish rap group to which I shall return in the next chapter, sold more than 300,000 copies of the album, called *Cartel*, in Turkey in 1995. There are dozens of Turkish music stores in Kreuzberg selling Turkish pop, arabesk, rap and folk music albums and arranging public concerts with the singers coming from Turkey.

In the Turkish discos of Berlin, the youngsters listen to these German-Turkish singers as well as the ones from Turkey. Listening to Turkish music, drinking Turkish *Efes* beer, and remembering the summer loves and vacations in Turkey, the youngsters construct a kind of imaginary journey back to Turkey. The infusion of Turkish pop music into the Turkish discos in Germany, and dancing to the rhythm of the Turkish pop singer *Yonca* as well as to *Madonna*, also gives the youngsters self-esteem – one which grows with one's own cultural capital (Trauffetter, 1995). The dancing spaces in the discos, which are dominated by what is Turkish, serve as a kind of imaginary remigration to the homeland and to the past. This imaginary remigration is the precondition of the solidarity network among the youngsters. This group setting also resembles a part-time diasporic community formation that excludes what is German. What these youth groups form in these spaces is a kind of part-time communitarianism that provides them with a political response to their exclusion from the public space in Germany.

Football is another crucial aspect of the orientation of the diasporic Turkish youth to their homeland. Most of the youngsters fanatically support one of the leading Turkish teams. When I was conversing with some of the youngsters in the *Naunyn Ritze* youth centre, talking about football warmed up the conversation quite rapidly. A thirteen year-old boy, a fan of *Galatasaray*, asked me which team I supported. When I said I was a fan of *Fenerbahçe*, the traditional rival of *Galatasaray*, we had a very lively conversation revolving around football. For a considerable number of Turkish youths, playing football provides a chance for social mobility. Although they may now play for a Berlin youth team, these youngsters aspire to playing in one of the first league teams of Turkey (Table 7).

Table 7: Major Turkish Football Teams in Kreuzberg

Football Team	Foundation Year	Total Members	Turkish Members
Altinordu	1995	100	100
Berlin Türkspor	1965	524	503
BSC Agrispor	1984	319	255
Hatayspor	1981	130	130
Hilalspor	1987	211	211
Karadeniz	1987	78	78
SG Anadoluspor	1978	343	211
Türkiyemspor	1978	455	441

Source: Der Bezirksbürgermeister von Berlin-Kreuzberg, 1.1.1996

Religion and Ethnicity

Apart from the orientation to homeland, there are other forms of cultural sources that shape the cultural identity of the Turkish hip-hop youth: religion, ethnicity and their reception in Turkey. Religion is a particularly influential cultural source of identity for the diasporic Turkish youth. The celebration of Islam among the diasporic Turkish youth springs, in part, from the German society's perception of them.

The majority society tends to employ Islam as a symbolic instrument to define the Turkish youth; and it is used in turn by the youngsters themselves. For instance, one of the rap groups, to which I shall return shortly, calls itself *Islamic Force*, although they have nothing to do with radical Islam. This kind of identity manifestation seems to indicate a growing kind of what Vertovec (1995: 13) calls 'cultural Muslim identity' among young Turks.[2]

The stress on religion is usually something they adopt from their parental culture as part of their negotiation with the majority society. The way the youth employs religion as a source of identity is quite distant from essentialist. This is a form of what Herbert J. Gans (1979: 6) calls 'symbolic ethnicity':

> [A]s the functions of ethnic cultures and groups diminish and identity becomes the primary way of being ethnic, ethnicity takes on an expressive rather than instrumental function in people's lives, becoming more of a leisure-time activity and losing its relevance, say, to earning a living or regulating family life. Expressive behaviour can take many forms, but often involves the use of symbols – the symbols as signs rather than myths. Ethnic symbols are frequently individual cultural practices that are taken from the older ethnic culture; they are abstracted from that culture and pulled out of its original mooring, so to speak to become stand-ins for it.

Gans' expression of symbolic ethnicity is quite applicable to the situational use of ethnicity and religion by the Turkish hip-hop youth in Berlin. As a response to the extreme right-wing German militancy, arson attacks and governmental integration policies towards the privileged *Aussiedler* and *Übersiedler* (ethnic German expatriates), working-class Turkish youths began to politicise themselves to win space in the urban landscape. In the process of politicisation, the youngsters have extensively invested in ethnic symbols such as religious and national days, ethnic foods, attachment to homeland, return to the history of homeland and religious and/or ethnic figures.

There are some other sources of identity for the diasporic Turkish youth i.e., ethnic symbols appearing in the form of either ornaments or tattoo. These symbols usually refer to a covert way of communication amongst the youngsters. Kreuzberg is a place where a stranger could gain the trust of the youngsters in a short while by means of ethnic symbols. Ethnic symbols make communication easier, since they express the distinction between 'us' and 'them.' But one should be careful in mapping out the symbolic meanings of these ornaments because they might be put on for fashion as well as for ethnic and political identifications.

Ethnic symbols are diversified according to ethnic and political allegiances. In this sense, the most popular ethnic symbols for right-wing Turkish nationalists are Turkish flag, grey wolf with a crescent moon, and Koran necklace; and for the *Alevis* the forked sword (*Zül-fükâr*), the picture of the *Chaliph Ali* and/or *Pir Sultan Abdal* (*Alevi* patron saint, 16th century) holding a *baglama*[3] in his hands. Before the Sivas affairs in 1993, *Alevis* used to keep these symbols in the form of picture on the walls of their rooms. Now, those symbols have become one of the main sources of identity for the *Alevi* youngsters. Previously *Alevi* youngsters also carried Turkish flags on their belt buckles, for instance. After the arson attacks in Mölln and Solingen, the *Alevi* youngsters used their Turkishness as the main base to articulate their reaction. Subsequently, in response to the killings of the *Alevi* intellectuals and people in *Sivas* and *Gazi Mahallesi*, they qualified this articulation by symbolically highlighting their *Alevism*.

Reception of Diasporic Youth in Turkey: German-Like (Almanci)

The identity formation of the diasporic youth results in a permanent dialogue between the country of settlement and the homeland. For instance, the reception of the Turkish diasporic youth in Germany and Turkey has an impact on their daily politics of identity. The overwhelming orientation of the Turkish youngsters to the homeland is both accelerated and disrupted by the official and popular discourses in Germany and Turkey. Considering how they are alluded to by the official German discourse ('*Gastarbeiter*', '*Ausländer*', '*Mitbürger*'), they are always represented either through their 'otherness' or through their 'displacement' (Çaglar, 1994: 97).

Turkish migrants and their children in Germany are officially defined in Turkey as either '*gurbetçi*', or '*Almanya'daki vatandaslarimiz*' (our citizens in Germany). German-Turks are stereotypically defined by the Turkish people in Turkey as either '*Almanyali*' or '*Almanci*'. Both terms carry rather negative connotations in Turkey. The major Turkish stereotypes about the German-Turks are those of their being rich, eating pork, having a very comfortable life in Germany, losing their Turkishness, and becoming more and more German. Çaglar (1994: 98) defines those stereotypes as:

[t]he heavily overloaded cars packed with household goods that they bring from Germany for their houses in Turkey; their pretentiousness and readiness to pay any price when shopping; their different styles of dress and such details as the way their girls walk; [...] [their] readiness to pay more than local inhabitants for land, apartments, and brides.

Implicitly derogatory in its markedness, in its explicit differentiation from a non-emigrant Turk, the label bears witness to a combination of difference, lack of acceptance, and rejection (Mandel, 1990: 158). Their Turkish language and the way they dress are also influential in the construction of an *'Almanci'* image. The youngsters are also subject to this labelling. Mehmet (18) explained one of the memories he had from Ankara:

I was buying some clothes in a shopping centre in Ankara. When I was talking to the salesperson, a girl whom I did not know suddenly approached me and asked a question. "Excuse me, are you from Germany because I bet with my friend over there that you come from Germany." I did not understand how they realised. I think because of the way I spoke to the salesperson, or the way I dressed up. I do not really know. I mean, here we are called *yabanci* (foreigner), and there in Turkey, in my own country, they call us *'Almanci'*. I am depressed about that moment.

"[H]ere we are called *yabanci* (foreigner), and there [in Turkey] [...] they call us *Almanci.*" Such a line remains a very common discourse amongst the German-Turkish youth. *Almanci* designates someone who has adopted Germany, and *yabanci* refers to being a foreigner in the country of adaptation. The youth considers these two given distinctions in the process of their identity formation.

The orientation to the homeland of the children of Turkish immigrants has always been a concern for scholars. Some of them argue that decreasing contact with the homeland will result in the loss of home (Kagitçibasi, 1987; Abadan-Unat, 1985). Explaining the alienation and exclusion of the first and second generations by the majority society, Kagitçibasi (1987: 199) differentiates the two generations:

Chapter 5

The first generation hangs on to his traditional culture and identity, often as a defensive reaction to rejection by the dominant culture. This tendency is further strengthened by frequent visits to the country of origin and continuing close ties with family and kin. He carries his original national cultural identity with him. The second generation 'foreigner,' born in Europe, however, does not really have such a distinct identity (at least not to the same degree) to hang on to. He may even lack the language of the original country being thus deprived of meaningful interpersonal ties through visits home. There is, in fact, no 'home' for the *deculturated* or *culturally impoverished* second generation in a state of alienation [italics mine].

Kagitçibasi, in her statement, seems to disregard the increasing impact of the global interconnectedness and symbolic links between the subject and homeland. What emerges out of all these symbolic bonds is an 'imaginary homeland.' What is more, she also tends to essentialise culture as a practice by defining the youth as 'deculturated' and 'culturally impoverished.' Furthermore, she seems to reduce the cultural identity of the diasporic youth to an essentialist form of 'Turkish culture.' Here, cultural identity is not seen as a process but as being something fixed and essential. In fact, cultural identity is rather acquired and renewed in a continuous dialogue between self and external world. It is a dialogical process in which self is constructed collectively in relation to the 'other.' Contrary to what Kagitçibasi claimed, the orientation of the Turkish diasporic youth to Turkey has not declined, rather increased. The growing cultural interaction between Turkey and the diaspora has undoubtedly facilitated the orientation of the diasporic communities to the homeland.

Working-Class Turkish Youth Leisure Culture

The leisure culture of the working-class Turkish hip-hop youngsters consists of various components originating either from their parental culture or from global hip-hop youth culture. These constituents are namely *'âlem'* (meeting with friends), *düğüns* (wedding ceremony), *arabesk* music, rap, graffiti, dance and 'cool' style. *'Alem,' düğüns* and *arabesk* are those leisure time activities deriving from their working-class and/or rural-origin parental culture. These events are the other forms of orientation to the homeland, whereas rap, graffiti and dance are the main constituents of the global hip-hop youth culture which a considerable number of diasporic Turkish youth have internalised. In what follows I shall describe both the particularist and universalist constituents of leisure culture among the working-class Turkish hip-hop youth living in Kreuzberg.

The working-class Turkish youngsters mostly 'hang around' together and entertain themselves in the group meetings taking place in one of the youngsters' house. They call these meetings *'âlem'* and themselves *'âlemci.'* *'Alem'* is a ritual that has been carried from *'sila'* (home) to *'gurbet'* (diaspora) by the migrants. In these ritualised meetings, they drink alcohol, listen to *arabesk* music, and experience imaginary journeys back home.[4] These events, organised among close circles of friends, provide the male youth groups with a ground for the construction of a 'part-time communitarianism.' Listening to *arabesk* music, talking about summer vacations, and drinking *'Raki'* or *'Efes,'* the youngsters recreate the homeland in their imagination.

Another aspect of their leisure culture is the wedding (*düğün*) ceremonies taking place in the specially designed Turkish wedding saloons such as *Dedem* (Wedding) and *Burcu* (Kreuzberg). Turkish wedding ceremonies in Berlin are not so different from their equivalents in Turkey. Both are very working-class oriented rituals and similar in terms of the performances of the folk music singers, *arabesk* singers, and folk dances with a double-sided drum (*davul*) and a double-reed instrument (*zurna*).[5] This type of wedding ceremony is a ritual brought by the rural migrants to the urban space. Dancing on *davul-zurna* for the migrants is, in fact, an imaginary journey back home and back to the previous rural life. The ritual is itself authentically performed in the open air in the villages and rural towns of Anatolia, because *davul-zurna* is such a combination of musical instruments that it should preferably be performed in the open air due to its high-volume. Thus, *davul-zurna* performances, which are accompanied by guests' folk dances in the wedding saloons, mostly bring about a kind of chaos. Urbanisation has transformed some rituals. Wedding ceremonies, which used to reproduce the communal pride in the rural space, have now been carried into the urban space.

There are some main reasons why the guests go to wedding ceremonies. Firstly, they want to entertain themselves; secondly, they conceive it as a duty to go to the weddings and to give a gift (mostly money and/or gold)[6] to the new couple with the consideration that their own children will get married some day; and sometimes to meet friends and/or relatives who live a long distance away. In one of the weddings, to which Yüksel, the owner of a music store in Adalbertstraße invited me, what was remarkable was the golden jewellery worn by the youngsters. It was an *Alevi* wedding of a couple originating from the city of Erzincan (eastern Anatolia), and the gold necklaces of *Zülfükâr* sword and of *Pir Sultan Abdal* in various sizes were obviously the most popular ornaments among the *Alevi* youngsters, reflecting their allegiance to ethnic symbols. Apart from symbolising the ethnic/religious/peer group values, gold is also a dramatisation of wealth.

Another crucial aspect of the wedding ceremonies worth mentioning is the selection of the singers and groups by the hosts. The selection of famous and popular groups and/or singers by paying big amounts yields a *distinction* to the parents of the couple, especially that of the groom. In most weddings, although the parents of the groom are not able to afford big expenses, they do their best in order to gain a superior social status within the community.

Folk dance is an indispensable part of the wedding ceremonies both in Turkey and in the diaspora. In modern urban Turkey, the circle folk dances (*halay*) are closely identified with the countryside and almost everywhere seen as a devaluation of country living. However, diaspora populations perceive these dances as bearers of ethnic identity. In Berlin, elegant and urban Turks take pleasure in dancing circle dances, whereas in Turkey, city people might prefer not to identify with this type of folk dancing. It seems that in the diaspora populations, the question of rural origin may be less significant than ethnic identification, and the positive and valued aspects of it, including dance, music and food. Besides providing a cultural distinction, circle dances also offer a sense of collectivism to the diasporic communities. Collectivism is literally embodied in the shape of the dance and the shared code of communication between the dancers.[7]

So far in this chapter I have outlined the particularist aspects of the working-class Turkish hip-hop leisure culture. Next, I shall outline the common aspects of the global hip-hop culture, which serves to integrate a significant number of working-class Turkish diasporic youths into the mainstream youth culture.

Hip-Hop Youth Culture and Working-Class Diasporic Turkish Youth

Hip-Hop is a youth culture that enables ethnic minority youths to use both their own 'authentic' cultural capital and the global transcultural capital in constructing and articulating their identities. It provides the diasporic youth with a ground where they can use their ethnicity as a strategising tool to articulate their identities in response to the majority nationalism and racism. It also serves as a mechanism to incorporate the ethnic minority youth into the global youth culture. The youngsters' use of 'authentic' culture as a strategising tool in the process of identity formation principally springs from their need to come to terms with the unpleasant present pervaded by racism, unemployment, exclusion and poverty. As Clifford (1988: 5) has rightly stated, the diasporic groups who are alienated by the system and swept up in a destiny dominated by the capitalist West, no longer invent local futures; what is different about them is that they remain tied to traditional pasts and ethnicities. Remaking, or recovering, the past serves at least a dual purpose for the diasporic communities. Firstly, it is a way of coping with the conditions of the present without being very critical about the *status quo*. Secondly, it also helps to recuperate a sense of self not dependent on criteria handed down by others – the past is what the diasporic subjects can claim as their own (Ganguly, 1992: 40).

However, Turkish youngsters, while having a sense of looking backward, also tend to transcend the exclusionist policies of the German nation-state by exhibiting a transnational articulation of culture. In fact, what makes these youngsters hip-hop youth are not those particularist cultural sources, but universalist constituents. There are various ways in the global hip-hop culture through which ethnic minority youths can resist the dominant regimes of representations and incorporate themselves into the mainstream. Rap, graffiti, dance, and the 'cool' look are some examples. All these particular aspects of hip-hop culture attempt to localise power and to create a distance between the already-excluded youth group and the legitimate forms of institutions such as police, education and media. These are the attempts by the youngsters to get away from the limited boundaries of the 'ghetto' life. This is a chance to broaden the living boundaries in a way that leads to the incorporation of the youth into the mainstream culture. By doing graffiti, rap, or breakdance, they all want to be 'da

King' ('da' is the vernacular of article 'the'). Roaming around the city, trying to discover the outskirts of the urban landscape, painting and tagging (signing) graffiti, attending break-dance competitions and parties, and fighting against rival youths, they do all these things with, and within, the gang.

Hip-Hop culture has become very popular among Turkish youngsters since the late eighties. Especially, Turkish youngsters living in Kreuzberg at around that time switched from gangsta group formation to hip-hop group formation.[8] Taner (26) is one of the main figures of the Turkish hip-hop scene in Berlin, who experienced this transformation:

Before the wall came down there were American discos where the American soldiers used to go to. They brought the life from America to Berlin. They brought here all those DJing, break-dance, white dancing gloves, and all those sorts of things. Hip-Hop started with the Americans here, with dance and music. Then we, the Turks, have found ourselves in this culture. We have grown up with two different musical tastes: *arabesk* at home and hip-hop in the American discos.

Hip-Hop has provided these youths with a ground to incorporate themselves into the mainstream global youth culture. In what follows I shall describe the common constituents of the global hip-hop youth culture as much as they relate to the Turkish hip-hop youth in Kreuzberg. As there will be a separate chapter on the rap music and the rappers, I shall leave rap out for the time. Graffiti, dance and 'coolness' are the aspects to be examined in the following section.

Graffiti

The word 'graffiti,' taken from Italian, served originally as the name of inscriptions scratched on walls. The word is related to the name of a particular technique of mural painting, that of *'sgraffito.'* Today, other techniques are used apart from scratching and/or carving: felt tip pens are used inside and on small areas, aerosol spray cans are used outside and on large areas. Regina Blume (1985) has defined the motives for producing graffiti as:

(a) a proof of existence – *scribo, ergo sum* (I write therefore I am);
(b) a need to express oneself;
(c) a sense of belonging to a group;
(d) a pleasure in aesthetic, creative and physical acts; and
(e) an expression of boredom.[9]

Having all these motives, graffiti, or tagging, becomes a way of resistance against the formal life, sanctions of the adults, and the legitimate world of the institutions. The world of graffiti is the youngsters' other world because grown-ups do not read them, and also this is the world in which the minority youth can express itself with its own vernacular language without any restriction or questioning.

Graffiti is a way of expression of the poverty of the urban 'ghetto,' of youngsters' territorial claims, and of their power. It is the freedom of writing *'Kanak'* instead of *'Kanake,'* or *'masaka'* instead of *'Massaker.'* Writing graffiti on the forbidden walls like the metro stations is a kind of covert war waged against the official authorities. Sneaking in the dark of the night with the spray cans and masks without being captured by the police sounds like the accomplishment of a 'mission impossible.' Graffiti, for the subaltern ethnic minority youngsters, refers to the 'bombing' of the institutional space. Constructing a counter-hegemonic space, the graffiti makers wage a war against the power of state. These youngsters are the 'spray warriors,' or the 'street heroes,' who fight against the official authorities for the localisation of power. The youth localise their power in their graffiti and street fights providing them with a sense of recognition by the public. This Hegelian sense of subjective recognition could have a 'productive' context:[10] a youngster, for instance, could come to transform himself as a thinking and active subject; and he could also achieve his self consciousness in a dialogue of mutual recognition with the public.

Recently, the local authorities have tried to legitimise graffiti by using it as an educational tool for the kids and youngsters. For instance, the graffiti on the walls of the *Admiralstraße* is an attempt to warn the youngsters against the dangers of drug and violence and to strengthen the feeling of neighbourhood (Figure 1, see p. 235).

Graffiti is also a source of *distinction* for the youth. To become famous, a graffiti marker must go beyond his local boundaries in the city. The more tags (personal signs) you have all around Berlin, the more popular you become within the hip-hop community. *'Slai'* is a

Chapter 5

tag which I have seen almost all around Berlin, in Schöneberg, Wedding, Kreuzberg and Tiergarten. *'JFK'* is the most popular graffiti group in Berlin.

They always prefer making graffiti in the most dangerous places: the walls of metro stations or high buildings. It is also quite normal to see a graffiti like *'36 Boys'* all around the city, so that the group called *'36 Boys'* may well be popular amongst the youngsters, and of course constitute a threat to the police force, who are the 'enemy' for these youngsters. Eyüp, a 22-year-old boy in *Chip*, quit making graffiti when he was let off by the police officers after his apprehension:

I was tagging around four o'clock in the morning in Kotbusser Tor metro station. After I finished my work, the police caught me on my way home. I mean, I was pissed off with myself, because they didn't see me tagging. They just saw the spray can in my hand. I should have better hidden it. Anyway, they took me to their car. I was extremely afraid that they were gonna beat me and tell my parents that I was tagging. Then I was surprised because they did not harm me; they just gave me a speech about the violation of the rules, and then gave me a lift up to my apartment. They even didn't tell my parents. I got shocked really. Then I decided to quit doing these things. But, I tell you, if the police had beaten me, I would carry on tagging much more than I used to.

The Berlin graffiti scene is composed of Germans as well as the minority youngsters. They have a bilingual graffiti magazine (German-English) called *BackJumps*. The magazine consists of written and figurative form of graffiti samples from Berlin and other urban centres such as New York, Paris, London and Melbourne. The graffiti artists also have a transnational connection with the hip-hop scene in the other European cities like Paris, Amsterdam and London. The language of graffiti is usually English. By using English as the graffiti language, the Turkish hip-hop youngsters have both the feeling of sharing a code of communication with the outside world, and of sustaining a resistance movement against the supremacy of the German language. On the other hand, in figurative graffiti, the common rule is to imitate others' figures, TV-cartoons, and comics. All the figures in the graffiti made in many different countries look like each other, with big eyes (as in the globalised Japanese TV-cartoons) and a style of dressing similar to that of the American-black hip-hop scene

(Figure 2, see p. 236).[11] Adapting various aspects and colours from their ethnic arsenal, the youngsters make their own additions to the globalised style of figurative graffiti, and build up their local style of graffiti. Then, graffiti turns out to be a field where culture is constructed on the basis of bricolage and hybridity with the global and local motives.

Sometimes the graffiti artists might go further and have their own peculiar style. This peculiar style provides them with the possibility to switch to painting. *Erhan*, or *Gino*, is one of them. *Erhan* used to be a graffiti artist. Now, he is a painter. Although he is just 18 years old, he has held many exhibitions in Germany. He works in a workshop in the attic of the *Naunyn Ritze* youth centre. The titles of his works are all English, e.g., 'Jump to the Future,' 'Disappearing Footsteps,' 'Eagle Eyes,' 'Birth of Virgin' and 'Dedicated to Hasan.' The use of English gives him a sense of being incorporated into the global culture. It is amazing to see the shift in his work from the figurative graffiti to painting. This artistic switch has given his work a postmodern look. What he is providing the audience with is a hybrid art composed of two distinct artistic forms: graffiti and painting.

Dance

Break-dance is another constituent of the hip-hop youth culture. The dance-floor has a threefold function for the diasporic youth. Firstly, the dance-floor provides the Turkish youth with a substantial ground for the homing of the diaspora because they appear to be the 'hosts' in the dance-floor. Secondly, the dance turns interethnic confrontations from fighting to dancing. As *Özcan* (19), a Turkish youngster in *Naunyn Ritze*, said 'there were previously fights in the streets, now there is dance, we compete on the stage. I show my superiority by way of dancing.' In doing so, hip-hop youth affirms the "sublimation of fight into dance, of conflict into contest, of desperation into style and a sense of self-respect" (Hebdige, 1988: 216). Finally, the dance is also another source of *distinction* that the boys tend to use against 'others.' Previously, breakdance as a distinction was convertible to economic capital: some of the *Naunyn Ritze* youngsters have made some money from participating in the break-dance competitions organised in Berlin.

CHAPTER 5

'Cool' Style

'Cool' is an American word which has become a very crucial motto of the contemporary hip-hop youth culture. It literally means "(2) not affected by passion or emotion [...] (3) lacking enthusiasm warmth of interest; lacking in cordiality [...] (5) (of jazz music, a jazz musician) restrained or relaxed in style [...]; characteristic of those who favour relaxed music; good, excellent, admirably up to date, stylish [...]."[12] Recently, especially since the early 1980s, the word 'cool' has been extensively used in hip-hop youth culture by blacks and Latinos living in the United States. Ruth Horowitz (1983: 87-88) has defined 'coolness,' in the context of Chicano youth in Chicago, as the ability to stand back from certain situations and rationally evaluate others' actions. The contextual use of 'cool' posits a distance between the object and the subject who is using the word. Being cool, looking cool, or staying cool has a critical connotation in itself. It is a way of expressing a transcending reality for the youngsters.

In hip-hop culture, a critical gaze is very crucial. It requires positioning oneself at a reasonable distance to the external world, so that one can keep the critical look. Unlike the recent techno, punk, or grunge cultures, one is never supposed to get lost in the artificial world of entertainment, and s/he should always keep her/his 'coolness.' An example is the way the rappers and their groupies move in the concerts, or in their daily lives, which looks very serious and masculine. This masculine posture symbolises resistance against subordination. It gives the impression that these ethnic minority youngsters have been consciously positioning themselves against cruelty, hostility and inequality springing from capitalism. Their cool style is a challenge against the hegemony of the dominant regimes of representations. By looking so, the youngsters are also challenging, at a symbolic level, the stereotypes of the outsiders about their indifference to life, which may come from both the majority society and from middle-class Turkish communities. The German society may have stereotypes about their violence and vandalism; on the other hand the middle-class Turkish groups may treat them as troublesome, lazy and non-integrationist. Thus, their cool style is, at the same time, a response to the stereotypes of both Germans and Turks.

The cool style which is performed in accordance with a critical posture has also something to do with the way the youngsters dress.

The clothes are chosen to represent both a sense of freedom and an 'authentic' working-class backlash. Wide and comfortable outfits are a major part of the cool style. It symbolises freedom and comfort as opposed to the traditional tight and stiff outfit. The way the rappers and the break-dancers dress also represents the celebration of working-class origin. Wearing wide overall trousers they resemble the mine workers, or the construction workers. Hebdige (1987: 123-124) previously defined the difference between the early youth cultures and their relation to each other in terms of class:

[P]unk style was perhaps interpreted by the teddy boys as an affront to the traditional working-class values of forthrightness, plain speech and sexual puritanism which they had endorsed and revived. Like the reaction of the rockers to the mods and the skinheads to the hippies, the Teddy boy revival seems to have represented an 'authentic' working-class backlash to the proletarian posturing of the new wave.

Departing from the statements of Dick Hebdige concerning the youth 'subcultures' of the earlier periods, hip-hop may well be considered the new form of youth culture representing an 'authentic' working-class backlash to the proletarian posturing of the 'new wave.' Yet, it goes beyond the notion of 'subculture' because the formation of ethnic minority hip-hop culture seems to retain a more complex process, which is characterised by globalisation and modern diasporic consciousness.

The word 'cool' has become a transcultural notion and the motto of a distinct youth style. It is evident that this word has quickly been adopted in many languages. Since culture is becoming more and more global and transnational, the national languages become incapable of creating new words to comply with such a rapid cultural change. German, French and Turkish are some of the languages to which the word, 'cool,' has infused without any resistance. German language has even produced the antonym with the prefix of *'un'*: *'un*cool.'

Although 'cool' is a very global word, it might have many local connotations in itself. The Turkish rappers' use of the word is, of course, a cultural translation. Thus, the word might lose some of its content as well as gaining some other connotations. MC Ünal, pronouncing the word with a very American accent, states that "what is cool in Berlin might not be considered cool in München, for instance."

Here, 'cool' refers to the acceptability of something within hip-hop youth culture in a local sense. It intimates a local cultural code depicting what might suit hip-hop culture. Incidentally, the word 'hip' is another American word, which likewise has an extensive use in the world. In slang, it literally means "(1) following the latest fashion in especially popular and jazz music, clothes, etc., stylish [...]."[13] 'Hip' is also a new word that has entered the German language. It depicts trendy and stylish, such as a 'hip concert,' 'hip colour,' or 'hip movie.'

Hip-Hop Youth Style: A Cultural Bricolage

German-Turkish youngsters, at first glance, might seem as if they are practising a conventional and essentialist form of cultural identity that they have taken out of the ready-made package of cultural attributes carried across from homeland by their parents. Such a conclusion would be misleading because the formation and articulation of cultural identity is a process, which is not free from the constant intercourse between various social groups, classes and cultures. As Czarina Wilpert (1989: 21) accurately states:

The significance of the concept of cultural identity within this framework derives from the assumption that, in the construction of a collective ethnic identity, culture becomes a resource. It is not that culture, which may be in continual transformation, is viewed as something static and fixed, nor that an immigrant 'community' is considered to live as a homogenous closed cultural entity within a foreign society. Rather, elements of culture, its signs and symbols, may be transformed or filled with new meaning and take on a new significance in this process. This is accomplished in a particular context at a specific moment in history in interaction with the conditions and principles which structure the lives of the immigrant descendants, and with reference to the resources they have at hand for understanding the world around them [...].

Hereby, Wilpert reminds us of two significant points. The first point to be considered is that reification of culture in the diaspora is a vital instrument to be employed in the process of identity formation. The second point to bear in mind is that the community culture formed in the diasporic space is not immune to the allure of the culture of the wider society, unchanging, or always clear and unambiguous. Kreuzberg is not a traditional little village cut off culturally, socially, and ecologically from the majority society; its community culture cannot be equated with that of *Gemeinschaft* (Töennies, 1957).

In this sense, there are at least three main landmarks that shape the cultural identification of the German-Turkish hip-hop youth in Berlin:

a) 'authenticity' which is the expression of imagined Anatolian culture;
b) global culture which is mainly the imitation of urban Black American symbols; and
c) German culture which refers to the life styles of German peer groups to which the German-Turkish youngsters desire to adapt themselves.

For instance, as outlined in the previous chapter, the language used by the German-Turkish youth in Berlin reflects a mixture of their Turkishness, Germanness and cosmopolitan identity. This refers us to the 'multiple cultural competence' of the descendants of migrants.[14] Modern diasporic communities like the Turkish diaspora in Europe should learn to inhabit at least two identities, "to speak two cultural languages, to translate and negotiate between them" (Hall, 1993: 310). People belonging to such cultures of hybridity tend to gravitate either to 'Tradition' or 'Translation.' Gravitating to tradition is an attempt to restore the former purity and authenticity which are felt as being lost, whereas choosing translation acknowledges that identity is subject to the play of history, politics, representation and difference rather than being subject to purity (ibid.: 309).

What German-Turkish youngsters construct is a form of cultural bricolage, or creolization, which literally means the interruption of the monolithic structure of the nation-state in a way that leads to the emergence of a 'third space' (Bhabha, 1994), or a 'third culture' (Featherstone, 1990). Cultural bricolage is also what Homi Bhabha calls a 'differential communality,' and what Felix Guattari (1989: 14) refers to as the 'process of heterogenesis.' By the *'processes of heterogenesis'* Guattari negates the Hegelian and Marxist dialectics whose aim is the 'resolution' of opposites. He argues that "our objective should rather be to nurture individual cultures, while at the same time inventing new contracts of citizenship: to create an order of the state in which singularity, exceptions, and rarity coexist under the least oppressive conditions" (ibid.: 14). He describes this formation "as a logic of the 'included middle,' in which black and white are indistinct, in which the beautiful coexists with the ugly, the inside with the outside, the 'good' object with the bad" (ibid.: 14).

Cultural bricolage is, in a sense, constitutes a 'third space' that enables other positions to emerge (Bhabha, 1994: 211). This creolization process brings about the emergence of a transnational identity, or what Gilroy (1987: 13) calls a 'syncretic culture.' As Gilroy (ibid.) states, "culture does not develop along ethnically absolute lines but in complex, dynamic patterns of syncretism." Cultural identity is not something fixed and permanent, "it refers to becoming as well as being, and is never complete, always in process" (Hall, 1991: 47). Thus, cultural identity of the German-Turkish youth is formed on the basis of continuous dialogue between past and future, between homeland and country of residence, between different worlds of meaning, between various life-worlds, between global winds and local resistance, between 'roots' and 'routes,' and between 'here' and 'there.' Gilroy's (1987, 1993) definition of a kind of duality of consciousness – with direct reference to W. E. B. Du Bois' notion of 'double consciousness' underlines diasporic individuals' awareness of multilocality which derives from their attachments to those given continuous dialogues. The 'double consciousness' of diasporic subject serves to bridge the gap between the local and the global.

* * *

To summarise, this chapter has indicated particularist and universalist aspects of the Turkish hip-hop youth living in Kreuzberg. It was concluded that the Turkish hip-hop youth has simultaneously developed a form of cultural nationalism and a syncretic 'third culture.' The sources of their cultural nationalism are twofold: the first one is the majority nationalism that has recently been quite hegemonic and even coercive in Germany. This point is enormously important in view of what I will argue in the following pages because it shows that ethnic identities are not simply the product of 'traditional mores,' but the result of an unequal conversation between majority and minority groupings. Sandra Wallman (1978) suggests that boundaries and social definitions are always the result of an encounter between at least two social agents. She puts the focus on the ethnic majority – not on the minority populations – because it is [majority] ethnicity, according to her, which determines the boundary of 'them' and 'us.' The second source of this cultural nationalism is the media, both German language media and Turkish language media. In Berlin, one will immediately realise that Turks, or other ethnic groups, are excluded in the German print media or radio-TV. In that way, the feeling of exclusion and segregation for Turks may increase. They are, in a sense, forced to get back to their own cultural and local settings by the structural adjustments. On the other hand, as explained in the third chapter, international Turkish media and Berlin-Turkish media insist on the notion of Turkishness to sustain the particularist ethnic sentiments of the German-Turks.

The syncretic 'third culture' of the Turkish hip-hop youths derives from their multicultural competence, which enables them to switch between various cultures such as minority culture, majority culture and global culture. To put it differently, they form their cultural identity through the hybridity of 'tradition' and 'translation,' authenticity and syncreticism, heritage and politics. The practice of cultural bricolage fosters a relationship among heterogeneous elements in a meaningful ensemble, which displays both harmony and tension. (Clifford, 1997: 12). This multicultural competence is acquired by means of transnational communications and transportation, sustaining the pace and density of relationships of the diasporic youth with the homeland and the entire world. The 'third culture' that is formed by the diasporic youth, at the same time, has a progressive nature. This syncretic culture, as Melucci (1989: 14) has correctly stated, is "the journey into unfamiliar territory [...] [which] teaches us to recognise ambivalence, encourages us to acknowledge different points of view, and thereby stimulates awareness of potential freedoms [...]."

Hip-Hop culture has emerged as a source of alternative identity formation and social status for the Turkish diasporic youth living in an ethnic enclave whose older local support institutions have been demolished. Alternative social identities were formed in fashions and language, and in establishing neighbourhood crews or posses. These crews, who are composed of hip-hop fans, artists, musicians, and dancers, are new kinds of families providing insulation and support in a complex and unyielding environment and may, in fact, contribute to the community-building networks that serve as the basis for new social movements (Rose, 1994: 34). As this chapter was an attempt to interpret the discourses of Turkish hip-hop fans, artists and dancers in Kreuzberg, I will explore those of the rappers in the next chapter.

Notes

1. Tarkan, Candan Erçetin, Özcan Deniz, Azer Bülbül, Sibel Sezal, Can Kat, *Cartel*, Erci-E, Karakan, Bay X, Rafet El Roman, Ahmet and Ünlü are some of these singers and/or groups. There are also some other singers coming from other countries such as BenDeniz (Switzerland), and Cemali and Özlem Tekin (USA). It is ironic that not only Turkish origin singers and/or groups are coming to Turkey to seize a share in the expanding Turkish pop music market, but also some non-Turkish singers are coming into the market with Turkish lyrics such as 'Endi ve Pol' (Andy and Paul are English pop singers and they print their names with Turkish vernacular). For further information, see Greve (1996, 1997) and Köhne and Kepenek (1997).
2. In his research on the young Muslims in Keighley, West Yorkshire, Vertovec (1995) drew our attention to two Asian football teams called 'Keighley Young Muslims' and 'Keighley Muslims' in order to expose the construction and articulation of 'cultural Muslim identity' among young Muslims.
3. *Baglama* is a musical instrument having a guitar-like body, long, and strings that are plucked or strummed with the fingers or a plectrum. *Baglama* has always been one of the main symbols of the *Alevi* culture.
4. The word '*âlem*' literally means amusement and/or entertainment.
5. *Zurna* is a kind of authentic Turkish musical instrument having a flute-like body with shrill pipe usually accompanied by a drum.
6. Çaglar (1994: 196) states that 'although the *hemsehri*s of the bride and groom do not feel obliged to pin gold on the bride any more, the amount of gold Turkish brides receive in Germany is higher in comparison with Turkey.' For the *hemsehri*s of the bride and groom, it is a symbolic capital to have gold pinned on them in public.
7. Gillian Bottomley (1987) touches on a similar tendency amongst the Greek diaspora in Australia. She points out that Greek *kalamatianos* (a circle folk dance that is very similar to Turkish folk dance halay) danced by young people in a Sydney club is not that danced by villagers in Greece. This is because, she states, such a traditional ritual gives a positive distinction to the diasporic youth from dominant Anglomorph population.

8   Gangsta groups in Kreuzberg drew great attention from both Turkish and German media in Berlin. For further information, see "Ghetto Sisters," *Brigitte* 19 (1990): 125-132; "Vereint Jagd auf Skinheads," *Der Tagesspiegel* Nr. 13562 (6 May 1990); "Der Haß darauf, als Nichts zu gelten," *Süddeutsche Zeitung* Nr. 184 (11/12 August 1990); "Die Barbaren kommen!" *Zitty* 4 (1993); and "Türk Kizlari Çetesi," *Tan* (9 March 1990 – Turkish).
9   In her work on graffiti, Blume (1985) has explored the historical aspects, sources, forms, functions and addresses of graffiti.
10 The notion of 'productive' is free from its Marxist connotations, which imprison the subject into an ideology of productionism. The term has rather a Lefèbvreian meaning transcending crude and brutal economism.
11 For further information, see Henkel et al. (1994).
12 See *The Oxford English Dictionary*. Oxford: Clarendon Press, 1993.
13 See *The Oxford English Dictionary*. Oxford: Clarendon Press, 1993.
14 Ålund (1992: 75) mentions 'double cultural competence' in the Swedish context to refer to cultural bricolage of the immigrant youth simultaneously fitting both into their own parental cultural identity and Swedishness.

Chapter 6

Aesthetics of Diaspora: Contemporary Minstrels

In the day time the radio's scared of me,
Cause I'm mad, plus I'm the enemy,
They can't c'mon and play with me in primetime,
Cause I know the time, plus I am gettin' mine.

Chuck D. (Public Enemy)

Hip-Hop as a form of aesthetics of diaspora enables the descendants of migrants to construct a syncretic culture entwined with diasporic consciousness and transculturalism through the method of collage and by means of globalism. The Turkish rappers in Berlin present an adequate example to expose the production of cultural bricolage among a group of Turkish diasporic youth. Accordingly, this chapter will map out the social identities and counter-hegemonic discourses of the Turkish rappers in Berlin, and the rise of the Turkish hip-hop community in Germany. There are many German-Turkish rap groups in Berlin, such as *Cartel, Islamic Force, Ünal, Erci-E, Azize-A*. The interviews held with the rappers will be often quoted in order to expose the way they narrate their stories as contemporary storytellers of the diasporic youth in the urban landscape. By doing so, the rappers will have the ground to express themselves as in a virtuoso verbal performance through an imaginative excursion. Besides describing the discourses of those storytellers and/or organic intellectuals, the interviews with the rappers are also essential to demonstrate the transcultural and transnational nature of some diasporic youth cultures.[1]

CHAPTER 6

Rappers as Contemporary Minstrels, 'Organic Intellectuals' and Storytellers

For someone who grew up listening to a very mixed variety of music ranging from western classical music to Turkish classical music, someone who idealised the sound of *Eric Clapton*, someone who felt attached to the Turkish protest music of the eighties such as *Zülfü Livaneli, Yeni Türkü* and *Ezginin Günlüğü*, and someone who always switched between the western and eastern forms of music, rap was not a natural transition for me. Although Turkey is a land of hybrid forms of music of any type, rap was a taste that was difficult to acquire at first. Recently, I have grown to greatly appreciate rap as an oppositional political practice. As it became an academic interest of mine, I began to be amazed by the narratives, stories and discourses of the rappers in particular.

The rappers I worked with during the course of my research in Berlin made me conscious about their own social identities. The more I analysed their lyrics and narratives, the more I realised that they are what Antonio Gramsci (1971)[2] called 'organic intellectuals' and/or what Walter Benjamin (1973) called 'storytellers' of their own local communities. These two terms are quite complementary in essence. Organic intellectual refers to the intellectual who originates in subaltern groups, as in the urban ghetto communities. Gramsci's (1971: 12) definition of 'organic intellectual' presupposes the existence of a dominant class or group, exercising hegemony and domination on the subaltern classes or groups, through the State and juridical government. The 'organic intellectual' serves to raise the interests of his/her newly organised class or group, who aim to be incorporated into the system and to take their place in the process of distribution of resources. They attempt to disrupt the social, political and cultural hegemony of the dominant groups. The Turkish rappers in Berlin try to contribute to the formation of a sense of unified community as opposed to the exclusion, segregation, misrepresentation and racism prevailing in the country of adaptation.

A storyteller, on the other hand, "is a man [sic] who has counsel for his readers [...] The storyteller takes what he tells from experience – his own or that reported by others. And he in turn makes it the experience of those who are listening to his tale" (Benjamin, 1973: 86-87). Benjamin also states that "the storyteller joins the ranks of the teachers and sages" (ibid.: 107). Hence, the rapper is an intellectual storyteller who has counsel for his/her audience and who wishes to mobilise his/her local community against the power of the hegemonic and/or coercive group. The rapper also reminds us of what we are already inclined to forget, i.e., the 'communicability of experience' which is destined to decrease. In this sense, rap turns out to be a critique of the modern urban way of life disrupting the 'communicability of experience.' In other words, rap helps to communicate symbols and meanings, articulating intersubjectively the lived experience of social actors.

Besides mapping out the rappers with these two terms – 'organic intellectuals' and 'storytellers,' I will also define some of the rappers as 'contemporary minstrels'. It is a preferable formulation in the context of the Turkish rappers because the notion of minstrel also has its equivalent in the Anatolian cultural context. The medieval Turkish minstrels (*halk ozani*) were the travellers who enlightened the masses with their lyrics accompanied by the sound of a stringed musical instrument *baglama*. In the sixteenth and seventeenth centuries, some of these minstrels used to write and sing poems against the supremacy of the Ottoman rule over the peasantry. They were the spokespersons of the degraded and undervalued Turkish popular culture against the Ottoman high culture, which was a mix of Byzantine, Persian, Arabic and Turkish.[3] Having been raised in a working-class and/or rural-based parental culture which was pervaded by the Anatolian minstrels' music and myths, most of the Turkish youngsters in Berlin might well feel themselves attracted by the educative nature of rap. Besides taking inspiration from the intellectual teaching of the Anatolian minstrels, the rappers also tend to borrow their lyrical structure: it is quite common for the Turkish rappers in Germany to state their names in the last part of the lyrics as the mythical Turkish minstrels used to. Thus, having such a cultural tradition makes the Turkish rappers more capable of contextualising themselves locally within the global hip-hop youth culture on which they receive an up-to-date flow of information via MTV, VIVA TV (German local form of MTV), music magazines, tapes, records and CDs.

Furthermore, the discursive similarity between the Turkish rap and Turkish 'traditional' folk music in the diaspora context should also be expressed. As the ethno-musicologist Martin Greve has recently stated the rap songs and folk songs produced by the German-Turks resemble

CHAPTER 6

each other. Comparing both music cultures, Greve points out that the discourses of the lyrics in both some rap songs and folk music songs are quite identical.[4] For instance, the discourse analysis of the lyrics written by Islamic Force, a Berlin based Turkish rap group, and Minstrel Shah Turna, a Berlin based female traditional minstrel, demonstrates that the diasporic experience of the Turkish migrants and of their descendants are perfectly matching.

German-Turkish hip-hop youngsters, like other minority hip-hop youth groups, tend to express themselves by means of protest music, break-dance and graffiti, which fit into the consumerist popular culture. This kind of expression facilitates the emergence of resisting identities. The youngsters develop these resisting identities within the 'areas of conversation' (Bottomley, 1992: 131) with those who have anti-Turkish prejudices; and aim discriminatory acts towards them. The racist attacks on the Turkish community members in Mölln and Solingen in 1992 and 1993 received an extensive reaction from within the Turkish diaspora throughout Europe. Turkish rap groups immediately reacted to the arson attacks in a very radical way. They have played a vital role in developing the anti-racist struggle by communicating information, organising consciousness and testing out, deploying, or amplifying the forms of subjectivity within the Turkish diaspora. In what follows, I shall portray the major rap groups/singers and delineate their counter-hegemonic discourses.

Cartel: Cultural Nationalist Rap

In summer 1995, a gangsta rap group called *Cartel* was introduced to the Turkish audience. Most of the public/private TV and radio channels and the print media focused their attention on this group, and their video and CD suddenly became Number 1 in the Turkish pop charts. These 'strange-looking' guys had come from Germany. In the video, they were walking in German streets with a number of groupies behind them. Their hit rap song, also called '*Cartel*,' was sending messages to the Turkish youth in Germany to unite against the rising racist attacks and killings. The way they walked in the video was not so different from its equivalent in American rap (jabbing towards the camera with their fingers); the anger and hatred in their faces against the murders of the Turks in Germany were easily readable; and they were calling everybody to join the 'movement' of *Cartel*: "Gel gel

Cartele gel / Carteldekiler kankardesler" (Come to *Cartel* / The ones with *Cartel* are bloodbrothers).

Cartel is a music project initiated by a Berliner producer called Ozan Sinan. The group is composed of three different rap groups originating in various regions of Germany: *Karakan* (based in Nürnberg), *Da Crime Posse* (based in Kiel), and a West-Berliner MC, *Erci-E*. The group consists of seven members: five Turkish, one German and one Afro-Cuban. They all dress austerely in black, with Turkish motives on the uniform T-shirts. The design of the CD/tape resembles the Turkish flag, with a red background and the initial letter 'C' of '*Cartel*' which imitates the crescent on the flag. The name '*Cartel*' on the cover is also decorated with Turkish ornamental shapes. The release of the group and the goods (*Cartel* T-shirts, caps, hats and coats) was extremely well timed. It was a time in Turkey when popular nationalism was prevailing. Thus, such a group immediately encountered a warm welcome from the Turkish audience. The group was also extensively promoted by the Turkish media to strengthen the hegemony of the state as a measure against centrifugal forces such as Kurdish nationalism.

Before the group went to Turkey to give concerts, the media promotion had already been done. Thus, *Cartel* had already had an impact on the national pride of a remarkable part of the Turkish audience. They were greeted by an ardent crowd of youths from the right-wing nationalist movement, *Milliyetçi Hareket Partisi*, MHP, which is active in both Turkey and Germany, and advocates Turkish and Pan-Turkish Nationalism.

This kind of support was present in all the concerts of *Cartel*, held in many major cities of Turkey, even in the south-eastern Anatolian cities. The fact that *Cartel*'s rap salute was very similar to the 'grey-wolf' salute of the MHP, turned the group into a new *totem* for the nationalist crowds. As Robins and Morley (1996: 252) pointed out,

What the ultra-nationalist youths were seeing and identifying with was the tough and angry mood of rap culture. These were young people who were insecure, often in a paranoid way and consequently aggressive, in the expression of their Turkish identity. These were the ones who were prepared to come to *Cartel*, drawn by its talk of bonding and belonging.

Being translated from the German to the Turkish context, *Cartel* suddenly became one of the main pillars of popular Turkish nationalism. Such a translation encouraged these crowds to do something about the 'enemies of the Turkish nation and race' at a time when the dream of Turkish *Turan* (Volk, greater Turkic world) was revisited. MC *Erci-E*, to whom I shall return shortly, expressed his surprise and shock at this enthusiastic reception by the extreme-right wing youths, and complained about the misunderstanding of the Turkish audience. Yet, whatever way they were interpreted in Turkey, the manager and the production company *Polygram* were satisfied with the result: in 1995 they sold more than 300,000 copies of the album in Turkey, displacing Michael Jackson from number one in the album-charts, and more than 20,000 copies in Germany.

The rap group *Cartel* is a form of 'playful cultural-nationalist rap.'[5] *Cartel* infuses rap with Turkish percussion, a blend of Turkish-German, English and Spanish lyrics, Turkish folk music sound, and cries against racists. *Cartel* rappers assert and construct a distant *pan-Turkish diasporic cultural identity* while acknowledging the African connections of rap art. Like many other Turkish rap groups, *Cartel* also acknowledges its 'authentic' Turkish folk music connection in the form of a lyrical structure which was used by the mythical Turkish minstrels (*halk ozani*). By doing so, the rappers also contextualise themselves both in their 'own authentic' culture and in the global youth culture. By means of hip-hop culture, the youngsters ironically both convince themselves of their involvement in the mainstream global culture, and feel attached to their own 'authentic' cultural and ethnic identities. It is a syncretic mode of demonstrating incorporation into the mainstream and attachment to the roots. As the elements of a surviving strategy, they are in need of incorporating into the mainstream culture, because the 'myth of return' is over; they are also in need of going back to their roots, because the past is one of the rare things they can claim as 'their own.' Rap is a resistance movement in itself, offering a shared code of communication as well as a sense of collectivism. Above all, rap culture, which is dominated by *Cartel*, tends to bridge the gap between the displaced Turkish diaspora community and the 'imaginary homeland.' In other words, it is an imaginative journey back home.

As the intellectual storytellers of their group, the members of the hip-hop nation form an 'imagined community' that is based less on its realisation through state formation than on a collective challenge to the consensual logic of Germany and to the majority German nationalism (Decker, 1992: 54). Hip-Hop nationalism as a variant of minority nationalism should be explored in relation to the majority nationalism. The use of ethnic symbols resembling the Turkish flag should not immediately be labelled as regressive, racist or exclusionist. Such a straightforward judgement would lead us to misinterpret the nationalist discourse of *Cartel*, and to underestimate the presence of German nationalism. Hennayake's notion of 'interactive nationalism' is unquestionably of good use to understand the major impetus behind minority nationalisms (Hennayake, 1992). Interactive nationalism simply refers to a kind of minority ethnic nationalism, which is formed in opposition to the simultaneous practice of hegemonic politics and exclusionary nationalist politics of the majority nation and/or of the dominant ideology. Paraphrasing John Berger (1972: 11), it is the fear of the present, which make the Turkish youth celebrate their 'past' and 'authenticity.' In this sense, the cultural nationalist discourse of *Cartel* provides Turkish youth with a ground to acquire a positive and optimistic politics of identity.

Music is said not only to express differences but also to articulate them creatively, affecting social and cultural realities while at the same time being shaped by them (Grenier, 1989: 137). Music-making and other forms of popular culture serve as a specific site for the creation of collective identity as well as shaping and reflecting dominant and subordinate social and cultural relations. In some cases, music might become a social force attempting to transform the existing social system. Rap is very instructive in this sense. *Cartel*, while being sustained by the Turkish cultural capital, attempts to construct a 'pan-Turkish' diasporic cultural identity. The rappers strongly adhere to a notion of community, and principally do not assume that this community is pre-given and exists naturally; rather, they consider that it must be constructed and created against all odds, in the face of the threat of decimation (Swedenburg, 1992: 58). In this way cultural-nationalist rappers can be considered the 'organic intellectuals' of their communities.

Accordingly, *Cartel* has a political message to announce both to the Turkish minority and the German majority, besides being the symbol of cultural pride. The rappers in Berlin aim to mobilise the masses against arson attacks, racism, xenophobia, exclusion, drug trade, drug abuse, materialism, capitalism, and antagonism between Kurds and Turks. They are also intent on praising the family institution, on celebrating the brotherhood of Turkish and Kurdish, on presenting Germany as the new homeland, and on criticising the perception of the diasporic youth as *'Almancı'* (German-like) in Turkey and *'Ausländer'* (foreigner) in Germany. They try to inform the audience about their own experiences and those of the others. The expression of the black French rapper, MC Solaar, gives the rationale behind rapping: 'if you rebel, you isolate yourself. If you explain, people learn' (*Newsweek*, February 26, 1996). Thus, the rationale behind the hip-hop nation is the quest for communication and dialogue with the hegemonic social classes/groups.

Kankardesler	Bloodbrothers
Allahim yine mi?	Oh my God, again?[6]
Kankardes cankardes demek	Bloodbrother is everything
Gerekirse kardes için ölmek	It is to die for your brother
Canini kanini vermek	It is to sacrifice
Gözünü kirpmadan herzaman iste	Always tell me what you want
Defol dazlak dedik	We said, "piss off skinhead!"
Biz Türküz deyince fasist bilindik	When we said we were Turks,
Yanindayim koçum sonuna kadar senin	We were labelled as fascist.
Sana edilen laf ayni anda bize	I am always with you boy.
Oynamaya bakma damarima basma	Screaming at you means screaming at me
Söylüyorum sana kaybedersin sonunda	Don't dare to fool me,
Meseleyi fazla uzatmaya gelmez	You will be the loser.
Hepberaber olursak bizi kimse yenemez	If we get together, no one can beat us
Hadi gülüm yandan yandan	C'mon guys!
Karakan geliyor çekilin yoldan	*Karakan* is coming.
Hadi gülüm yandan yandan	C'mon guys,
Biz korkmayiz ondan bundan	Nothing can scare us.
Kan kan kankardesler	Blood blood bloodbrothers
Hepberaber bizi yenemezler	They can't beat us
Kan kan kankardesler	Blood blood bloodbrothers
Hepberaber iste sana *Cartel*	This is *Cartel*
Üç tane harf kan, alti tane harf daha kardes	Five letters 'blood,' seven more letters 'brother'

Bu ne demek acaba, küçük bir sözcük	What is this, a little word
Ama anlami büyük	But with a strong meaning
Ne ateslere biz körükle yürüdük	We walked through many troubles
Bazen kaybettik bazen kazandik	Sometimes lost, sometimes won
Kankardesimizi yalniz birakmadik	We never left alone our bloodbrother
Anca beraber kanca beraber	Forever together
Arkadasin çok olur gelirler giderler	Your friends come by and leave
Kankardesim seni hayatinca severler	They love you
En kötü gününde bile yaninda gezerler	They hang around with you to death
Karsinda *Cartel*, bilmiyorsan eger sana söylerler	This is *Cartel*, if you don't know someone can tell you
Çocuk ögrende gel, ugrasimiz rap	Go and find out, our business is rap
Çünkü pop bize yaramaz	Cos pop is no use for us
Sarmaz bize yakismaz bizi açmaz	It isn't for us
Kursun gibi sözler deler geçer	Words can kill like a bullet
Refrain	Refrain
Soracaksin kim diye, ben Kerim	My name is Kerim
Kâbus ilk adim bunu böyle bilin	I am known as nightmare
Kara kemiklerle bizim Alper	Next to me Alper with black bones
Seksi kanakeden nefret eder	He hates sexy *'kanake'*
Sadece o degil bizim hepimiz	Not only him, all of us
Birimiz hepimiz, hepimiz birimiz	One for all, all for one
Türk, Kürt, Laz ve Çerkez	Turk, Kurd, Laz and Circassian[7]
Ayrimcilik yaparsak kaybedecegiz	We will lose if we disunite
Uyanmak çok kapisinda kahpeler	Lots of traitors behind
Toz pembe bakmasin gelecege	Don't dream
Zannettigin arkadaslik bu degil	What you think of is not friendship
Daha da öte daha da ileri	It is something further, stronger
Hep beraber olup kiracagiz zincirleri	All together we will break up the chains
Kankardeslere yakisir bir sekilde	In a way that suits the bloodbrothers
Eger hazirsaniz simdi sira sizde	If you're ready, it's your turn now.
Refrain	Refrain
Karakan (Cartel)	*Karakan (Cartel)*

This particular rap song by *Cartel* demonstrates the need to unite across the diaspora of the German-Turks that consist of various ethnic groups such as Kurd, Laz and Circassian. By this song, MC *Kerim* (*Cartel*) invites his Turkish 'bloodbrothers' to fight racist arson attacks. This song also displays that the flow of the lyrical structure resembles that of the Turkish minstrel tradition. In the last part of the song, MC *Kerim* first introduces himself, and sharply gives his message: "One for all, all for one."

The rise of the local rap sound amongst the German-Turks is an indication of the cultural nationalism that is sustained by the processes of racialisation, assimilation and 'acculturation.' The sources of Turkishness which have appeared as components of rising cultural nationalism have offered the German-Turkish youngsters a positive sense of identity in the face of negative pressures towards assimilation and racism. Here, "ethnicity is used as a source in the struggle for social status, in particular, to counteract the negative representations of immigrant workers, and those with minimal power in their 'host' societies" (Bottomley, 1992: 57). The minority hip-hop youth culture is an attempt to constitute a form of counterculture. What the ethnic minority youth constructs is no more a kind of passive 'sub-culture.' Ethnic minority youngsters have become aware of the contradiction between the prevailing ideologies of equal opportunity and the reality of discrimination and racism in their daily lives. This, as Castles and Miller have stated, can lead to the emergence of countercultures and political radicalisation (Castles and Miller, 1993: 33). What are the main constitutive parts of the minority youth counterculture and political radicalisation? There is not a straightforward answer to this question. It seems that ethnicity is the primary instrument for the German-Turkish youth to construct a counterculture and a fruitful sense of identity. *Cartel* as a form of gangsta rap presents a form of diasporic cultural politics; and it also positions itself against cultural displacement, racism and capitalist exploitation.

Islamic Force: Universalist Political Rap

Islamic Force was founded in 1986 by the self-initiatives of *Boe-B* (male Turkish) and the manager Yüksel. Besides *Boe-B*, there are three more members: *Killa Hakan* (male Turkish), DJ *Derezon* (male, German mother and Spanish father), and *Nelie* (female, German mother and Albanian father). What they make is conceived as *oriental rap* and anti-racist rap in Berlin. *Boe-B* writes the lyrics, DJ *Derezon* is the technical expert in mixing melody, beat and rhythm. The name, *Islamic Force* was chosen to provoke the Germans who have a stereotypical image of Islam; otherwise the group has nothing to do with radical Islam. Recently, in order to release their works in Turkey, they have changed their name to *Kan-Ak*. The reason for this change is the concern surrounding the probability that the Turkish audience in Turkey might well misinterpret the name Islamic Force. The previous misinterpretation of *Cartel*'s discourse by the Turkish audience in Turkey has also made them conscious about probable unjust critiques in Turkey.[8]

By changing their name to Kan-Ak, the rappers believe to have a more gangsta-type of name for the Turkish market: *Kan-Ak* literally means 'running blood' in Turkish. On the other hand, the reason for choosing the new name *Kan-Ak* is also the acceptance of an offensive word used by the right wing Germans to identify the Polynesians (*Kanake*). There is a parallelism between the use of *nigga* instead of the racist word 'nigger' by the blacks in the USA and the use of *Kan-Ak*, or *Kanak*, instead of the offensive word *Kanake* by the Turks. The choice of such a name, in a way, springs from their feeling of being '*white-niggers*'. Tommy L. Lott's analysis of the term *nigga* is instructive in this context (Lott, 1994: 246). He rightly claims that gangsta rap has creatively reworked and recoded the social meaning of the term in a socially transgressive and politically retaliatory manner. Similarly, Peter McLaren offers an illuminating explanation for the revision of the term *nigger* by the blacks in New York, or Los Angeles:

When gangsta rappers revise the spelling of the racist version of the word *nigger* to the vernacular *nigga* they are using it as a defiant idiom of a resistive mode of African American cultural expression which distinguishes it from the way that, for instance, white racists in Alabama might employ the term (McLaren, 1995: 37).

The term *Kan-Ak* is the Turkish vernacular of the original racist version of *Kanake*. "If you take negative racist identifications like *Kanake*, and make them positive for your own use," says MC *Soft-G*, "then the racist groups have to produce new concepts to insult you. And it is always difficult to produce new concepts." It is a term that has very specific bounds of acceptable usage – it could only be used by the working-class Turkish youth.⁹

The term *Kanak* also permits a form of class-consciousness among the working-class Turkish youth in the sense that it distinguishes Turkish urban working-class youth from those middle-class Turkish youths that feel denigrated whenever the term is used. Besides the fact that Turkish rap has evolved in the binary-coded struggle against the hegemony of the German nation-state and rising racial attacks, it has also developed as a relatively independent expression of Turkish male artistic rebellion against the newly emerging Turkish bourgeoisie and the Turkish media. In doing so, the youngsters tend to romanticise the ethnic enclave as the fruitful root of cultural identity and authenticity. MC *Boe-B* pointed out that the Turkish media have always represented the 'successful' and 'well-integrated' middle-class Turkish youngsters rather than the working-class youth in Kreuzberg who had no 'achievement.' Thus, the working-class Turkish youngsters are to imagine themselves in opposition to the 'white' German society, and also to the other 'blacks' who aspire to integrate themselves into the dominant German culture (Robins and Morley, 1996: 249).

Islamic Force Is the first Turkish rap group to combine a drum-computer rhythm of Afro-American tradition with melodic samples of Turkish *arabesk*¹⁰ and pop music.¹¹ By mixing some traditional Turkish musical instruments such as *zurna*, *baglama* and *ud* with the Afro-American drum-computer rhythm, they transculturate rap music. Transculturation is a two-way process whereby elements of international pop, rock, and rhythm-and-blues are incorporated into local and national musical cultures, and indigenous influences contribute to the new transnational styles (Wallis and Malm, 1984: 300-301). What happens in practice is that individual music cultures pick up elements from transcultural music, but an increasing number of national and local music cultures also contribute to transcultural music. Through the transculturation process, music from the international music industry can interact with virtually all other music cultures and subcultures in the world due to the world-wide penetration of music mass-media (Wallis and Malm, 1990/1984). In *oriental rap*, the global rhythm and beat of rap infuse into local Turkish folk music, pop music and *arabesk* music. *Oriental rap* becomes the music of the state of bricolage, or hybridity, as in *Islamic Force*.

MC *Boe-B* defines their rap style with an illustrative example: "The boy comes home and listens to hip-hop, then his father comes along and says 'Come on boy, we're going shopping.' They get into the car and the boy listens to Turkish music on the cassette-player. Later, he gets our record and listens to both styles in one" (quoted in Elfleim, 1996). Transculturation, in the form of mixing *arabesk* and hip-hop in one, is, at the same time, the expression of a 'double diasporic consciousness.'[12] This consciousness stems from the double migration experience that the migrants experienced both in Turkey and in Germany. Before migrating to Germany, most of the migrant parents had already lived a diasporic experience (*gurbet*) by leaving their villages to work in the big industrial cities of Turkey. *Arabesk* has been the expression of their parental culture. They have been raised in such a cultural climate at home. The pessimism of *arabesk* music has dominated their musical taste. What Ferdi – a 16-year-old boy in the *Chip* youth centre – has said is very illustrative to understand the impact of *arabesk* on the diasporic youth: "When I listen to Ferdi Tayfur I feel that I am back home, especially that song, you know which one I mean: '*Hadi gel köyümüze geri dönelim*' ('Come on, let's go back to our village')."[13] On the other hand, they have experienced the problems of being an ethnic minority in Germany away from their homeland. In diaspora they have taken hip-hop as an expression of their alienation and resistance to the capitalist system. Arabesk also provides these working-class youngsters with a symbol of solidarity, but not in more than a weak and implicit sense of solidarity against anybody else. Arabesk is not threatening, and so the Turkish diasporic youth can keep its mystique meaning to themselves.[14]

Thus, *arabesk* and hip-hop are the two musical styles which some of the youngsters prefer listening to as an expressive form of their 'double diasporic identity.' They employ *arabesk* as a musical and cultural form to express their imaginary nostalgia towards 'home,' 'being there,' or the 'already discovered country of past;' and, on the other hand, they consider hip-hop a musical and cultural form to express their attachment to the 'undiscovered country of the future.' To put it differently, both *arabesk* and hip-hop represent the symbolic expression of the dialogue which the diasporic youth have between 'past' and 'future,' between 'tradition' and 'translation,' between 'there' and 'here,' between the local and the global.

Chapter 6

Selaminaleyküm

Köyden Istanbul'a vardilar

Alman gümrügünde kontrol altinda kaldilar
Sanki satin alindilar
Bunlari kullanip kovariz sandilar

Ama aldandilar
Bizimkiler onlarin hesaplarini bozdular
Köylü dedikleri kafalari kullandilar

Çalisip edip kosturdular
Her köseye bir firin ya da imbiss kurdular
Ama bu kadar iyi haberin acisi da var
Kaybediyoruz can kaybediyoruz kan
Evler yaniyor bazen deliriyor insan
Ben bunlari anlatmak için seçildim

Hepsi bagiriyor *"Boe-B* söyle"
Ben de hip-hop seklinde sunuyorum Kadiköy'de

Selaminaleyküm aleykümselam
Selaminaleyküm aleykümselam
Müzigimize devam

Burda olanlari size anlatiyoruz
Haberlerimizi size evet sunuyorum
Bizim semtten Kadiköy'e bir baglanti kuruyoruz
Harbi hip-hop duyuruyoruz
Burdan size yolluyoruz
Turlarsin artik sesle mahallelerde
Altinda bir Benz ya da bir BMV, ya da Golf, ya da Audi, ya da herhangi
Nebileyim, ne bileceksin, polis arkanda

Selaminaleyküm

They arrived in Istanbul from their villages
And got searched in the German customs
It is as if they got purchased
Germans thought they'd use and kick them off

But they failed to
Our people ruined their plans
Those peasants turned out to be clever

They worked hard
Opened a bakery or an *imbiss* on each corner
But they paid a lot for this success
We are losing life, losing blood
Homes are on fire, we get mad
I was chosen to explain these things

Everybody screams "Tell us *Boe-B*"
And I am telling our story as hip-hop in Kadiköy[15]

Selaminaleyküm aleykümselam
Selaminaleyküm aleykümselam
Let's go on rapping

We tell you our experiences
We present you the news
We connect our neighbourhood and Kadiköy
We are doing real hip-hop
And we tell it to you
You drive with high-decibels in the streets in either Benz, or BMW, or Golf, or Audi, or whatsoever.
The police is behind you

Takip ediyorlar seni	They are following you
Ama sen farkina varmadin daha	You haven't yet realised
Bakmadin daha	You haven't yet looked behind
Sinyal vermeden dönüyorsun	You are turning without signalling
Aniden her yerde polis görüyorsun	Suddenly everywhere gets full of police
In diyor, indiriyor	He says, "get out!"
Araban çalinti diyor	He says "you stole this car"
Bir kagidin eksik diye karakola götürüyor	He is taking you to the police station just because of the lack of a document
Hiç acimiyor	He doesn't have any mercy at all
Adam isini biliyor	He knows his business
Sayiyor, aliyor ve kontrol ediyor	He is counting, taking and controlling
Senin de insan oldugunu görmüyor	
Hafiften haksizlik oluyor	He doesn't know, you are also human
Ve bunu *Boe-B* size Kadiköy'e kadar duyuruyor.	This is unjust
	And I am telling this story in a far land, Kadiköy.
Refrain	Refrain
Boe-B (*Islamic Force*)	Boe-B (*Islamic Force*)

Islamic Force attempts to bridge the gap between the diaspora and the homeland. Their rap song '*Selaminaleyküm*,' following the traditional Turkish minstrel genre with the name of the poet in the last part of the song, for instance, undertakes to inform the Turkish youth in Turkey about their own experiences in the diaspora away from 'home.' MC *Boe-B* narrates in this rap that they have been raised in families who have been twice migrants. This song is the expression of double diasporic identity as well as that of the quest for homeland. By referring to Kadiköy in the song, he holds on to his roots. He defines himself as a 'messenger' chosen by his community in Berlin to express their state of being to their Turkish compatriots in the homeland. He tells a 'true' story to his 'imaginary' Turkish compatriots about the life-worlds of the German-Turks who are subject to institutional racism, harassment, arson attacks and discrimination. This song is quite illustrative of two crucial points: firstly, it exposes how "a diaspora can be created through the mind, through cultural artefacts and through a shared imagination in the age of cyberspace" to use Cohen's words (1996: 516); and secondly, how the diasporic youth use an emerging global cultural form (hip-hop) and a granted local cultural form (*arabesk*) for their own expressive purposes. This syncretic 'double diasporic consciousness' simultaneously points at Turkey and Berlin, past and present as well as local and global.

MC Boe-B's narrative in the given song resembles that of the Turkish minstrels. In fact, the rapper as a 'storyteller' and/or an 'organic intellectual' has its equivalent in Anatolian culture. Though having completely different musical tastes, rhyming and storytelling are the common denominators of both artistic forms. Thus, the working-class Berlin-Turkish youth, who have been raised with the sound of Turkish folk music, could easily relate to the rap form of art. The key concept in what follows will be the transcultural form of *Islamic Force*. I have reproduced the personal narratives of the group members to be able to demonstrate their individual discourses and politics of identity.

DJ Derezon (26):
He was born in Kreuzberg. He is the son of a German mother and a Spanish father. He feels alienated in Germany, and akin to the Turkish minority. He is partly assimilated to the minority Turkish youth culture; he actually defines himself as Turkish. For him Turkishness is a state of mind and an equivalent of feeling in minority: "We are all foreigners. We are Turkish." While saying this, he immediately adds, "Brooklyn is similar to Kreuzberg." After receiving his *Abitur* from high school, he became involved in hip-hop culture, tagging on the walls all over Berlin. Then he started DJ-ing. He went to Brooklyn and did some DJ-ing with Black Americans in 1992. He picked up a Black American accent there. After returning to Berlin he became one of the most important figures in the Berlin hip-hop scene. He got in touch with the Turkish rapper *Boe-B* (Bülent) and the manager Yüksel in 1993 and later with *Killa Hakan* and *Nelie*. After listening to some Turkish samples, he decided to mix the Turkish melodies with beat and rhythm. He also convinced *Boe-B* that he should rap on Turkish samples: "I said: it is your roots, *Boe-B*, you should do that. Everybody is doing that." He always refers to the Black American origin of hip-hop. His presence in *Islamic Force* and his transnational links with

the East Coast hip-hop community confirm the transcultural character of hip-hop culture.

DJ *Derezon* also defines the role of the rapper as a medium establishing communication between various segments of the community:

Rappers are the speakers of the streets [...] They are the politicians of the community [...] We live here in Kreuzberg and have many friends. We always talk to our friends and have a continuous exchange of ideas. At the end of the day, we construct our own vision, and then express it to society [...] We are doing culture rap and political rap [...] Rap is a chance for the subordinated minorities to appear on the stage of art.

Boe-B (24):
He came to Germany when he was 8 and finished *Hauptschule* in Kreuzberg. His friends called him Bobby (*Boe-B*) in the primary school due to his resemblance to Bobby in the American TV series *Dallas*. Then he recovered this name for the stage, changing it to *Boe-B* (B is the initial of his forename, Bülent). Having been involved in gangsta groups in the past, he is afraid that some day Kreuzberg might turn into another New York in terms of the crime rate:

We are the voice of the streets. The media do not present life in the streets. What we do is to bring the street life onto the stage [...] We express ourselves through rap.

As the songwriter of the group, *Boe-B* composes lyrics against racism, drug abuse, materialism, police terror, exclusion, youth bands and rap theft. He favours East-Coast rap, which gives priority to lyrics and political messages. His favourite rap group is *Wu Tang Clan* (*WTC*) because he sees a resemblance between *WTC* and themselves. *WTC* is an East-Coast rap group who displays a bohemian way of life and a gangsta profile like *Islamic Force*. Since *Boe-B*'s group has begun to be involved in the commercial rap business, he is shifting towards West-Coast rap laying the emphasis on beat and rhythm rather than lyrics.

Boe-B's rap is a clear exponent of the fact that the beauty of the rap experience does not only spring from the mix and the beat, but also from the quality of the rhyme and of the voice. The point is not to show that one can rhyme but that one can rhyme differently. While stating the peculiarities of good rapping, he underlines the competition between *Islamic Force* and *Cartel*. One of his main concerns is rap theft. It is said that *Cartel* and *TCA Microphone Mafia* have stolen some of their Turkish samples.

Killa Hakan (23):
He was born in Kreuzberg. He dropped out of the *Oberschule*. He is a fan of hardcore rap and *arabesk* (especially Müslüm Gürses).[16] He used to be a *gangsta* before joining *Islamic Force*. He defines the rapper as a 'storyteller,' or a narrator, who utters various stories. He attributes a broad meaning to hip-hop:

Real hip-hop does not exist in Turkey. We are trying to take it there. The rappers are gonna change the Turkish youth in Turkey. After the introduction of hip-hop, Turkey will improve itself much further.

He often complains about racism in Germany, and he seems quite keen on returning to Turkey for good:

When the Germans see a black-haired Turkish youth driving a brand-new car, they stare at him with questioning eyes. They don't like the Turks with leather jackets at all.

Hakan's discourse on racism reminds us that biological racism is still quite significant for the diasporic Turkish youth. By aligning himself with 'hardcore' rap, Hakan attempts to renegotiate his own ethnicity through proclaiming a specific musical taste. By positioning himself in the marginal space of hardcore rap, he also aims to disavow the dominant regimes of representation and to incorporate himself into the global youth culture. In the meantime, he seems to complain that having an advantageous economic position is not enough to get rid of racial harassment.

Nelie (26):
She was born in Kreuzberg, too. Her mother is German and her father Kosovo-Albanian. She is a Muslim. Having been raised with the Turks in her childhood, she attended the Koran courses in a Turkish mosque and learned to speak fluent Turkish from her Turkish friends. Now, she is making soul music in Turkish.

Erci-E: Party Rap

Erci-E (23) is one of the rappers of *Cartel*. He was born in Berlin outside Kreuzberg. Erci first encountered rap when he was 13 years old. His first acquaintance with rap was a crucial moment for him. Rap meant, for him as well as for many other rappers, transcending the pessimism of pop music at first sight:

Rap is my favourite music. I have loved that coolness since the age of 13. The other music styles have become boring for me. For instance, pop music was very stable without any change. What fascinates me in rap is its dynamism and power.

After giving up university for music, he began making *oriental* or *alternative* rap. Like many other Turkish rappers, he relates better to East Coast rappers. He is well aware of the changes in rap music all around the world, especially in the United States. Like all the Turkish rappers, *Erci-E* gives reference to the American differentiation of rap sound as East-Coast and West-Coast. *Erci-E* underlines the creative and progressive character of the rap music for the Turkish diaspora as well as for the other minority youth all around the world. He sees hip-hop as a ticket out of the 'ghetto':

In rap, rhythm and melody are as important as lyrics. *Cartel* gave something to the Turkish youngsters living in Europe. Now I want to give something else to them. Rap should be progressive. I don't want to talk about the problems any more, I want them to enjoy themselves by listening to optimistic rap and having positive feelings. The message of my new solo long-play, which I will give to the Turkish youngsters in minority all around Europe, is to struggle against violence and to seek solidarity [...] Wherever there is a minority, hip-hop is there. It is a rebellion culture. It is not necessarily a revolt against the political government. American-Blacks have grown up in the ghetto. Hip-Hop has become a way for them to get out of the ghetto. By means of Hip-Hop they have the chance to do more creative things in their leisure time.

He is planning to have his solo long-play produced all over Europe and even in the United States of America:

Turks in Europe have been forgotten; they should communicate with each other. Turkish youngsters in France should know that they are living the same things as the Turkish youngsters in Germany [...] I want to explain something new to them in their own 'broken' Turkish accent [...] Turkish pop is not for us. It is just talking about love, that is it. There is, for instance, sea in those pop songs, but there is no sea in Germany. I repeat it: Turkish pop is not for us.

Erci-E tends to see hip-hop in a much broader context which leads him to the conclusion that rap may well create what we might call a 'diasporic interchange' and 'diasporic intimacy' among Turkish peoples in the diaspora struggling against racism and capitalist exploitation in their countries of settlement. The progressive and resisting role of music is not only limited by national boundaries. The existing network of global capitalism and communication technology takes the message of the diasporic form of organic intellectuals beyond the national territories (Decker, 1992). He also attempts, on the other hand, to break up the 'rhythmic obedience' of the pop and *arabesk* music by providing an alternative to the Turkish audience.[17] By saying so, he also underlines the fact that rap has reversed the established pattern of pop music by dictating a strong and progressive lyrical content beyond the much more common passivist romanticism.

For *Erci-E*, back to basics is one of the main aspects of hip-hop culture in terms of ethnic symbols, music taste and images. Accordingly, he attempts to add Turkishness to rap. He is aware of the fact that, while making rap music, it is vital to have a sample melody. For instance, in the USA, almost all the songs of James Brown have been made into samples for the rap songs. *Erci* does not like to take James Brown's songs as samples because:

He is not Turkish; he is black. I thought samples should be from our own music. Baris Manço is the James Brown of Turkish rap. There is also Erkin Koray and Mogollar. They were making soul-funk in the seventies. We used to listen to their songs during the journeys to Turkey by car when I was nine, or ten years old; and we were proud of their bass sound.

Those were the Turkish popstars of the seventies, who were, in a way, providing a contact with the West, in a musical sense, for the Turkish audience in Turkey. It is quite amazing to be witness to the fact that these musicians have had an essential meaning in the diasporic Turkish youngsters' imagination. Those popstars have given them a safe bridge, or a reference point, to combine two different cultures without any contradiction.

Erci, as an intellectual of his own community, is trying to find some correlation between the radical, or rebellious, character of the Turkish youth and their representation in the media:

I have grown up in Berlin. I haven't seen any other place apart from Germany. I speak German. Germans don't like me, and I don't like them. There is poverty in Turkey; Germany seems reasonably better than Turkey. We have always been misrepresented here in the German media. For instance, Turkey represents poverty and Islamic fundamentalism for the German televisions. Turkish children grow up with these images and with a kind of reactionary feeling that explodes in adolescence. What we can do is to protect ourselves against them and not to bother them. We are capable and able to do this. Since most of the Turkish children are in the *Hauptschule*, what else can the Germans think about the Turks? The parents didn't look after their children. The result is that the children haven't seen their parents as important as they are, and they take them for granted. Then, they conclude that we have poverty, because we are Turks. No, we are here and we are gonna stay here. We have to change things. We are paying taxes, so we have the right to get something in return. This is the reason why the Kreuzberg people are so miserable [...] We must change the image of Turkey. *Cartel* was a good example. We have joined the European Football championship finals in England this year, and there are many German tourists going to Turkey. On top of all these things, we want to make a contribution to the new image of Turkey.

By doing so, *Erci-E* wages a war against the formal representation of Turkey and Turks in the German media, which he considers the main source of tension between Germans and Turks. Furthermore, Erci's narrative makes one point very clear: the welfare of the diasporic youth is directly related to the image of the homeland in the country of settlement. What he aims to achieve is to be able to give a positive sense of identity to the diasporic Turkish subjects by means of informal networks of communication such as rap.

Chapter 6

Ünal: Gangsta Rap

Ünal (27) was born in Kreuzberg. He was sent to Turkey by his parents to have a 'better' education when he was seven years old. He stayed in Turkey until the age of fifteen. Then he obtained his university degree from the School of Audio Engineering at the Berlin Technical University. Now, he is living in Steglitz, a district of Berlin with a very small Turkish population. He is both a rapper and a producer. He is called *Soft-G* on the stage. He first founded *Ypsilon Music* with Yüksel, the manager of *Islamic Force*. After the *Ypsilon Music* project ended, he started to run the *Orient Express* Music Company producing basically for the Turkish market. The pop-music singers Can Kat, Ahmet and Bay-X are his productions for Turkey. He is recently running another project for the Turkish market in collaboration with a Turkish female soul singer living in New York and a songwriter from Istanbul. He is the producer in the middle, using the global network of electronic mail, fax and telephone.

He has made a video for Can Kat as well. In the video, *Ünal* is rapping in a tenor voice wearing an Italian-American gangster suit of the twenties. The video was a big success in Turkey. In contrast to the other Turkish rappers, he is more attracted by the Italian-American rap style. Besides the music production for the Turkish market, he is making music for the Turkish youngsters living in Germany as well. *Azize-A*, for instance, is a Turkish woman rapper working with *Ünal* to break into the German music market.

Ünal often draws attention to the politics of rapping. He points out that the rapper is an intellectual, and at the same time the microphone is the rappers' 'lethal weapon.' On that account, in the hip-hop scene he is called *Soft-G*, where the letter G refers to 'gangsta.' *Ünal*'s picture on Can Kat's CD, which contains some of his rap pieces, is very illustrative in this sense. He holds a big microphone in his hands as if he is gripping a 'lethal weapon.'[18] His politics of rap is identical to that of Ice-T: Ice-T declares in the song that his 'lethal weapon' is his mind.[19]

Ünal depicts the major differences between the youth cultures since the sixties. The main difference of hip-hop culture from the others, to him, is its local character:

The difference of hip-hop from the previous youth cultures is that hippie and punk were global, whereas hip-hop is very local. Every epoch has its own particular problem. Hippies were concerned with some global problems such as sexual freedom, peace and nature. Punk culture was a bit closer to hip-hop due to its concern with some local concerns such as revolt against the dominant social values. Hip-Hop springs from the minorities unlike the Hippie and Punk cultures. Hip-Hop youngsters living all around the world have various problems and concerns. For instance, an American rapper doesn't necessarily have to get on well with the Turkish rapper in Berlin. Hippies were different; they had a global communication through the common idols that they used to listen to such as The Beatles [...].

Ünal also points out the 'Turkification of rap' through the mixing of instruments and melodies. By saying so, he acknowledges the 'bricolage' character of rap transcending the cultural boundaries in music:

In a sense, we Turkify the rap. We are, for instance, trying to mix *Zurna* and rock in our own melodies. Günay is an example of this.[20] We must create a *Turkish Community* in rap like the East-Coast or West-Coast. In a very near future, I will produce a tape including two rap songs from each Turkish rap group in Berlin.

Like many other Turkish rap groups such as *Cartel, Islamic Force* and *Erci-E* he also underlines his objection to pop music which is repetitive and leading to 'narcotic passiveness'[21] and/or 'rhythmic obedience':

Rap is rebellious music, whereas pop is commercial music. This is the difference between rap and pop. Rap is usually a social critique. When a rebellious rap becomes too popular, it shouldn't be conceived as pop music, because it still keeps its critical nature.

His claim on popular-critical rap, in fact, undercuts the perspectives of Adorno by arguing that repetition in rap is not always connected to the commodity system of late capitalism in the same way as other popular musical forms are. Adorno's interpretation of popular music as an ideological instrument leading to 'rhythmic obedience' (Adorno, 1990/1941) is challenged by *Ünal*'s interpretation of popular rap which may well lead to a form of collective resistance.

CHAPTER 6

Azize-A: Woman Rap

Azize-A (26) is a woman rapper from Berlin. She is living in Steglitz with her parents. She completed the *Realschule*. Although she does not want to be considered a feminist rapper, she does feminist rap. Besides rapping, she appears in a children's programme, *Dr. Mag*, made for ZDF TV. Her taste of music is dominated by American black music, such as jazz, funk and soul. She is very critical of Turkish *arabesk* music due to its pessimism. She is trying to break the traditional image of the Turkish woman in Europe, and wants to show that the second and third generation Turkish youngsters have become very 'multi-kulti' and cosmopolitan. She attempts to play with the multicultural capital in order to be accepted by the majority society.

She calls her rap *oriental rap* because she mixes some Turkish and Arabic musical instruments such as *Ney*, *Ud* and *Saz* with the western ones. She also uses some Turkish samples for her rap:

> I used a song of Ibrahim Tatlises as a sample.[22] Turkish people have forgotten their roots because of imitating the West too much. We want to reverse this flow. We are trying to use our own treasures. We turn towards Turkey, and they (the Turks) turn towards the West. In the end, we meet in the middle.

The letter A in *Azize-A* refers to the initial of the Turkish word *Abla*, which means elder sister. *Azize-A* is like her equivalents Sister Souljah (a member of *Public Enemy* between 1990 and 1992) and Schwester-S (a German woman rapper). *Azize-A* adds a crucial meaning to rap:

> Rap sends subliminal messages to the people. I want to explain to the people (German and Turkish) that the Turkish woman has many other values and talents. I want to demonstrate that we are not sitting at home and doing housework all day. I also attempt to erase the question of "are we Turkish or German?," and announce that we are multi-kulti and cosmopolitan. I want to show that we are no more sitting between the two chairs, we have got a 'third chair' between those two chairs [...].

The whole process, which is embodied by Azize-A and other German-Turkish rappers, illustrates the formation of cultural bricolage by modern diasporic subjects. Cultural bricolage which is grounded on the lines of local-global, 'tradition'-'translation,' and past-present negates many of the ill-defined concepts about the state of ethnic minority youths such as 'in-betweenness,' 'lost generation' and 'degenerated.' Negating the so-called state of 'in-betweenness,' Azize-A draws a new picture of the diasporic youth. Her insistence on multiculturalism seems to be the main pillar of her politics of identity. She does not invest in the cultural boundaries imprisoning culture as a distinct, self-contained and essentialist form. By stating that she wants to erase the question: "are we Turkish or German?," she denies the classical understanding of culture and reconfirms what Rosaldo (1989: 26) said: "Cultures are learned, not genetically encoded."

* * *

To reiterate, rap has become the urban popular art of a remarkable number of Turkish youths in Berlin. The Turkish rappers in Berlin are substantial constituents of the diasporic cultural form developed by a considerable amount of working-class Turkish youths. Using the traditional Turkish musical genre as the source of their samples and having been guided by the traditional Turkish minstrels in terms of lyrical structure, these contemporary minstrels, or storytellers, tend to be the spokespersons of the Turkish diaspora. What Ünal's 'Turkish community' attempts to provide is an informal network of communications which will shape popular knowledge in a manner that contests German nationalism and hegemony from within the Turkish diaspora. In this sense, Turkish rappers do not merely constitute a form of protest like hippies and punks, but also initiate a 'class politics' along the lines of Gramsci's notion of 'organic intellectuals.'

As organic cultural intellectuals, the rappers transform 'common-sense' knowledge of oppression into a new critical awareness that is attentive not only to ethnic but also to class contradictions. These organic intellectuals attempt to build a 'historical bloc' – a coalition of oppositional groups united around counter-hegemonic ideas – against the 'traditional elite' who try to 'manage consent' by making domination appear natural, voluntary, and inevitable. The efforts by Turkish rappers in Berlin to enter the mainstream by forming a 'Turkish community' reflect their struggle to assemble a 'historical bloc' capable of challenging the ideological hegemony of German cultural domination. Furthermore, rap music, as a popular cultural form, becomes a powerful vehicle, which allows today's Turkish youth to gain a better understanding of their heritage and their present identities when official channels of remembering and identity formation continually fail to meet their needs. What Azize-A calls the 'third chair' illustrates how the diasporic subject crosses over the cultural borders and constructs a syncretic cultural identity. In his poem *'Doppelmann,'* Zafer Senocak writes of his Germany as:

> I carry two worlds within me
> but neither one whole
> they're constantly bleeding
> the border runs
> right through my tongue.[23]

The diasporic subject who is defined in this poem is someone experiencing a constant tension between homelessness/rootlessness and diasporic home. "The split," as Senocak states, "can give rise to a double identity. This identity lives on the tension. One's feet learn to walk on both banks of the river at the same time" (Suhr, 1989: 102). The discourses of the Turkish rappers in Berlin, which I presented, affirm what Hall (1994) pointed out that contemporary diasporic identities are developed on two paramount dimensions: universalism and particularism. The universalist axis refers us to the model of interculturalism in the form of 'third space' – or 'process of heterogenesis,' or 'third culture' – (Guattari, 1989; Bhabha, 1990; Featherstone, 1990). On the other hand, the particularist axis presents the model of cultural essentialism. Cultural identity of the diasporic subject is simultaneously grounded both on an 'archaeological' form that entails the rediscovery of an essential and historical culture, and a 'retelling of the past' that claims the production of a positional, situational and contextual cultural identity. In other words, the whole question of diasporic cultural identity is a tense interaction between essence and politics and between 'Tradition' and 'Translation.'

This chapter has also displayed that the music of the diaspora constitutes a philosophical discourse because they reject "the modern, occidental separation of ethics and aesthetics, culture and politics" (Gilroy, 1993: 38). The musical genre of the diaspora is, at the same time, the indication of the emergence of a global culture transcending national boundaries. This new notion of global culture contradicts the conventional notion of culture that is thought to be territorial, and belonging to nations, regions and localities (Smith, 1990, 1995). The nature of the existing culture is syncretic. This 'cultural syncreticism' is facilitated by global capitalism, which disrupts the national boundaries. The emergence of modern diasporic cultures and identities is consistent with current scholarship in cultural studies, which suggest that the concept of culture must be looked at in new ways "that are capable of somehow operating against its own inner character, which was defined long ago by the notions of rootedness, stasis, and fixity that are intrinsic to its original meanings in the fields of crop management and animal husbandry" (Gilroy, 1995: 18).

Notes

1. The rap group *Cartel* is represented in a slightly different way from the others, as most members of the group originate outside Berlin. The only member of the group from Berlin is *Erci-E* whom I interviewed separately.
2. Gramsci (1971) makes a differentiation between the 'professional intellectuals' and 'organic intellectuals.' Professional intellectuals are attached to the state, whereas organic intellectuals aim to improve socio-economic, political and cultural interests of their communities. Professional intellectuals are the deputies of the State, and they have a 'mandarin consciousness.' Organic intellectual, on the other hand, must be an organiser of the centrifugal forces. It should also be pointed out that the term 'organic intellectual' was first used by Gilroy (1987: 196) to define the black London rapper Smiley Culture. For further information, see also Decker (1992).
3. Some of the mythical Turkish minstrels in the seventeen century were Karacaoglan, Köroglu and Pir Sultan Abdal. Arif Sag, Musa Eroglu, Mahsuni Serif, Yavuz Top and Mazlum Çimen are some of the contemporary minstrels in Turkey. These minstrels are often invited to European cities by Turkish communities to perform their art and to 'preach.'
4. Martin Greve calls the Turkish folk music minstrels in diaspora as the 'transnational minstrels.' For a detailed explanation on this issue see, Martin Greve (2000).
5. Swedenburg (1992) classifies the rap groups into four sub categories in the Anglo-American context: a) hard or serious nationalist rap of, say, *Public Enemy*; b) playful cultural-nationalist rap

of, say, *Jungle Brothers*; c) gangsta rap of, say, *Ice-T*; and d) women's rap of, say, *Queen Latifah*.

6 'Allahim yine mi?' (Oh my God, again?) is the cry of a woman in the background, which echoes the image of the 'caring mother.' Her cry is for the Turkish families who were killed in the arson attacks in Mölln and Solingen.

7 Laz and Circassian are just two of the major ethnic groups in Turkey. For a detailed map of ethnic composition of Turkey, see Andrews (1989).

8 Islamic Force, or Kan-Ak, could not achieve going to Turkey. The group disintegrated after the sudden death of Boe-B in 1999. Now, Killa Hakan is doing solo rap; and Derezon is Djing for some other groups.

9 Mapping out the creation of black-British youth identities, Claire E. Alexander (1996: 56-58) raises similar issues concerning the use of the term 'nigga' by the working-class black youth.

10 The history of *arabesk* music in Turkey starts with the internal migration from rural spaces to urban spaces since early 1960s. It is an epiphenomenon of urbanisation. *Arabesk* is primarily associated with music, but also with film, novels and foto-roman (photo dramas in newspapers with speech bubbles). *Arabesk* music is a style, which is composed of western and oriental instruments with an Arabic rhythm. This syncretic form of music has always borrowed some instruments and beat of the traditional Turkish folk music. The presence of the *arabesk* music on TV was banned by the state until the early eighties. The conservative-populist government of Turgut Özal set it free in the mid-eighties. The main characteristic of *arabesk* music is the fatalism, sadness and pessimism of the lyrics and rhythm. Hitherto, the lyrics were composed of an irrational and pessimist reaction of people with a rural background to the capitalist urban life. Recently, the composition of the lyrics has extensively changed. Instead of expressing pessimism in the urban space, lyrics tend to celebrate the beauty of the pastoral life, which has been left behind. In other words, it has become a call to the people to go back to basics. It should be pointed out that there is an extensive literature on the sociological dimensions of the *arabesk* music in Turkey (Özbek, 1994; Stokes, 1994; Güngör, 1993).

11 The group is using the old popular Turkish melodies from Baris Manço, Zülfü Livaneli and Sezen Aksu as their samples.
12 The term 'double diasporic consciousness' derives from Gilroy's notion of 'double consciousness' – a term which he reinterpreted from W.E.B. Du Bois (Gilroy, 1987).
13 This song is a critique of urbanisation and industrialisation, and narrates the longing and nostalgia of the *'gurbetçi'* for the pastoral way of life.
14 Similarly, Ulf Hannerz (1968) has defined the concept of 'soul' as a solidarity symbol among the Black 'ghetto' youth which is not threatening to anybody.
15 Kadiköy is a district of Istanbul in the Anatolian side. MC Boe-B states the name of Kadiköy because he was born there.
16 Müslüm Gürses is one of the main figures, or schools, of the *arabesque* music in Turkey. A remarkable number of his 'groupies,' on ecstasy, tend to harm themselves with razor blades during the concerts. A similar trend has also been noticed in Berlin amongst a group of Turkish youth living in the ethnic enclave.
17 Theodor Adorno (1990/1941) used the notion of 'rhythmic obedience' to refer to the 'pseudo individualisation' aspect of popular music.
18 Can Kat (1995). Çek Git, Berlin: E.M.Y. Records.
19 Ice-T (1989). "Lethal Weapon." *The Iceberg/Freedom of Speech ... Just Watch What You Say*. Sire Records.
20 Günay is the Turkish solo in a multi-cultural music group composed of an American, a Cameron, a German and three Turkish musicians. They try to improvise the Turkish folk music by mixing the instruments and sounds.
21 I borrowed the term 'narcotic passiveness' from Umberto Eco. In fact, he uses the term in the context of media: 'Liberated from the contents of communication, the addressee of the messages of the mass media receives only a global ideological lesson, the call to *narcotic passiveness*. When the mass media triumph, the human being dies' (Eco, 1986: 137; italics mine).
22 Ibrahim Tatlises is a very popular *arabesk* singer in Turkey and in the Middle East.
23 Quoted in Suhr (1989: 102).

Conclusion

This study has explored four inter-related theoretical concepts: diasporic consciousness, diasporic youth, globalisation and cultural bricolage with reference to the Berlin-Turkish hip-hop youth. This work primarily suggests that the contemporary diasporic consciousness is built on two contradictory axes: particularism and universalism. The presence of this dichotomy derives from the unresolved historical dialogues that the diasporic communities experience between continuity and disruption, essence and positionality, tradition and translation, homogeneity and difference, past and future, 'here' and 'there,' 'roots' and 'routes,' and local and global (cf. inter alia Clifford, Hall, Gilroy, Cohen and Vertovec).

By the same token, it should also be stated that the particularist constituents of diaspora identities such as inheritance, tradition, religion and ethnicity are all deferred and altered in the diaspora as spiritual, cultural and political metaphors. Hence, losing their essentialist nature, these particularist constituents are put into play by the diasporic subject as key ingredients for a politics of identity. For instance, the idea of 'going back to basics' among the working-class Turkish diasporic youth is, in fact, a counterculture of self-defence. As we saw, Neco's attempt to reify the Ottoman past in his paintings as the very essence of his Turkishness is, by and large, a fiction or a form of mimicry which is far from essentialism, because what we call Ottoman culture does not have a fixed essence in the sense that Neco is referring to. Contrarily, the Ottoman culture was a hybrid culture, which was comprised of Turkish, Roman, Greek, Seljuk, Arabic and Persian components.

Secondly, this work has claimed that the processes of cultural identity formation among the working-class Berlin-Turkish male hip-hop youth have principally revolved around their attempt to form a diasporic consciousness. The working-class Berlin-Turkish hip-hop youths are active agents in the construction and articulation of the di-

CONCLUSION

asporic consciousness. Being raised in Kreuzberg, which I presented in this work as a prototype of diasporic space (*Kleines* Istanbul), these youths have created a new home there as well as an identity grounded in more than one location: Berlin and Turkey. Kreuzberg as a diasporic space has provided these ethnic minority youths with a *symbolic wall* or *fortress* protecting them against racialisation, unemployment, misrepresentation, exclusion and discrimination. Accordingly, the sense of being a member of a 'different' people with historical roots and destinies outside the time/space of the 'host' nation provides them with a distinction and pride.

The third key term that I have considered is globalisation, which appears here as an individual consciousness of the global situation. The construction of modern diasporic consciousness does not merely depend upon the rigid incorporation regimes of the country of settlement; it also owes a lot to globalisation. The wide networks of communication and transportation between German-Turks and Turkey play a crucial role in the formation and maintenance of a diasporic identity among the transnational communities. The modern circuitry connects the diasporic youth both to the homeland and to the rest of the world. This is the reason why it becomes much easier for them to live on 'both banks of the river' at the same time. Turkish hip-hop youth in Berlin, as explored in this work, exemplify a growing stream, of what Brecher et al. (1993) have called '*globalisation from below.*' This constitutive entanglement has become a characteristic of modern diaspora networks. The expansion of economic, cultural and political networks between German-Turks and Turkey, for instance, points to this growing stream. In the context of the diasporic condition, 'globalisation from below' refers to the enhancement of the access of transnational migrants and their descendants to those social, cultural, political and economic mechanisms which enable them to transcend the conditions imposed upon them by the transnational capitalism which is organising them into a system of international and hierarchical division of labour. To put it differently, diasporic consciousness enables the diasporic subject to overcome the limitations and oppression of the global capitalism.

The fourth crucial concept that I explored throughout the book is cultural syncreticism, or cultural bricolage. It is globalisation that gives birth to the processes of cultural bricolage among the diasporic youth. What emerges out of this cultural syncreticism is what we might call 'third space' or 'third culture' (cf. Bhabha, 1990). As I demonstrated in the previous chapters, these 'third cultures,' that are formed in the 'border zones' and that Azize-A called 'third chair,' might contribute to the disruption of the conventional binarism of 'migrant culture' versus 'host culture.' Thus, knowing that such new cosmopolitan forms, or 'glocalised' identities, spring from presumed discrete cultural traditions, we might open ourselves up to a relationship that transcends us, that exists beyond and apart from us instead of fully explaining and assimilating the other, thereby reducing her/him to our world.

Among other things, Berlin-Turkish youth that simultaneously experience various life-worlds, also acquire a multicultural competence to behave appropriately in a number of different social spaces. There are linguistic, social and cultural borders between their distinct life-worlds, which I presented in Chapter 4 as youth centre, street, school and household. These youngsters always have to translate and negotiate within and between these rigidly defined spaces. Accordingly, diasporic youths construct their cultural identities in the intersection line of these separate social spaces, or in what Rosaldo (1989) calls 'border zones.'

The aesthetics of diaspora such as rap music and literature that are produced within the Turkish diaspora might give us some clue about the characteristics of these newly emerging cosmopolitan and transnational *third cultures*. For instance, 'Oriental' rap as a form of popular art is produced through a blend of particularist and universalist constituents such as the mix of traditional Turkish samples and lyric structures with an Afro-American drum-computer rhythm. This unique form of cultural bricolage in the context of the Turkish diasporic youth negates those conventional and stereotypical assumptions made by many scholars on the descendants of transnational migrants, which include, for instance, 'caught betwixt and between,' 'lost generation,' 'inbetween,' 'acculturated' and 'assimilated.'

As far as the working-class Berlin-Turkish hip-hop youth is concerned, the stereotyped definitions of German-Turkish youth made by various scholars have been disproved by the youths themselves. The terms such as 'deculturated' and 'culturally impoverished,' which have been attributed to the descendants of transnational migrants undermine the increasing impact of global interconnectedness and symbolic links between the subject and the homeland. Rather, these youngsters are subject to an enriched condition, which springs from being both inside and outside the West, or from what Du Bois called 'double consciousness.' The state of 'double consciousness' conjures up the very nature of diasporic identity, i.e. particularism and universalism.

This fruitful objectivity of the diasporic youth can also be explicable through Georg Simmel's notion of 'stranger.' The stranger is a constitutive element of the group itself – an element that is both inside and outside the group. The stranger develops a unity of closeness and remoteness in her/his human relationships: as Simmel (1971/1908: 143) pointed out, the distance within this relation indicates that one who is close by becomes remote, but his/her strangeness indicates that one who is remote becomes near. Although the stranger is excluded, and distances himself/herself, from the receiving society, s/he imports qualities into it, which do not spring from the group. Accordingly, his/her distance to the group itself enables him/her to develop objectivity.

Yet, the diasporic cultural identity of the Turkish hip-hop youth is not only limited to the state of *double consciousness*,' it goes beyond this factual predicament. These youngsters construct and articulate a state of what I call *double diasporic consciousness* in their imagery. This consciousness springs from the double migration experience of their parents, which they encountered both in Turkey and in Germany. As I outlined in Chapter 6, this double diasporic consciousness has become evident in the youths' expressive culture. *Arabesk* and hip-hop are the two major cultural forms that the Turkish hip-hop youth employed to express their own 'double diasporic condition.'

Additionally, this work has brought to attention ways in which a diaspora can be created through cultural artefacts and a shared imagery, which symbolically connect the diaspora to homeland. As I demonstrated in the case of the rap group *Islamic Force* (see Chapter 6), MC Boe-B tries to develop an imaginary intimate relationship with his people in Kadiköy, Istanbul. This corresponds to an important fact of the world we live in today: many persons on the globe live in what, extending Benedict Anderson (1983), Arjun Appadurai has called 'imagined worlds' (1990: 296-97). Such 'imagined worlds' which are constituted by the historically situated imaginations of persons and groups can, in some cases, demonstrate the fact that diaspora might also be an imaginary fiction as well as an actual condition.

This study has also examined Turkish migratory processes; incorporation regimes of the Federal Republic of Germany; ethnic-based political participation strategies of Turkish migrants; notions of ethnic minorisation and culturalisation; features and discontents of multiculturalism in the city of Berlin; Turkish ethnic associations; and cultural identity of the middle-class Berlin-Turkish youths. All of these complex issues have been raised to comprise a competent theoretical ground in order to formulate the major components of the modern diasporic identity. In addition to this, it was concluded that modern diasporic identities are historically conditioned according to the patterns of migratory processes in question, to the immigration policies of 'host' states, to the transnational networks of communication and transportation, and to the conscious intervention of social actors. It was also demonstrated that, creating a community consciousness, diaspora discourse constructs a network of solidarity and confinement among transnational migrants and their descendants. In this sense, diasporic discourse appears to be replacing, or at least supplementing, migrant and minority strategies.

Modern diaspora identities are those that are constantly producing and reproducing themselves anew, through transformation and difference. They are not defined by essence or purity, but by the recognition of heterogeneity, diversity, divergence, multiplicity and syncreticism. This is why I have refrained myself from locating the Turkish diasporic youth in a continuous space between diaspora and homeland without reinscribing an ideology of cultural difference. In this sense, the notion of diaspora conveys an identity that is not a fixed, essentialist and authorised totality, but is always in a constant process of change and transformation. Accordingly, this work has outlined the whole question of identity as a matter of politics and process, but not of essence and inheritance. Although it was phrased that modern diasporic identities have been grounded on both essentialist and situationalist pillars, it was made clear that the essence, in the final analysis, has become a principal source of identity politics for the transnational migrants and their descendants.

Hence, the diasporic cultural identity of the Berlin-Turkish hip-hop youth corresponds to a particular time and space. It delimits itself within this certain time and space. It is highly unlikely that we will see a similar snapshot of these youngsters in the near future, representing their cultural identity. However, the future generations will carry on forming new identities and 'third cultures' that transcend conventional binarism and dominant regimes of representation.

Appendix

Glossary

Alem — Universe, world; having parties with friends.

Alemci — Someone who has amusing parties with his/her friends.

Alevism — Anatolian version of *Shiism*, but it is a more hybrid form of belief consisting of many different rituals and religious undertones such as Sufism, Shamanism, Christianity, Judaism as well as Islam. Turkish *Alevi*s used to be concentrated in central Anatolia, with important pockets throughout the Aegean and Mediterranean coastal region and the European part of Turkey. Kurdish *Alevi*s were concentrated in the northwest of the Kurdish settlement zone. Both Turkish and Kurdish *Alevi*s have left their isolated villages for the big cities of Turkey and Europe since 1950s.

Almanci, Almanyali — German-like; stereotypical definition of German-Turks in Turkey. The major Turkish stereotypical images of German-Turks are those of their being rich, eating pork, having a very comfortable life in Germany, losing their Turkishness, and becoming more and more German.

Arabesk — It is mostly known as a music style, which is composed of western and oriental instruments with an Arabic rhythm. This syncretic form of music has always borrowed some instruments and beat of the traditional Turkish folk music. The main characteristic of *arabesk* music is the fatalism, sadness and pessimism of the lyrics and rhythm. It also corresponds to a fatalistic and pessimistic life style, which emerges in the urban spaces of Turkey.

Appendix

Ausländerbeauftragte	Commissioner for Foreigners' Affairs
Ausländergesetz	Foreigners' law in Germany.
Ausländerliteratur	Foreigners' literature in Germany.
Aussiedler	Ethnic Germans who repatriate from Eastern Europe; resettlers.
Baglama	A musical instrument having a guitar-like body, long, and strings that are plucked or strummed with the fingers or a plectrum.
Berufsschule	Vocational school
Bombing	A hip-hop term, which refers to the tagging and/or painting of several locations in one go.
CDU	Christian Democratic Union – Conservative Party in the FRG
CSU	Bavarian Sister Party of the CDU
Dügün	Wedding ceremony
Efes	Popular Turkish beer.
FDP	Free Democratic Party
Gastarbeiter	Guest worker.
Gesamtschule	Comprehensive school; grades 5-13.
Grüne (Green Party)	Ecological Party in the FRG
Grundschule	Primary school; grades 1-6
Gurbet	An Arabic word, which derives from *garaba*, to go away, to depart, to be absent, to go to a foreign country, to emigrate, to be away from one's homeland, to live as a foreigner in another country.
Gurbetçi	Someone who is in *gurbet*.
Gymnasium	Academic secondary school; grades 5-13
Hauptschule	Lower secondary school; grades 5-9 (or 10)
Hemsehri	Fellow villager.
Imbiss	German word for '*döner kebab*' kiosk.
Isyan müzigi	Rebellion music, protest music.
Kanak	Turkish vernacular of the German word *kanake*, which is an offensive word used by the right wing Germans to identify the Africans.
Kanak Sprak	A creole language spoken and written by the working-class German-Turkish youth.

Länder	The 16 constituent political-administrative units of the Federal Republic of Germany.
Mitbürger	Fellow citizen.
Oberschule	Grammar school; grades 5-13
PDS	Partei des Demokratischen Sozialismus – Left-Socialist Party in the FRG
Raki	Popular Turkish alcoholic beverage, made of grape and aniseed.
Realschule	Intermediate secondary school; grades 5-10
Sila	Home
Sonderschule	A different kind of primary school with specialist classes for children with 'learning difficulties;' grades 1-9
SPD	Socialdemocratic Party
Sunni	The dominant school in Islam religion.
Tagging	A pseudonym signature made with one colour marker pen or spray can.
Übersiedler	East Germans who migrated to the Federal Republic of Germany during the Cold War.

Bibliography

ABADAN, N. (1964). *Bati Almanya'daki Türk Isçileri ve Sorunlari*. Ankara: DPT Yayinlari.

ABADAN-UNAT, N. (1976). "Turkish Migration to Europe 1960-1975: A Balance Sheet of Achievements and Failures." In: N. Abadan-Unat (ed.), *Turkish Workers in Europe 1960-1975*. Leiden: E.J. Brill.

ABADAN-UNAT, N. (1985). "Identity Crisis of Turkish Migrants." In: I. Basgöz and N. Furniss (eds.), *Turkish Workers in Europe* (Indiana University Turkish Studies).

ABADAN-UNAT, N. (1988). "The Socio-Economic Aspects of Return Migration in Turkey." *Migration* 3: 29-59.

ABADAN-UNAT, N. AND N. KEMIKSIZ (1986). *Türk Dis Göçü 1960-1984: Yorumlu Bibliyografya*. Ankara.

ADLER, P.A. ET AL. (1986). "The Politics of Participation in Field Research." *Urban Life* 14, No. 4 (January): 363-376.

ADORNO, T.W. (1990/1941). "On Popular Music." In: S. Frith and A. Goodwin (eds.), *On Record*. New York: Pantheon.

AKSOY, A. AND K. ROBINS (1997). "Peripheral vision: cultural industries and cultural identities in Turkey." *Paragraph* 20, No. 1 (March): 75-99.

ALASUUTARI, P. (1995). *Researching Culture: Qualitative Method and Cultural Studies*. London: Sage Publications.

ALEXANDER, C.E. (1996). *The Art of Being Black: The Creation of Black British Youth Identities*. Oxford: Clarendon Press.

ÅLUND, A. (1992). "Immigrant Youth: Transnational Identities." In: C. Palmgren et al. (eds.), *Ethnicity in Youth Culture* (Stockholm: Stockholm University Press): 73-94.

ÅLUND, A. (1994). "Ethnicity and modernity: On 'tradition' in modern cultural studies." In: J. Rex and B. Drury (eds.), *Ethnic Mobilisation in a Multi-Cultural Europe*. Aldershot: Avebury.

ÅLUND, A. (1995). "The Quest for Identity: Modern Strangers and New/Old Ethnicities in Europe." *Unpublished Workshop Paper on Nationalism and Ethnicity* (Bern, 2-4 March).

ÅLUND, A. (1996). "Multiethnic Sweden: Youth in a Stockholm Suburb." *Migration Papers* No. 7. Esbjerg: South Jutland University Press.

ÅLUND, A. AND C.U. SCHIERUP (1991). *Paradoxes of Multiculturalism: Essays on Swedish Society*. Aldershot: Avebury.

AMIT-TALAI, V. AND WULFF, H. (EDS.) (1995). *Youth Cultures: A Cross-Cultural Perspective.* London: Routledge.

ANDERSON, B. (1983). *Imagined Communities: Reflections on the Origin and Spread of Nationalism.* London: Verso.

ANDREWS, P.A. (1989). *Ethnic Groups in the Republic of Turkey.* Wiesbaden: Dr. Ludwig Reichart.

ANIK, H. AND F. SENGÜN (1995). "Turkish-German Code Switching: Turkish teenagers and students in Berlin." Unpublished Working Paper. Freie Universität Berlin.

APPADURAI, A. (1990). "Disjuncture and difference in the global cultural economy." In: M. Featherstone (ed.), *Global Culture: Nationalism, Globalisation and Modernity.* London: Sage.

APPEL, R. AND P. MUYSKEN (1987). *Language, Contact and Bilingualism.* London: Edward Arnold.

ASAD, T. (1993). *Geneologies of Religion: Discipline and Reasons of Power in Christianity and Islam.* Baltimore: The Johns Hopkins University Press.

ATACAN, F. (1993). *Kutsal Göç: Radikal Islamci Bir Grubun Anatomisi.* Istanbul: Baglam Yayinlari.

BARKER, M. (1981). *The New Racism.* London: Junction Books.

BARTH, F. (1994). "Enduring and emerging issues in the analysis of ethnicity." In: H. Vermeulen and C. Govers (eds.), *The Anthropology of Ethnicity: Beyond 'Ethnic Groups and Boundaries'.* Amsterdam: Het Spinhuis.

BARTH, F. (ED.) (1969). *Ethnic Groups and Boundaries: The Social Organisation of Cultural Difference.* London: Allen & Unwin.

BASH, L. ET AL. (1994). *Nations Unbound.* Switzerland: Gordon and Breach Publishers.

BASH, L. ET AL. (1995). "From Immigrant to Transmigrant: Theorising Transnational Migration." *Anthropological Quarterly* 68: 48-63.

BAUDRILLARD. J. (1993). *The Transparency of Evil*, translated by J. Benedict. London: Verso.

BAUMANN, G. (1996). *Contesting Culture: Discourses of Identity in Multi-Ethnic.* London: Cambridge University Press.

BAYKAN, A.C. (1993). "Islam as an Identity Discourse." *Arena Journal* 1: 45-61.

BECKER, H. (1997/1963). "The Culture of a Deviant Group: The 'jazz' musician." In: Ken Gelder and Sarah Thornton (eds.), *The Subcultural Reader.* London: Routledge.

BELL, D. (1975). "Ethnicity and Social Change." In: Nathan Glazer and Daniel P. Moynihan (eds.), *Ethnicity: Theory and Experience*. Harvard University Press.

BELL, D. (1978). "Modernism and Capitalism." *Partisan Preview* 45: 206-222.

BENJAMIN, W. (1973). "The Storyteller: Reflections on the Works of Nikolai Leskov." In: Hannah Arendt (ed.), *Illuminations*. London: Fontana Press.

BERG, B. L. (1995). *Qualitative Research Methods for the Social Sciences*. Boston: Allyn and Bacon.

BERGER, J. (1972). *Ways of Seeing*. London: Penguin Books.

BERGER, J., J. MOHR AND S. BLOMBERG (1975). *The Seventh Man*. Middlesex: Penguin Books Ltd.

BERMAN, M. (1983). *All That Is Solid Melts Into Air*. London: Verso.

BHABHA, H. (1988). "The Commitment to Theory." *New Formations* 5 (Summer): 5-23.

BHABHA, H. (1990). "The Third Space." In: J. Rutherford (ed.), *Identity: Community, Culture, Difference*. London: Lawrence & Wishard.

BHABHA, H. (1994). *The Location of Culture*. London: Routledge.

BLASCHKE, J. (1983). "Ethnische Koloniebildung in westeuropäischen Industrie-Gesellschaften am Beispiel der Türken in Berlin." *B.I.V.S. Working Paper*, Berlin.

BLUME, R. (1985). "Graffiti." In: Teun A. Van Dijk (ed.), *Discourse and Literature: New Approaches to the Analaysis of Literary Genres*. Amsterdam: John Benjamins.

BOTTOMLEY, G. (1987). "Cultures, Multiculturalism and the Politics of Representation." *Journal of Intercultural Studies* 2: 1-9.

BOTTOMLEY, G. (1992). *From Another Place: Migration and Politics*. Cambridge: Cambridge University Press.

BOURDIEU, P. (1984). *Distinction*. Cambridge/MA: Harvard University Press.

BOURDIEU, P. (1993). *Sociology in Question*. London: Sage Publications.

BOYARIN, D. AND J. BOYARIN (1993). "Diaspora: Generation and the Ground of Jewish Identity." *Critical Inquiry* 19 (Summer): 693-725.

BRAH, A. (1996). *Cartographies of Diaspora: Contesting Identities*. London: Routledge.

BRAKE, M. (1980). *The Sociology of Youth Culture and Youth Subcultures*. London: Routledge.

BRANDT, B. (1996). "The Politics of Exclusion: The German Concept of Citizenship." *Migration* 37.

BRECHER, J. ET AL. (1993). *Global Visions: Beyond the New World Order*. Boston: South End Press.

BRENNAN, T. (1994). "Off the Gangsta Tip: A Rap Appreciation or Forgetting about Los Angeles." *Critical Inquiry* 20 (Summer): 663-693.

BRUBAKER, R. (1992). *Citizenship and Nationhood in France and Germany*. Cambridge/MA: Harvard University Press.

BRUINESSEN, M.V. (1996a). "Aslini inkar eden haramzadedir." *Birikim* No. 88 (August): 38-51.

BRUINESSEN, M.V. (1996b). "Kurds, Turks and the *Alevi* Revival in Turkey." *Middle East Report* (Summer): 7-10.

ÇAGLAR, A. (1990). "The Prison House of Culture in the Studies of Turks in Germany." *Working Paper*. Berlin. Department of Social Anthropology. Free University.

ÇAGLAR, A. (1994). *German Turks in Berlin: Migration and Their Quest for Social Mobility*. PhD. Thesis. Montréal. Department of Anthropology. McGill University.

ÇAGLAR, A. (1998). "Verordnete Rebellion: Deutsch-türkischer Rap und türkischer Pop in Berlin." In: R. Mayer and M. Terkessidis (eds.), *Global Kolorit: Multikulturalismus und Populärkultur*. St. Andrä/Wördern: Hannibal.

ÇAKIR, R. (1990). *Ayet ve Slogan: Türkiye'de Islami Olusumlar*. Istanbul: Metis.

CASTLES, S. (1985). "The Guests Who Stayed – The Debate on 'Foreigners Policy' in the German Federal Republic." *International Miration Review* XIX, No. 3: 517-534.

CASTLES, S. (1993). "Migration and Minorities in Europe. Perspectives for the 1990s: Eleven Hyphostheses." In: John Solomos and John Wrench (eds.), *Racism and Migration in Western Europe*. Oxford: Berg Publishers: 17-34.

CASTLES, S. AND G. KOSACK (1973). *Immigrant Workers and Class Structure in Western Europe*. London: Oxford University Press.

CASTLES, S. AND M.J. MILLER (1993). *The Age of Migration*. Basingstoke: MacMillan.

CASTLES, S., B. HEATHER AND T. WALLACE (1984). *Here for Good: Western Europe's New Ethnic Minorities*. London: Pluto Press.

CHEESMAN, T. (1998). "Polygot Politics: Hip hop in Germany." *Debatte*, Volume 6, No. 2.

CLARKE, J., S. HALL, T. JEFFERSON AND B. ROBERTS (1975). "Subcultures, Cultures and Class." In: S. Hall and T. Jefferson (eds.), *Resistance Through Rituals: Youth Subcultures in Post-War Britain*. London: Hutchinson.

CLIFFORD, J. (1994). "Diasporas." *Cultural Anthropology* 9, No. 3: 302-338.

CLIFFORD, J. (1988). *Predicament of Culture*. Cambridge/MA: Harvard University Press.

CLIFFORD, J. (1992). "Traveling Cultures." In: L. Grossberg, C. Nelson and P. Treichler, *Cultural Studies*. New York: Routledge: 96-116.

CLIFFORD, J. (1997). *Routes: Travel and Translation in the Late Twentieth Century*. Cambridge/MA: Harvard University Press.

COHEN, P. (1972). "Subcultural Conflict and Working-class City" *Working Papers in Cultural Studies* 2 (Spring): 5-51.

COHEN, R. (1995). "Rethinking 'Babylon': iconoclastic conceptions of the diasporic experience." *New Community* 21, No. 1: 5-18.

COHEN, R. (1996). "From Victims to Challengers," *International Affairs* 72, No. 3 (July): 507-520.

COHEN, R. (1997). *Global Diasporas: An Introduction*. London: UCL Press.

CRESSEY, P.G. (1932). *The Taxi-Dance Hall*. New York: Greenwood Press.

CROSS, B. (1993). *It's Not About a Salary...: Rap, Race and Resistance in Los Angeles*. London: Verso.

DECKER, J. (1992). "The State of Rap: Time and Place in Hip-hop Nationalism." *Social Text* 34: 53-83.

DERRIDA, J. (1981). *Positions*, translated by Alan Bass. London: The Athlone Press.

DICK, H. (1987). *Subculture: The Meaning of Style*. London: Routledge.

ECO, U. (1986). *Travels in Hyperreality*. London: Picador.

ELFLEIM, D. (1998). "From Krauts with Attitude to Turks with Attitude: Some Aspects of German Hip-Hop History." *Popular Music*, 17(3): 255-265.

FAIST, T. (1991). "Schooling, Work, and Ethnicity: The Impact of Public Policy on the Incorporation of Young Turks in the Federal Republic of Germany in the 1980s." *Working Paper*. Presented at the 1991 Anual Meeting of the American Political Science Association.

FAIST, T. (1995). *Social Citizenship for Whom?* Aldershot: Avebury.

FAIST, T. (2000a). "Border-Crossing Expansion of Spaces in and between Germany and Turkey." *Working Paper*, German-Turkish Summer Institute, University of Bremen.

FAIST, T. (ED.) (2000b). *Transstaatliche Räume. Politik, Wirtschaft und Kultur in und zwischen Deutschland und der Türkei.* Bielefeld: transcript.

FEATHERSTONE, M. (1990). *Global Culture: Nationalism, Globalization and Modernity.* London: Sage Publications.

FOUCAULT, M. (1979). "Governmentality." *Ideology and Consciousness* 6: 5-21.

FRIEDMAN, J. (1994). *Cultural Identity and Global Process.* London: Sage Publications.

GANGULY, K. (1992). "Migrant Identities: Personal Memory and the Construction of Selfhood." *Cultural Studies* 6, No. 1: 27-49.

GANS, H. (1979). "Symbolic Ethnicity: The Future of Ethnic Groups and Cultures in America." *Ethnic and Racial Studies* 2, No. 1 (January): 1-20.

GIDDENS, A. (1990). *The Consequences of Modernity.* Cambridge: Polity Press.

GILLESPIE, M. (1996). *Television, Ethnicity and Cultural Change.* London: Routledge.

GILROY, P. (1987). *There Ain't no Black in the Union Jack.* London: Hutchinson.

GILROY, P. (1993). *Black Atlantic: Double Consciousness and Modernity.* Cambridge/MA: Harvard University Press.

GILROY, P. (1994). "Diaspora." *Paragraph* 17, No. 3 (November): 207-210.

GILROY, P. (1995). "Roots and Routes: Black Identity as an Outernational Project." In: H.W. Harris et al. (eds.), *Racial and Ethnic Identity: Psychological Development and Creative Expression.* London: Routledge.

GITMEZ, A. AND C. WILPERT (1987). "A Micro-Society or an Ethnic Community? Social Organization and Ethnicity amongst Turkish Migrants in Berlin." In: John Rex et al. (eds.), *Immigrant Associations in Europe.* Hants: Gower.

GÖKDERE, A.Y. (1978). *Yabanci Ülkelere Isgücü Akimi ve Türk Ekonomisi Üzerindeki Etkileri.* Ankara: Is Bankasi Yayinlari.

GORDON, M. (1947). "The Concept of the Sub-Culture and its Application." *Social Forces* (October).

GRAMSCI, A. (1971). *Selection From the Prison Notebooks*. London: Lawrence & Wishart.

GRASS, G. (1981). "Kreuzberg fehlt ein Minarett." In: H. W. Richter (ed.), *Berlin, ach Berlin*. Berlin: Severin und Siedler.

GRENIER, L. (1989). "From Diversity to Difference: The Case of Socio-Cultural Studies of Music." *New Formations* 9 (Winter): 125142.

GREVE, M. (1996). "Deutsche Exportschlager." *Daily Taz* (20 August).

GREVE, M. (1997). *Alla Turca: Music aus der Turkei in Berlin*. Berlin: Die Ausländerbeauftragte des Senats.

GREVE, MARTIN (2000). "Kreuzberg und Unkapaný: Skizzen zur Musik türkischer Jugendlicher in Deutschland." In: I. Attia and H. Marburger (eds.), *Alltag und Lebenswelten von Migrantenjugendlichen*. Frankfurt: IKO.

GUATTARI, F. (1989). "The Three Ecologies." *New Formations* 8 (Summer): 131-147.

GÜNGÖR, N. (1993). *Arabesk: Sosyokültürel Açidan Arabesk Müzik*. Ankara: Bilgi Yayinevi.

GÜRSOY-TEZCAN, A. (1992). "Introduction." In: Aras Ören, *Please No Police*, Novel translated from the Turkish by Teoman Sipahigil. Austin: Center for Middle Eastern Studies: ix-xxxvii.

HALL, S. (1988). "New Ethnicities." In: K. Mercer (ed.), *Black Film, British Cinema*, ICA Document No. 7. London: Institute of Contemporary Arts.

HALL, S. (1989). "Ethnicity: Identity and Difference." *Radical America* 23, No. 4: 9-20.

HALL, S. (1991a). "The Local and the Global: Globalization and Ethnicity." In: Anthony King (ed.), *Culture, Globalization and the World System*. London: Macmillan Press.

HALL, S. (1991b). "Old and New Identities, Old and New Ethnicities" in Anthony D. King (ed.), *Culture, Globalization and the World-System*. London: Macmillan Press.

HALL, S. (1993). "The Question of Cultural Identity." In: S. Hall et al. (eds.), *Modernity and Its Futures*. Cambridge: Polity Press: 274-325.

HALL, S. (1994). "Cultural Identity and Diaspora." In: P.Williams and L.Chrisman (eds.), *Colonial Discourse and Post-Colonial Theory* New York: Columbia University Press.

HALL, S. (1997). "The Work of Representation." In: S. Hall (ed.), *Rep-

resentation: Cultural Representations and Signifying Practices. London: Sage.

HALL, S. AND JEFFERSON, T. (EDS.) (1976). *Resistance Through Rituals: Youth Subcultures in Post-War Britain.* London: Hutchinson.

HAMMERSLEY, M. AND P. ATKINSON (1983). *Ethnography: Principles in Practice.* New York: Tavistock.

HANNERZ, U. (1968). "The Rhetoric of Soul: Identification in Negro Society." *Race* IX, 4: 453-465.

HANNERZ, U. (1989). "Culture Between Centre and Periphery: Toward a Macroanthropology." *Ethnos* 54: 200-216.

HANNERZ, U. (1992). *Cultural Complexity.* New York: Columbia University Press.

HANNERZ, U. (1996). *Transnational Connections.* London: Routledge.

HARRIS, C. (1997). "No Blacks, Please, We're British." *Working Paper.* Coventry. Centre for Research in Ethnic Relation. University of Warwick.

HEBDIGE, D. (1979). *Subculture: The Meaning of Style.* London: Routledge.

HEBDIGE, D. (1988). *Hiding in the Light.* London: Routledge.

HEINEMANN, L. AND F. KAMCILI (2000). "Unterhaltung, Absatzmärkte und die Vermittlung von Heimat. Die Rolle der Massenmedien in Deutsch-Türkischen Räumen." In: T. Faist (ed.), *Transstaatliche Räume. Politik, Wirtschaft und Kultur in und zwischen Deutschland und der Türkei.* Bielefeld: transcript.

HEITMEYER, W. ET AL. (1997). *Verlockender Fundamentalismus.* Frankfurt am Main: Suhrkamp.

HENKEL, O. ET AL. (EDS.) (1994). *Spray City: Graffiti in Berlin.* Berlin: Akademie der Künste.

HENNAYAKE, S.K. (1992). "Interactive Ethnonationalism: An Alternative Explanation of Minority Ethnonationalism." *Political Geography* 11, No. 6 (November): 526-549.

HOLZNER, L. (1982). "The Myth of Turkish Ghettos: A Geographic Case Study of West German Responses Towards a Foreign Minority." *The Journal of Ethnic Studies* 9: 4 (Winter): 65-85.

HOROWITZ, R. (1983). *Honor and the American Dream: Culture and Identity in a Chicano Community.* New Brunswick: Rutgers University Press.

HOROWITZ, R. (1986). "Remaining an Outsider: Membership as a Threat to Research Rapport." *Urban Life* 14, No. 4 (January): 409-430.

HORROCKS, D. AND E. KALINSKY (1996). "Migrants or Citizens? Turks in Germany between Exclusion and Acceptance." In: D. Horrocks and E. Kolinsky (eds.), *Turkish Culture in German Society Today*. Oxford: Berghahn Books: x-xxviii.

HORROCKS, D. AND E. KALINSKY (1996). *Turkish Culture in German Society Today*. Oxford: Berghahn Books.

INNENAUSSCHUSS DES DEUTSCHEN BUNDESTAGES (1999). *Reform des Staatsangehörigkeitsrechts: Die parlamentarische Beratung*. Berlin: Deutscher Bundestag.

IRELAND, P.R. (1994). *The Policy Challenge of Ethnic Diversity: Immigrant Politics in France and Switzerland*. Cambridge/MA: Harvard University Press.

ITZKOWITZ, K. (1978). "Differance and Identity." *Research in Phenomenology* 8: 127-143.

JANMOHAMED, A. AND D. LLOYD (EDS.) (1990). *The Nature and Context of Minority Discourse*. London: Oxford University Press.

KAGITÇIBASI Ç. (1987). "Alienation of the Outsider: The Plight of Migrants." *International Migration* XXV, No. 2 (June): 195-210.

KAYA, A. (1998). "Multicultural Clientalism and Berlin-Alevis." *New Perspectives on Turkey*, No. 18 (July).

KAYA, A. (1999). "Cultural Bricolage and 'Double Diasporic Cultural Identity' Amongst Turkish Hip-hop Youth in Berlin." *Popular Cultures*. Izmir: British Council and Ege University.

KAYA, A. (2000). *Sicher in Kreuzberg: Berlin'deki Küçük Istanbul*. Istanbul: Büke Yayinlari.

KAYA, A. (2000). "The Construction of Ethnic Group Discourses and Second Generation German-Turks in Berlin." G.G. Özdogan and G. Tokay (eds.), *Redefining State, Nation and Citizen*. Istanbul: Eren Yayincilik.

KEITH, M. (1995). "Making the Street Visible: Placing Racial Violence in Context." *New Community* 21, No. 4: 551-565.

KLUSMEYER, D.B. (1993). "Aliens, Immigrants, and Citizens: The Politics of Inclusion in the Federal Republic of Germany." *Daedalus* 122, No. 3 (Summer): 81-114.

KNIGHT, J. (1986). "Confinement and Isolation: Video in West Germany's Turkish Community." In: *Independent Media* 60.

KNÖDLER-BUNTE, E. (1987). *Kreuzberger Mischung: Die Innerstädtische Verflechtung von Architectur, Kultur und Gewerbe*. Berlin: Internationale Bauausstellung.

Köhne, G. and A. Kepenek (1997). "Hiphop für Atatürk." *Zeit Magazin* 18: 16-22.

Lefèbvre, H. (1989). *The Production of Space*, translated by D. Nicholson-Smith. Oxford: Blackwell.

Lévi-Strauss, C. (1966). *The Savage Mind.* Chicago: University of Chicago Press.

Levinas, E. (1986). "The Trace of the Other," translated by A. Lingis. In: M. Taylor (ed.), *Deconstruction in Context.* Chicago: University of Chicago Press.

Levinas, E. (1987). *Collected Philosophical Papers*, translated by A. Lingis. The Netherlands: Kluwer Academic Publishers.

Liebkind, K. (ed.) (1989). *New Identities in Europe: Immigrants and the Ethnic Identity of Youth.* Aldershot: Gower.

Lipsitz, G. (1994). "We Know What Time It Is: Race, Class and Youth culture in the Nineties." In: A. Ross and T. Rose (eds.), *Microphone Friends: Youth Music and Youth Culture.* New York & London: Routledge.

Lott, T.L. (1994). "Black Vernacular, Representation and Cultural Malpractice." In: David Theo Goldberg (ed.), *Multiculturalism: A Critical Reader.* Oxford: Blackwell: 230-258.

Mandel, R. (1989). "Turkish Headscarves and the 'Foreigner Problem': Constructing Difference Through Emblems of Identity." *New German Critique* No. 46: 27-46.

Mandel, R. (1990). "Shifting Centres and Emergent Identities: Turkey and Germany in the Lives of Turkish *Gastarbeiter*." In: D.F. Eickelman and J. Piscatori (eds.), *Muslim Travellers: Pilgrimage, Migration, and the Religious Imagination.* London: Routledge: 153-171.

Mandel, R. (1996). "A Place of Their Own: Contesting Spaces and Defining Places in Berlin's Migrant Community." In: B.D. Metcalf (ed.), *Making Muslim Space in North America and Europe.* Berkeley: University of California Press.

Marcuse, P. (1996). "Of Walls and Immigrant Enclaves." In: N. Carmon (ed.), *Immigration and Integration in Post-Industrial Societies.* London: MacMillan.

Marshall, B. (1992). "Migration into Germany: Asylum Seekers and Ethnic Germans." *German Politics* 1, No. 1 (April): 124-134.

Marshall, T.H. (1950). *Citizenship and Social Class.* Cambridge: Cambridge University Press.

MARTIN, D.C. (1995). "The Choices of Identity." *Social Identities* 1, No. 1: 5-20.

MARTIN, P.L. (1991). *The Unfinished Story: Turkish Labor Migration to Western Europe with Special Reference to the Federal Republic of Germany.* Geneva: International Labour Office.

MCLAREN (1995). "Gangsta Pedagogy and Ghettoethnicity: the Hip-Hop Nation as Counterpublic Space." *Socialist Review* 2: 9-55.

MCROBBIE, A. (1991/1978). "The Culture of Working-Class Girls." In: A. McRobbie (ed.), *Feminism and Youth Culture*. London: Macmillan.

MELUCCI, A. (1989). *Nomads of the Present: Social Movements and Individual Needs in Contemporary Society*. London: Hutchinson Radius.

MESETH, C. (1996). *Daily Taz* (Friday, 20 September).

MORLEY, D. AND K. ROBINS (1993). "No Place like Heimat: Images of Home(land) in European Culture." In: E. Caster et al. (eds.), *Space and Place: Theories of Identity and Location*. London: Lawrence & Wishart: 3-31.

MURPHY, K. (1990). "Made Men." *Film Comment* 26, No. 5 (September/October): 25-30.

MUSHABEN, J.M. (1985). "A Crisis of Culture: Isolation and Integration Among Guestworkers in the German Federal Republic." In: I. Basgöz and N. Furniss (eds.), *Turkish Workers in Europe*. Bloomington: Indiana University Press.

NAGEL, J. (1994). "Constructing Ethnicity: Creating and Recreating Ethnic Identity and Culture." *Social Problems* 41, No. 1 (February): 152-176.

NAUCK, B. (1988). "Migration and Change in Parent-Child Relationships: The Case of Turkish Migrants in Germany." *International Migration* 26: 33-55.

NECO (1994). "Wir haben Geschichte gemacht ...." In: O. Henkel et al. (eds.), *Spray City: Graffiti in Berlin*. Berlin: Akademie der Künste: 52-53.

NEGUS, K. (1996). *Popular Music in Theory*. Cambridge: Polity Press.

OCAK, A.Y. (2000). *Alevi ve Bektasi Ynanclarinin Islam Oncesi Temelleri*. Istanbul: Iletisim Yayinlari.

ÖNDER, Z. (1996). "Muslim-Turkish Children in Germany: Sociocultural Problems." *Migrationworld* XXIV, No. 5: 18-24.

ÖZBEK, M. (1994). *Popüler Kültür ve Orhan Gencebay Arabeski*. Istanbul: Iletisim Yayinlari.

ÖZCAN, E. (1994). *Türkische Immigrantenorganisationen in der Bundesrepublik Deutschland*. Berlin: Hitit.

PAMGREN, C. ET AL. (EDS.) (1992). *Ethnicity in Youth Culture*. University of Stockholm.

PAREKH, B. AND H. BHABHA (1989). "Identities on Parade." *Marxism Today*, June: 24-29.

PARK, R.E. ET AL. (1925). *The City*. London: University of Chicago Press.

POPLACK, S. (1988). "Sometimes I'll start a sentence in English y termino en Español." *Linguistics* 18: 581-616.

RADTKE, F.O. (1994). "The formation of ethnic minorities and the transformation of social into ethnic conflicts in a so-called multicultural society: The case of Germany." In: J. Rex and B. Drury (eds.), *Ethnic Mobilisation in a Multi-Cultural Europe*. Hampshire: Avebury.

RATH, J. (1993). "The Ideological Representation of Migrant Workers in Europe: A Matter of Racialisation?." In: J. Solomos and J. Wrench (eds.), *Racism and Migration in Western Europe*. Oxford: Berg Publishers: 215-232.

REX, J. (1986). "The Concept of a Multicultural Society." Coventry: Centre for Research in Ethnic Relations, University of Warwick, *Occasional Papers in Ethnic Relations* No. 3.

REX, J. (1991). "The Political Sociology of a Multicultural Society." *Journal of Intercultural Studies* 2, No. 1: 7-19.

REX, J. (1994). "Conceptual and Practical Problems of Multi-Culturalism in Europe." *Unpublished manuscript*. Presented in the 'Symposium on Multicultural Society.' Sweden: Vasteras, Swedish Ministry of Culture.

ROBERTSON, R. (1992). *Globalization*. London and Newbury Park: Sage.

ROBINS, K. (1991). "Tradition and Translation: National Culture in its Global Context." In: J. Corner and S. Harvey (eds.), *Enterprise and Heritage*. London: Routledge: 21-44.

ROBINS, K. AND D. MORLEY (1996). "Almanci, Yabanci." *Cultural Studies* 10, No. 2 (May): 248-253.

ROSALDO, R. (1989). *Culture and Truth: The Remaking of Social Analysis*. London: Routledge.

ROSE, T. (1994). *Black Noise: Rap Music and Black Culture in Contemporary America*. London: Wesleyan University Press.

RUSHDIE, S. (1990). "In Good Faith," *Independent on Sunday*, 4 February.

RUSHDIE, S. (1991). *Imaginary Homelands*. London: Granta.

RUSSON, J. (1995). "Heidegger, Hegel, and Ethnicity: The Ritual Basis of Self-Identity." *The Southern Journal of Philosophy* XXXIII: 509-532.

SAFRAN, W. (1991). "Diasporas in Modern Societies: Myths of Homeland and Return." *Diaspora* 1, No. 1 (Spring): 83-99.

SAMUEL, R. (1988). "Little Englandism Today." *Newstatesman & Society* (21 October): 27-30.

SANSONE, L. (1995). "The Making of a Black Youth Culture: Lower-Class Young Men of Surinamese Origin of Amsterdam." In: V. Amit-Talai and H. Wulff (eds.), *Youth Cultures: A Cross-Cultural Perspective*. London: Routledge.

SCHIERUP, C.U. (1994). "Multi-Culturalism and Ethnic Mobilisation: Some Theoretical Considerations." In: J. Rex and B. Drury (eds.), *Ethnic Mobilisation in a Multi-Cultural Europe*. Aldershot: Avebury.

SCHIFFAUER, W. (1997). "Islamic Vision and Social Reality: The Political Culture of Sunni Muslims in Germany." In: S. Vertovec and C. Peach (eds.), *Islam in Europe: The Politics of Religion and Community*. London: MacMillan Press.

SCHWARTZ, T. (1992). "The Turkish Community Berlin: Youth Cultures in the System of the German Welfare System." In: C. Pamfren et al. (eds.), *Ethnicity in Youth Culture*. University of Stockholm Press.

SEIDEL-PIELEN, E. (1995). *Unsere Türken: Annäherung an ein gespaltenes Verhältnis*. Berlin.

SENDERS, S. (1996). "Laws of Belonging: Legal Dimensions of National Inclusion in Germany." *New German Critique* 67 (Winter): 147-176.

SIMMEL, G. (1971/1908). "The Stranger." In: D.N. Levine (ed.), *Georg Simmel: On Individuality and Social Forms*. Chicago: The University of Chicago Press.

SKLAIR, L. (1991). *Sociology of the Global System*. Hertfordshire: Harvester Wheatsheaf.

SKLAIR, L. (1993). "Going Global: Competing Models of Globalization." *Sociology Review* (November).

SMITH, A.D. (1995). *Nations and Nationalism in a Global Era*. Cambridge: Polity Press.

SMITH, A D. (1990). "Towards a Global Culture?." In: M. Featherstone (ed.), *Global Culture: Nationalism, Globalisation and Modernity*. London: Sage.

STOKES, M. (1994). "Turkish Arabesk and the City: Urban Popular Culture as Spatial Practice." In: Akbar S. Ahmed and H. Donnan (eds.), *Islam, Globalisation and Postmodernity*. London: Routledge.

STOREY, J. (1993). *Cultural Theory and Popular Culture*. London: Harvester & Wheatsheaf.

SUHR, H. (1989). "*Ausländerliteratur*: minority literature in the Federal Republic of Germany." *New German Critique*, No 46 (Winter).

SWEDENBURG, T. (1992). "Homies in the hood: Rap's Commodification." *New Formations* 18 (Winter): 53-66.

TAYLOR, C. (1994). "The Politics of Recognition." In: A. Gutmann (ed.), *Multiculturalism*. Princeton: Princeton University Press.

TBB, Türkischer Bund in Berlin-Brandenburg (1996). *Türkçe Danisma Yerleri Kilavuzu*. Berlin: Karma.

TERAOKA, A.A. (1990). "Gastarbeiterliteratur: The Other Speaks Back." In: A.R. Janmohamed and D. Lloyd (eds.), *The Nature and Context of Minority Discourse*. Oxford University Press: 294-318.

TERENCE T. (1993). "Anthropology and Multiculturalism: What is Anthropology that Multiculturalists should be mindful of it?." *Cultural Anthropology* 8, No. 4: 411-29.

TERTILT, H. (1996). *Turkish Power Boys: Ethnographie einer Jugendbande*. Frankfurt am Main: Suhrkamp.

TÖNNIES, F. (1957). *Community and Society*, translated and edited by C. Loomis. New York: Harper and Row.

TÖLÖLIAN, K. (1991). "The Nation State and its Others: In Lieau of a Preface." *Diaspora* 1, No. 1: 3-7.

TOPRAK, B. (1981). *Islam and Political Development in Turkey*. Leiden: E.J. Brill.

TOURAINE, A. (1977). *The Self-Production of Society*. Chicago: The University of Chicago Press.

TRAUFFETTER, G. (1995). "Wer ist schon Madonna? Wir wollen Yonca." Daily *Süddeutsche Zeitung* Nr. 133 (12 June).

TRAUTNER, B. (2000). "Türkische Muslime und Islamische Organisationen als Soziale Träger des Transstaatlichen Raumes Deutschland-Türkei." In: T. Faist (ed.), *Transstaatliche Räume. Politik, Wirtschaft und Kultur in und zwischen Deutschland und der Türkei*. Bielefeld: transcript.

TÜRKISCHER ELTERNVEREIN IN BERLIN-BRANDENBURG E.V. (1995). *10 Jahre Elternarbeit 1985-1995: Eine Documentation des Türkischen Elternvereins in Berlin-Brandenburg e.V.* Berlin.

VASSAF, G. (1982). *Daha Sesimizi Duyuramadik: Avrupa'da Türk Isçi Çocuklari.* Istanbul: Belge Yayinlari.

VERTOVEC, S. (1995). "Young Muslims in Keighley, West Yorkshire: Cultural identity, context and 'community'." *Unpublished Research Paper.* Coventry: Centre for Research in Ethnic Relations. University of Warwick.

VERTOVEC, S. (1996a). "Berlin Multikulti: Germany 'Foreigners' and 'World-Openness.'" *New Community* 22, No. 3: 381-389.

VERTOVEC, S. (1996b). "Comparative Issues in, and Multiple Meanings of, the South Asian Religious Diaspora." *Conference Paper* presented in the 'Conference on The Comparative Study of the South Asian Diaspora: Religious Experience in Britain, Canada and USA.' London: School of Oriental and African Studies, 4-6 November.

VERTOVEC, S. (1997). "Diaspora," in E. Cashmore (ed.), *Dictionary of Race and Ethnic Relations.* London: Routledge.

WALLIS, R. AND K. MALM (1984). *Big Sounds From Small Peoples: The Music Industry in Small Countries.* London: Constable.

WALLIS, R. AND K. MALM (1990). "Patterns of Change." In: S. Frith and A. Goodwin (eds.), *On Records.* New York: Pantheon.

WALLMAN, S. (1978). "The Boundaries of 'Race': Processes of Ethnicity in England." *Man* 13, No. 2.

WATER, C. (1981). "Badges of Half-formed, Inarticulate Radicalism: A Critique of Recent Trends in the Study of Working-class Youth Culture." *International Labour and Working-class History*, No. 19 (Spring): 23-37.

WILLIAMS, R. (1977). *Marxism and Literature.* Oxford University Press.

WILLIAMS, R. (1983). *Keywords.* London: Fontana.

WILPERT, C. (1989). "Ethnic and Cultural Identity: Ethnicity and the Second Generation in the Context of European Migration." In: K. Liebkind (ed.), *New Identities in Europe: Immigrant Ancestry and the Ethnic Identity of Youth* (Aldershot: Gower): 6-24.

WOLF, E. (1982). *Europe and the People Without History.* University of California Press.

YOUNG, J. (1971). *The Drugtakers: The Social Meaning of Drug Use.* London: Paladin.

ZAIMOGLU, F. (1995). *Kanak-Sprak: 24 Misstöne vom Rande der Gesellschaft*. Berlin: Rotbuch.
ZAIMOGLU, F. (1998). *Koppstoff: Kanake Sprak vom Rande der Gesellschaft*. Berlin: Rotbuch.

Newspapers and Magazines

Der Spiegel 47 (1990). "In Kreuzberg kommandieren wir."
Der Spiegel 16 (1997). "Ausländer und Deutsche: Gefährlich fremd. Das Scheitern der multikulturellen Gesellschaft."
Die Tageszeitung (7 January 1997). "Gebetsrufe? -Ja bitte!."
Focus 31 (1997). "Gefährliche Ausländer."
Brigitte 19 (1990): 125-132. "Ghetto Sisters."
Zitty 4 (1993). "Die Barbaren kommen!."
Süddeutsche Zeitung (11/12 August 1990). "Der Haß darauf, als Nichts zu gelten."
Tagesspiegel (6 May 1990). "Vereinte Jagd auf Skinheads."
Tan (9 March 1990). "Türk Kizlari Çetesi."
Taz (2 May 1989). "DGB zählte 610.000 beim Tag der Arbeit."
Taz (4 December 1992). "Gurke des Tages: Moschee in Bobingen."
Taz (6 March 1995). "Einübung in mehr Toleranz."
Taz-Berlin (2 May 1989). "Steine in die Senatskosmetik."
Time (24 February 1997). "No Rest in the Ruhr."

Discography

Azize-A (1996). *Demo Cassette*. Berlin: GGM Orient Express.
Azize-A (1997). *Oriental Hip-Hop: Es ist Zeit*. GGM Orient Express.
Cartel (1995). *Cartel*. Istanbul: Polygram.
Erci-E (1997). *Sohbet*. Istanbul: Raks.
Islamic Force (1991). *My Melody/Istanbul*. Berlin: Orange Shark Music.
Islamic Force (1993). *The Whole World is Your Home*. Berlin: Orange Shark Music.
Islamic Force (1994). *Hip'N'Hop Tharpot*. Berlin: Orange Shark Music.
Islamic Force (1995). *Halt Keine Gewalt*. Berlin: Orange Shark Music.
Islamic Force (1997). *Mesaj*. Berlin, Kreuzberg: De De Records.
King Size Terror (1994). *Cehenneme Hosgeldin*. Nürnberg.
Orientation (1997). *Bosporus Bridge*. Berlin: GGM Orient Express.
Microphone Mafia (1994). *Stop Rassismus*. Köln.